Hounds and Hunting
Through the Ages

THE AUTHOR'S PACK IN ABANDONED COTTON FIELDS IN NORTH CAROLINA
From the Painting by Percival Rosseau

HOUNDS AND HUNTING
Through the Ages

JOSEPH B. THOMAS, M.F.H.
with a foreword by Mason Houghland, M.F.H.
and a new introduction by Norman M. Fine, editor of *Covertside*

THE DERRYDALE PRESS
LANHAM AND NEW YORK

THE DERRYDALE PRESS

Published in the United States of America
by The Derrydale Press
4720 Boston Way, Lanham, Maryland 20706

Distributed by NATIONAL BOOK NETWORK, INC.

Copyright © 1928 by Joseph B. Thomas
Copyright © 1933 by Windward House, Inc.

All rights reserved. No part of this publication may be reproduced,
stored in a retrieval system, or transmitted in any form or by any
means, electronic, mechanical, photocopying, recording, or otherwise,
without the prior permission of the publisher.

Library of Congress Cataloging-in-Publication Data

Thomas, Joseph B. (Joseph Brown). 1879-1955.
    Hounds and hunting through the ages / Joseph B. Thomas
      p. cm.
  Originally published: 1928.
    ISBN 1-58667-059-X (cloth : alk. paper); ISBN 1-56416-194-3
(leatherbound : alk. paper)
    1. Hunting. 2. Hounds. 3. Fox hunting. 4. Foxhounds. I. Title.

SK285.T5 2001
799.2'34—dc21   00-060139

♾™ The paper used in this publication meets the minimum requirements of
American National Standard for Information Sciences—Permanence of
Paper for Printed Library Materials, ANSI/NISO Z39.48-1992.
Manufactured in the United States of America.

DEDICATION

My dear Boy:

When you were a tiny baby, Mary, your old nurse, most often lulled you to sleep by singing in a minor key the old Irish hunting-song:

> *Hark Tally Ho! Hark Tally Ho!*
> *Hark Tally Ho! We'll chase him*
> *Hark Tally Ho! before we go*
> *We'll surely kill or earth him.*
>
> *Hark! Fifer, Fiddler, Jonah,*
> *Giggler, Dido, Fanny, Farmer,*
> *Spanker, Spoker, Tanker, Joker,*
> *Gaylass, Miller, Ranger.*

This song together with the hunting scenes painted on your crib and the walls of your room by your mother had you well "entered" to hunting atmosphere before you could toddle. Later, you were wont to see your mother and daddy go a-hunting, sometimes on foot with beagles, more often ahorse with foxhounds. The poignant smell of the saddle room with its shining steel, the furious scourings of cleaning rooms, the "doing" of scarlet coats, the glint of top hats as they passed the vigilant eye of Albert Alabaster, the arts of horse and hound management as practiced by James Stuart and Charlie Carver, not forgetting the admonitions of Frank Stuart in the hunting of "Banker," your first beagle; in short, the entire machinery of the chase has been an open book to you from infancy. Regarding riding whips, do you remember when I took a whip to school and asked Mr. Manders to use it on you if you were not as keen at your lessons as you were at shouting, "Gone away!" A puppy that does not stick to the line, or runs riot, is not much use, is he?

Sometimes, you must wonder why your forebears and so many of their friends apparently have gone mad about hunting; so, my boy, I shall try to

DEDICATION

tell you all I can about it, that you may profit just a little from what the "old man" has gleaned during the ups and downs of his hunting experience, and then apply or correct the observations.

Many hunt, but few have knowledge of hounds,—the reason for this, the history of that; hence without such knowledge, they lose much pleasure. If you really study all phases of hunting in its historical background, the game, the hounds, the horses, you will attain a life-long mental resource, and will thus enhance your knowledge of literature, art, and history.

In hunting, there is much more than mere beauty to enchant the eye or promote the physical exhilaration of perfect enjoyment. There is, above all, the lesson to be learned from qualities so necessary in the first-class hound, qualities which are also so essential in the first-class man:

Honesty — Sagacity — Determination — Drive.

Adversely, there are certain hound vices from which you should take warning, to wit,—

Skirting (philandering) — Babbling — Dwelling (dawdling).

Astute observation of hunting technique should tend to form a firm foundation to help you face your personal as well as the more serious problems of the modern industrial world with its chaotic struggle.

Men, especially in America, are prone to imagine that machinery, invention, efficiency systems, are about to free them from all drudgery and care, and make it possible for them to conquer the earth and all it has to offer. There is, perhaps, a danger that without proper counter spiritual influence, such as the love of the beautiful in nature derived from contact with God's green fields and woods, each new invention, instead of making man more free, is in reality enslaving him by mechanizing his very soul.

Individuality today is, perhaps, in a measure becoming atrophied by stereotyped enjoyments. In the maelstrom of so-called progress, many men play the part of submissive individuals. A human being wholly under the influence of modern industry is in danger of losing qualities of initiative, judgment, certain fundamental instincts of moral and physical courage, and the capacity for appreciation of much that is delightful in life. The hunting field should help maintain the proper balance between man and machine, between business routine and the physical freedom of primitive living.

The general technique of the chase, and the human qualities necessary for its successful pursuit, have changed little during the ages. It still demands the same courage, horsemanship, and a proper understanding of nature and animals as it did when practiced by our remote ancestors. The thrill today of a mounted pageant flashing across a delightful country, the cry of hounds ahead, a blue sky above, is the same thrill that made the great Char-

DEDICATION

lemagne, over a thousand years ago, alternate the governing of an immense empire with weeks in the hunting field.

Dear Boy, I hope a clear understanding and love of the chase may always be a source of increasing interest and a refuge to you, as it has been to me.

    Your affectionate,

FATHER.

STAG HUNT, FROM THE 'CUEVA DEL MAS D'EN JOSEP', ATTRIBUTED TO THOUSANDS OF YEARS B.C.

PREFACE

In its inception, this work was intended to comprise only a simple series of letters to my young son, which would impart something of the romance and practice of hunting. Looking forward to the day when

> *"Dappled hounds would run for him*
> *And horses jump like deer,"*

I hoped, as is the way of fathers, to spare him some of the mistakes I have made. Then, urged by friends who felt that a book of broader scope addressed to hunting men, and to laymen as well, was much needed, I have gradually enlarged the work to its present form.

During the four years that have elapsed since the writing was begun, many valuable suggestions have been received. To those who have so kindly encouraged the work, as well as to those who have contributed important data and illustrations, deep appreciation is herewith most gratefully rendered.

In England, especial acknowledgment is due the Duke of Beaufort, M.F.H., The Earl of Lonsdale, M.F.H., Sir Edward Curre, M.F.H., Dr. Howard Carter, Major E. Beddington Behrens, and Mr. W. Smithson Broadhead. In America, the list includes Mesdames Thomas Hitchcock, M. D. Crawford, N. S. Bell, and the following Masters of Foxhounds and gentlemen: A. Henry Higginson, Henry G. Vaughan, R. E. Danielson, J. M. Houghland, James W. Appleton, Samuel D. Riddle, William Warner Justice, Jr., Charles E. Mather, Plunket Stewart, M. Roy Jackson, Oakleigh Thorne, Samuel L. Wooldridge, J. Churchill Newcomb, P. A. Rockefeller, Percival Rosseau, Ernest R. Gee, E. M. Ward, Jr., and Harry W. Smith, who many years ago did much to inspire in me the love of hounds and hunting.

August, 1928.

TABLE OF CONTENTS

Introduction xvii
   By Norman M. Fine

Foreword xxi
   By Mason Houghland, M. F. H.

Chapter I. 1
   Fundamentals and Traditions.

Chapter II. 25
   Limners and Bards of the Chase.

Chapter III. 39
   Hounds and Horns of Yore.

Chapter IV. 51
   Present Day Hounds.

Chapter V. 73
   Attributes of a Good Hound.

Chapter VI. 100
   Comments on Hunting a Pack.

Chapter VII. 124
   The Eccentricities of Scent.

Chapter VIII. 137
   Kennels and Stables.

Chapter IX. 150
   Riding to Hounds and Hunt Uniforms.

Chapter X. 170
   Hunt Countries and Quarry.

LIST OF ILLUSTRATIONS

THE AUTHOR'S PACK IN ABANDONED COTTON FIELD
IN NORTH CAROLINA . . . . Frontispiece
  From the painting by Percival Rosseau
  Colour plate

                 Facing Page

HUNTING SCENES FROM RELICS IN THE TOMB OF
TUT-ANKH-AMEN 2

GREEK HUNTER WITH FOX, HARE AND HOUND 3

HOUNDS, HORSE, AND FALCON OF WILLIAM THE CONQUEROR . 3
  From the Bayeux Tapestry

FRENCH KENNELS OF THE XIVTH CENTURY 14
  Painting by Clara Fargo Thomas, after the MS. of Gaston de Foix

FRENCH FOXHUNTING SCENE OF THE XIVTH CENTURY . . 14
  Painting by Clara Fargo Thomas, after MS. of Gaston de Foix

EARLY VIRGINIA HUNTING SCENE 15
  From a frieze in an old Virginia Mansion

MR. PERCIVAL ROSSEAU'S HOUNDS KILLING A PANTHER . . 30
  From Mr. Rosseau's painting

SCENTING HOUNDS, ABOUT 1597 31
  From a frieze at Hardwick Hall

ANCIENT HORNS 39
  A PLATE SHOWING TEN ANCIENT HUNTING HORNS

WHITE HOUNDS OF KING HENRY II, XVITH CENTURY . . . 44

HOUNDS OF THE GLOUCESTER FOX HUNTING CLUB, ABOUT 1800 44

BALTAZAR, FRENCH HOUND BY DESPORTES, ABOUT 1700 . . 44

HOUNDS BRED BY PETER BECKFORD 44
  From painting by Sartorius

HUNTING HORNS 45
  A PLATE SHOWING FOURTEEN ANCIENT AND MODERN HUNTING HORNS

TYPES OF MODERN HOUNDS 54
  A PLATE SHOWING EIGHT MODERN HOUNDS

xiii.

LIST OF ILLUSTRATIONS

	Facing Page
French Stag Hounds of the Duchesse d'Uzès' Hunt	55
The Axe Vale Harriers of Devonshire	55
Kerry Beagles, imported by Mrs. W. Goadby Loew, M.F.H.	55
Mr. Thomas' Flier, '26	66
Photogravure from an etching by Bert Cobb	
Mr. Thomas' Frantic, '20	67
Photogravure from an etching by Bert Cobb	
The Correlation of Hound Qualities	76
A diagram	
Examples of Natural and Artificially-shaped Feet	77
A plate showing foot-prints of red and grey foxes, coyote, wolf, Virginia foxhound, Peterborough type foxhounds, etc.	
Squire Osbaldeston's Famous Foxhound Sire, Furrier	88
From a painting by Ferneley	
Meynell Waverly, '09,	
champion dog hound at Peterborough, 1911	88
From a painting by Cuthbert Bradley	
A Cast in America	108
From a drawing by W. Smithson Broadhead	
Drawing Woodlands	109
From a drawing by W. Smithson Broadhead	
Huntland, Loudoun County, Virginia	138
showing Huntland House, kennels and stables	
Kennels Built by Mr. P. A. Rockefeller	
for the Overhills Hunt	139
A diagram	
Kennels Designed by the Author	
for his Young Hound Pack	139
A diagram	
Huntland Kennels, Loudoun County, Va.	144
From a photograph	
Courtyard of Huntland Stables	144
From a photograph	
Lord Lonsdale at Barley Thorpe in the Cottesmore Country	158
From a photograph	

LIST OF ILLUSTRATIONS

	Facing Page
Cottesmore Fixture Card and Hound Lists	158
Hunt Uniforms, Horns, Hounds and Horses of the XVIIIth Century *From a Gobelin Tapestry*	159
A Typical French Hunting Forest THE ALLÉES OF THE FOREST OF CHANTILLY	176
A Typical English Hunting Country	176
Negotiating a Virginia Stone Wall MRS. THOMAS ON PIPE DREAM	177
The Snake or Worm Fence, with Stakes and Riders MRS. THOMAS ON COMMODORE GAUNT	177
The Red Fox (*Vulpes fulvus*)	188
The Grey Fox (*Urocyon cinereo-argentatus*)	188

INTRODUCTION

Hounds and Hunting through the Ages was one of Derrydale's best-selling titles. First published in 1928, the entire initial print run—50 deluxe editions and 750 trade editions—were out of print within a year, leaving a backlog of orders. Two hundred fifty more books were printed to meet the backlog. In 1933 Derrydale founder Eugene V. Connett issued the Windward House edition. The book was reprinted by Garden City Publishing Company in 1937 and again in 1939.

It was the first comprehensive book on hunting with hounds written by an American. Ancient hunting history, art and literature as well as the nuts and bolts of every facet of contemporary mounted foxhunting were covered. And the author's dedication, signed simply, "Father," in which he offers a lesson in living to his son by examining the virtues and vices of the foxhound—honesty, sagacity, determination, drive, skirting, babbling and dwelling—has long been one of my favorite pieces.

The introduction for the original Derrydale edition was written by the Earl of Lonsdale (the "Yellow Earl"), ex-M.F.H. of the Cottesmore (UK). Mason Houghland, M.F.H. and founder of the Hillsboro Hunt (TN), wrote his famous and oft-reproduced foreword for the Windward House edition. (Mr. Houghland must have liked what he wrote, because sixteen years later he used the very same foreword for his own book, *Gone Away*, published by the Blue Ridge Press.) Mr. Houghland's foreword is included in this edition.

Now that almost three-quarters of a century have passed since the books' debut, and we are able to view the author through the telescope of perspective, I decided to take a different approach from those of my legendary predecessors and devote this commentary to the man. Joseph B. Thomas was born in Boston in 1879, but pursued his career as an architect in New York. A proponent of the American foxhound, he was a leader among sportsmen and one of the twentieth century's foremost hound breeders.

In 1912, because the Masters of Foxhounds Association under A. Henry Higginson's presidency refused to keep studbook records of American foxhounds, Mr. Thomas called together nine other sportsmen and founded the American Foxhound Club "to encourage the systematic breeding and general use of American foxhounds in the United States." (Notwithstanding Mr. Higginson's love for English hounds and disdain for American hounds, he did have a measure of justification for refusing to keep studbook records of the latter; the accuracy and authenticity of American foxhound pedigrees of the period was certainly not up to the standards of the pedigrees of English foxhounds.) The AFC was the precursor of today's Foxhound Club of North America, the organization that sanctions and supports the major hound shows across North America (and the recently-instituted foxhound performance trials), its principal goal being the improvement of the breed.

One year earlier, Mr. Thomas had bought a farm in Middleburg, Virginia—Huntlands—and had begun construction of a major kennel and stable complex. Inspired by his Massachusetts friend, Harry Worcester Smith, Mr. Thomas began to assemble his pack of foxhounds with the help of his new huntsman, Charlie Carver (*The American Foxhound, 1747–1967*, Alexander Mackay-Smith, The American Foxhound Club, 1968). From 1911 to 1919, he supplied the hounds for both the Piedmont and the Middleburg packs. He became Master of the Piedmont Fox Hounds in 1915 and for the next four years fielded the finest pack of American foxhounds in the country and "showed sport of a caliber perhaps unequaled in the history of organized foxhunting in North America" (*American Foxhunting Stories*, Alexander Mackay-Smith, Millwood House, 1996, page 142).

The Middleburg-Piedmont hunting country, however, seems to have bred discord and dissension then as now. In a dispute with his former friend, Dan Sands, ex-Master of the Piedmont and the Middleburg hunts, Mr. Thomas resigned as Master of the Piedmont in 1919. He established Mr. Thomas' Hounds at his summer kennels at Ashby's Gap in the nearby Blue Ridge Mountains and, with his superb huntsman, Charlie Carver, began a program of hound breeding on a prodigious scale. At any given time, he often owned as many as one thousand foxhounds.

How did he manage this staggering number of hounds? He placed many of his bitches, bred to his stallion hounds, with night hunting farmers across Northern Virginia. He paid board for these hounds and their puppies to the farmers, who used them for their own sport, but he reserved the right to buy back any puppies he wanted for $50 each. These were prosperous times; new hunts were being started around the country; and Mr. Thomas was able to provide entire packs of entered hounds to new hunts. In 1926, for example, he helped to start five new packs!

Finally, in 1931 the MFHA published its first *Foxhound Kennel Studbook* listing American hounds in addition to the English. Mr. Thomas submitted 182 hounds, the largest number of any of the twenty-nine packs which maintained American hounds. According to entries in that and subsequent *Foxhound Kennel Studbooks*, hounds directly from Joseph B. Thomas were to be found in thirty-two organized packs of the time.

Joseph B. Thomas's influence on the American foxhound was enormous. His foundation bloodlines, which he bought and bred, were mostly old Virginia and Bywaters strains. He acquired hounds of the Brooke strain from Maryland and later out-crossed to Trigg hounds, both of which undoubtedly infused the bloodlines of Mountain and Muse, the famous and highly prepotent Irish hounds imported to Maryland in 1814. Today, the progeny of Mr. Thomas's breeding still thrive in the finest packs of American and Crossbred hounds in the country.

Norman M. Fine
Editor, *Covertside*
June 2000

FOREWORD

Fox-hunting is not merely a sport—and it is more nearly a passion than a game. It is a religion, a racial faith. In it are the elements that form the framework upon which beliefs are built: the attempt at escape from life as it is to life as we would have it; an abiding love of beauty; and an unconscious search for the eternal verities of fair play, loyalty and sympathetic accord, which are so clouded in our mundane existence.

It is a primitive faith, a "survival" the sociologist would term it, and harks back to the clear and simple outlook of our tribal gods. Through the years it goes on because, after the flush of many dawns, the thrill of never-ending pursuit, the sweet spice of danger, the simple tragedies of the field, and the weary darkness of long roads home, a few always become attuned to Nature's wondrous harmony of which they themselves are a part.

Like all religions it has many sects. There are the very "High Church" hunters with carefully observed ritual, who need form to guard the spirit and ceremonial to nourish belief. It is these Brahmans of the chase who make the picture the world sees, the scarlet coats on green fields, the great leaps, the beautiful backgrounds. They play a great part and merit the recognition of great effort. But in shadowy outline beyond them, outnumbering them a hundred to one, are legions of Fox-hunters, like Franciscan Brothers, whose profession of faith neither poverty nor sacrifice can dim, some who must even deny themselves the necessities in order to keep a couple of hounds.

On horseback, on mule back, or more often afoot, every night of the year, somewhere in every state in the Union, the horns of this great army of "hill-toppers" awaken the echoes of field and of forest.

I sometimes wonder if there have ever been but three great books written upon any subject we call Sport. I am convinced that this book is one of them. It belongs to all Fox-hunters alike, the "Meltonian" and the "Hill-Topper."

Mason Houghland, M. F. H.

September 26, 1933.
  Green Pastures,
    Brentwood, Tennessee.

CHAPTER I.

FUNDAMENTALS AND TRADITIONS

WHY should people of our day enjoy hunting when there are so many other diversions? The answer must be, it is in the blood—hereditary instinct impels, for the *genus homo* has been a hunter since man began, first from necessity, then for pleasure, and without doubt will so remain until he ceases to exist. History through the ages is interspersed with most vivid and impressive references to the definite appeal of hunting. In all countries, all sorts and conditions of men, from princes to peasants, have since time immemorial been imbued with the lure of the chase, coupled with the struggle for existence.

Granted, that man first had to hunt to live, anthropologists have sought to attain definite chronological data regarding the antiquity of hunting. Deposits found with skeletal remains of Paleolithic man show that animals were hunted one hundred and twenty-five thousand years ago. The so-called "hunting race," Neanderthal man, who lived forty thousand years ago, left relics notably in the caves of Dordogne, relics which indicate that the chase had progressed to the point where its influence was expressed in the rudiments of craftsmanship—even thoughts of hunting in the after life had developed, as proved by the implements found buried with their dead.

Though the Bible rarely mentions hunting, the name *Nimrod* has become almost the generic name for huntsman. His kingdom was Babel, Erech, Accad, and Calneh in the land of Shinar; he built Nineveh, and of him it is written:

. . . and Nimrod . . . began to be a mighty one in the earth . . . he was a mighty hunter before the Lord: wherefore it is said, even as Nimrod the mighty hunter before the Lord.—GENESIS x, 8-12.

Many are the hunting myths of the Golden Age of Greece: Adonis, beloved by Venus, slain by a boar while hunting; Orion, the great hunter, transformed into the constellation so conspicuous in November, the month of the Hunter's Moon; Actaeon, victim of Diana's wrath, changed by her into a stag because he, while hunting, chanced to see her bathing; Acastos and Meleager, heroes of the famous Calydonian boar-hunt.

In the heyday of Greece, stress was laid on sport as a school for war; Lycurgus ordered children to be sent out hunting, to avoid becoming unfit and lazy; Xenophon, in the fifth century before Christ, urged hunting for all men, as prompting them to rise early, inuring them to heat and cold, sharpening their wits, being good for the health, perfecting the sense of observation and hearing, delaying senile decay, and generally keeping them fit and prepared for military duty.

The Greeks seem to have passed on to the Romans their art of hunting, and many famous Romans were great hunters, among whom were Scipio and Pliny II. Caesar mentions, apparently with surprise, that the Gauls "coursed for the sport and not to live by what they caught." Caesar also records that those young Gauls were most honored who brought home the greatest number of trophies of the chase, such as antlers and horns of stags and aurochs. These trophies were offered as sacrifices to the glories of Diana and Apollo. Another Roman, Juvenal, referring to the City of Cynopolis, attests:

Oppida tota canem venerantur, nemo Dianam.

The press of the present century daily informs us of current events, not the least of which is progress in sporting activities. The general public is never so tensely thrilled as when an international event is to be staged; leaders in every form of sport are lauded. This is no modern innovation, for in classic times similar public enthusiasm for sport existed, and honors seem to have been divided between the Gods of War and the Goddess of the Chase.

Exhaustive research brings us to more recent times through successive references to general enthusiasm for the chase. Certain records point out the fact that in far off India, the Rajputs, descended from the same stock as the Greeks and the Gauls, are to this day mighty hunters. Old Tod, in his classic, *Antiquities of Rajasthan*, mentions the famous Prithi Raj as being so addicted to the sport that he was a poacher of the first magnitude, and thus began many wars with his neighbors; hunting, as training for character, is so highly thought of that the first "kill" made by the sons of a Rajput family is celebrated in state.

Throughout Asia, the chase was held in high esteem, even among the Scythic Tartars; the heir of Genghis Khan was appointed chief huntsman, that being the highest position that the state could offer. This enthusiasm for hunting was handed down through the Mogul Empire, among the descendants of the great Khan, to modern times, viz., a hunting excursion of Asoph Ul Doulah, Grand Visier and Nabob of Oude, is described by an English eye witness, in India, in 1785:

A circuit of from four to six hundred miles was covered during the cool season, from December to March. The personnel consisted of the court, the

The Gold Fan. The king hunting ostrich for plumes used in the fan.

Hunting scene on a cosmetic jar.   The King with his slughi hound, slaying a lion.

HUNTING SCENES FROM RELICS IN THE TOMB OF TUT-ANKH-AMEN.

GREEK HUNTER WITH FOX, HARE, AND HOUND.

HOUNDS, HORSE, AND FALCON OF WILLIAM THE CONQUEROR.
From the Bayeux Tapestry.

FUNDAMENTALS AND TRADITIONS

entire household, and a vast number of retainers, mounted musicians, mounted troops and artillery, estimated at twenty thousand souls in all. The animals included four or five hundred elephants for riding, fighting, carrying baggage, and clearing the jungle; five or six hundred beautiful Persian and Arabian horses, and about three hundred dogs, principally greyhounds; at least two hundred hawks, and trained swift leopards, called *cheetahs*, for catching deer. The equipment included carts for the women, a couple of English chaises, a buggy, a chariot, and several palanquins; tents of luxurious character, and paraphernalia for hot baths; vast quantities of matchlocks, pistols, bows and arrows, swords, sabres, and daggers composed the arms. A complete moving town attended the Nabob's camp, and every luxury was transported, even ice for the drinking water and making sherbets; the fruits of the season and fresh vegetables were sent on daily from the capital by relay bearers who traveled day and night, at a pace of four miles an hour. As divertisements, in addition to fighting elephants, there were fighting antelopes, fighting buffaloes, fighting rams, and gamecocks.

In Africa and Central America, historic records of hunting still exist, carved in stone monuments of lost civilizations.

In Europe, from the beginning of its history, all phases of the chase have been enthusiastically followed. In the sixth century, the Merovingian kings of France hunted extensively, and even lost their lives in the sport, as when Theodubert was gored by an aurochs. Poaching was severely punished, as is shown by the incident which occurred in the reign of Gontran, son of Clotaire, who, finding the remains of an aurochs in the Vosges forest where he was hunting, was informed by the gamewarden that the poacher was his chamberlain. Gontran put the chamberlain to death.

In the eighth century, perhaps the outstanding feature in the development of the chase was the definite association of the Christian religion with hunting, through the famous romance of St. Hubert, Christian patron saint of the hunt (as Diana was pagan protectress of the chase), whose story often appears in romance and art. Hubert, the "Brightwitted," held a prominent place in the court of the Frankish king, Theodoric. He was passionately fond of hunting, but with the death of his wife he retired to the monastery of Stavelot, and was appointed Bishop of Liège and of Tongres, by Pope Sergius I. He died in 727, and his remains were put in a Benedictine cloister in the Ardennes, ultimately a resort of pilgrims. St. Hubert's Day, November the third, is still celebrated by huntsmen in France and Belgium. His conversion to Christianity was brought about while he was hunting on Good Friday, by the miraculous appearance of a milk-white stag bearing between his horns a beaming cross. As patron of hunters, he is invoked in cases of hydrophobia; and the Bavarian, Bohemian, and Cologne orders of knighthood have been under his protection.

HOUNDS AND HUNTING

On through the Middle Ages, hunting was almost a mania. Many are the intriguing tales indicative of continued general enthusiasm for this sport, including continued close association with religion. The pious son of Charlemagne, Emperor Louis, was unable to prevent the high clergy and the priests, even abbesses, from hunting. In 968, the Evêque Archambault seized an abbey from which he violently expelled the Sisters, in order to make room for his hounds and hawks. It is recounted that the animals perished, struck by celestial vengeance. This form of ardor for the chase seems to have reached a climax when Gaston de Foix (to us the best-known hunter of the Middle Ages, because of his *Livre de Chasse*, 1387) argued that a good hunter is by far more likely to enter paradise than any other man. The views of the clergy seem to have been in accordance with this opinion, for when Francis I arranged the famous *Concordat* with Pope Leo X, the king was obliged to introduce an article curbing their sporting ardor. The Holy Father himself, who was a very keen "Chasseur," hunted in spectacles, clothed in a manner which scandalized not a little the more devout Romans.

Throughout Europe, from the time of Charlemagne, hunting and war were the two favorite pursuits of great personages. Innumerable are the historic characters from Roland and the Emperor Maximilian to Louis XVI, not to mention saints and many famous sinners who were devotees of the chase.

In the First Crusade, the knights traversed Europe and Asia Minor preceded by their packs of hounds, and with falcons on their wrists. The chronicle mentions the death of these noble hawks in the desert of Phrygia, where five hundred Crusaders died in a single day, the balance of the army being saved only because the hounds discovered water. At the time of the Second Crusade, in 1142, the Pope, Eugene III, found it necessary to forbid the Christian knights to take any hunting equipment with them, but it is not known to what extent this rule was obeyed. In any case, in the following Crusades, we find Philip-Augustus, Richard Cœur de Lion, and the companions of St. Louis, proceeding to Palestine with hounds and hawks. One chronicler states:

They hunted in Syria as in France, they hunted everywhere, in the open, at religious festivals, between battles, between church services; they hunted even in their sleep.

This habit of combining war with hunting outlived the crusades. We are told that when the English invaded France, in 1359, King Edward III had for his private use thirty mounted falconers, more than sixty couple of large hounds, and as many greyhounds, while many of the noblemen with him also had hounds and hawks of their own.

Equally interesting hunting data are identified with succeeding wars, significant of the unabated attention given to this sporting art. Coming to the

FUNDAMENTALS AND TRADITIONS

campaign of Salamanca, in 1812, when the Duke of Wellington was commander-in-chief of the Spanish army, we read:

Amid all the necessities which pressed on him from the beginning of the siege of Burgos, Wellington yet had thoughts to spare for lighter matters. Always a keen foxhunter, he encouraged his officers to follow hounds, which he kept during this campaign. On October 14, he wrote his adjutant general, who had gone home on sick leave, 'Goodman is now doing the duty of the office, poor Waters being very ill. I hope we shall soon have Waters again, particularly as the hunting season is going on apace. The hounds are on the road, and I shall want Waters for the earth-stopping business.' Again, on November 3, when in full retreat before Soult, 'If you should be pressed by the enemy, and if you should move, take care that all our stores and people (including my hounds at Arevalo) move off.' Wellington kept eight good hunters, besides seven chargers, sixteen couple of hounds,—an uneven lot, carried no head, and seldom killed a fox, owing to the difficulty Colonel Waters found in stopping the country effectively . . . but Wellington, who cared little for scientific hunting and only wanted lots of exercise, was quite content with the character of the sport.

Again, directly following the downfall of Napoleon, when Wellington was in command of the occupation of France, there were two packs of hounds hunted from his quarters at Cambrai, one, the Duke's own pack, and the other belonging jointly to Sir Harry Smith and Major William Havelock.

Even during the late World War, in several instances, packs were kept by British regiments in France, and one British regimental pack got as far as the plains of Italy. Also, the A. E. F., when stationed at Coblentz, under that best of sportsmen, Major-General Henry T. Allen, had their pack of hounds, some of which I sent them from the States. At Coblentz, much polo and sports of all kinds were abetted by the Commanding General, who had, when still a subaltern military attaché at St. Petersburg, imported some of the first Russian wolfhounds (*borzoi*) to America. Later, this same officer fought gallantly and successfully for polo and sports in the army.

Throughout history, patrons of art and literature who loved the chase have constantly endeavored, by commanding the bards, artists, and artisans of their times, to immortalize their favorite sport by means of the arts, and thus have ended by immortalizing themselves. Of such princely patrons, Francis I, of France, was perhaps the greatest—his ardor for the arts was only exceeded by his passion for hunting.

He had formed what he called 'the little Band' of the court ladies, who seemed to him the prettiest and most agreeable. With these ladies he frequently went on hunting trips. The Dauphiness [Catherine de Medici] begged to be allowed to go along, and she proved to be such a good sportswoman that he finally gave her standing permission to hunt with him whenever she wished to do so. She was a bold rider and looked well in the saddle. She apparently introduced into France

[5]

something like the modern side-saddle. Brantôme says that it was suggested to him by some of her ladies-in-waiting that she did this in order to make the best possible use of her natural advantages for the display of the fine hosiery for whose quality and proper adjustment she took the greatest care. But then Brantôme was more than inclined to take gossip for gospel. On one of these parties, her horse bolted with her, broke the horn of the saddle against the roof of a shed, and threw her to the ground so hard that she was very badly bruised. The king took such affectionate care of her that Catherine could hardly have regretted this first of a number of accidents which befell her because of her fondness for riding.

The King rode in a stag hunt nearly every day in the week. He used to say that, when he was old and sick, he would be carried after the hounds in a litter, and even added perhaps he would give orders for his dead body to be carried a-hunting in a coffin. His eldest son, Henry, was a tireless hunter, and one of the best young men in France at the dangerous game of the tournament.

Hounds and falcons, from the earliest times, have been considered the most complimentary gifts between sovereigns. For example, Lord Hastings, Minister of Edward IV, on behalf of his king, presented to Louis XI "greyhounds, an Irish pony, and a quiet hackney." Oftentimes, feudal obligations were paid in hounds and hawks, custom, in some cases, requiring that a vassal maintain the hunting equipment of the lord.

In the private life of feudal times, hunting was of much import. In the frequent banquets of the nobility, suggestions of the chase were often made a part of the entertainment. In the fifteenth century, during a state banquet given by Philippe le Bon, of Burgundy, a heron was loosed in the air from one end of the great hall. At the same time, from the other end of the hall a falconer flew a hawk which attacked the heron in mid-air with such *élan* that together they fell to the floor in the center of the great hall, and were, according to the etiquette of falconry, presented to His Grace. During the same feast, there was heard from the inside of a gigantic decorative pastry the sound of a hunt, the cry of hounds, the huntsman's cheer and horn.

In olden days, hounds and hunting were interwoven with the daily lives of all classes of landed proprietors to an extent unknown to-day. Up to the seventeenth century, it was often customary not only to allow hounds to enter the houses at any time, but to live habitually in the great hall, doubtless often to the distress of the chatelaine. A particular protest, describing in detail what the hounds did in the house that they should not do, has come down to us in quaint French. The hounds of Louis XIII often slept in his chamber. The duc de Vendôme, conqueror of Viciosa, even went further in this respect: "The dogs slept *en masse* in his bed; bitches had their puppies there," says Saint-Simon. His brother, the *grande prieur*, had the same custom. To this day, in England, one may see ancient dog gates at the foot of stairways to prevent ill-timed canine intrusions to the master's sleeping quarters.

FUNDAMENTALS AND TRADITIONS

Custis relates that one of Washington's French hounds, named *Vulcan* (on whose back Custis had often ridden when a child), was permitted to enter the house. On one occasion, it happened that upon a large company sitting down to dinner at Mt. Vernon, the lady of the mansion discovered that the ham, the pride of every Virginia housewife's table, was missing from its accustomed post of honor. Upon questioning, Frank the butler—this most polite and accomplished of all butlers—observed that a very fine ham had been prepared according to Madam's orders, but that *Vulcan* had entered the kitchen while savory ham was smoking in the dish, and without more ado had fastened his fangs in it. Although they of the kitchen fought the old spoiler desperately, yet *Vulcan* had finally triumphed and borne off the prize. The lady uttered remarks by no means favorable to old *Vulcan*, while the chief, having heard the story, communicated it to his guests and with them laughed heartily.

In Italy, hunting existed, although perhaps not so strenuously practiced as in other countries. Isabella d'Este, writing to her husband on the 27th of August, 1492, gives a delightful picture of Italian hunting in mediaeval days as follows:

To-day we went out hunting in a beautiful valley which seemed as if it were expressly created for the spectacle. All the stags were driven into the wooded valley of the Ticino, and closed in on every side by the hunters, so that they were forced to swim the river and ascend the mountains, where the ladies watched them from under the pergola and green tents set up on the hillside. We could see every movement of the animals along the valley and up the mountain-side, where the dogs chased them across the river; but only two climbed the hillside and ran far out of sight. Afterwards came a doe with its young one, which the dogs were not allowed to follow. Many wild boars and goats were found, but only one boar was killed before our eyes, and one wild goat, which fell to my share. Last of all came a wolf which made fine somersaults in the air as it ran past us, and amused the whole company. And so, with much laughter and merriment, we returned home, to end the day at supper, and give the body a share in the recreations of the mind.

Paramount love for the chase has always been a characteristic of Britishers of high and low estate, and hunting has been held in honor from the earliest period, but remote records are few and far between. Strabo, in the first century, notes the excellence of British hounds. As early as the ninth century, and possibly before, hunting constituted an essential part of the education of a young nobleman, as in the early days of Greece. Asser, writing of the Saxons, says that Alfred the Great, before he was twelve years of age, was a most expert and active hunter, and excelled in all the branches of that most noble art. Edward the Confessor delighted "to follow a pack of swift hounds in pursuit of game, and to cheer them with his voice," William of Malmesbury relates.

HOUNDS AND HUNTING

From the time of the first pirate duke of Normandy, the science of venery held a high rank in the ducal house, and William the Conqueror, in the eleventh century, may be said in a sense to have been the father of modern English hunting; at all events, his enthusiasm bore lasting results. He included in his domain all the large forests in the kingdom, and reserved exclusive hunting rights. He ordered that anyone who killed a dog should have his eyes put out, and in a similar manner he protected all game. Poachers, in the cruel manner of the times, could be killed without compunction by the gamewardens, and the dogs of neighboring nobles were not permitted to trouble the king's preserves. Not satisfied with the immense extent of his forests, he destroyed thirty-six parishes, drove out the inhabitants, and planted with trees a vast tract of over thirty miles between Salisbury and the sea, which tract is still known as the New Forest. It will be remembered that William Rufus, son of the conqueror, met his death at the hands of an enraged peasant whose home had been destroyed, in order to make this same preserve.

The following "paraphrase" from an English romance-poem of 1360 indicates that hunting was then highly developed:

The cunning huntsman coupled the hounds (greyhounds) opened the kennel doors and called them out, and blew three bold, clear notes on the bugles. The hounds the hunters stirred, a hundred hunters of the best . . . Before the cackling cock had crowed three times, the Lord leapt from his bed and all the people who would go a-hunting. Uncoupled among the thorns the hounds did race (forty bloodhounds), and all the hounds swayed together between a pool in the wood and the cliff . . . The fox tricked them with many quick turns and dodged in and out, and would pause and listen by many a hedgerow . . . and ever the hounds were at his tail that he might not tarry . . . and there in front of the horse they all fell on him and worried the wily fellow to death with a loud noise. The lord alighted, tore him out of the mouths of the dogs, and held him high over his head, hallooing, the while many a brave hound bayed him there. With jest the hounds they did reward.

Foxhunting in England is again mentioned in a charter given to the Abbot of Peterborough in the reign of Richard II (1377-1399), but did not become at all general till the eighteenth century.

As a reflection of this universal interest among Britons in hunting, Somerville, in 1735, fires the imagination in his immortal poem, *The Chace*, with such words as these:

>*While crowded theatres, too fondly proud*
>*Of their exotic minstrels, and shrill pipes,*
>*The price of manhood, hail thee with a song*
>*And airs soft warbling; my hoarse sounding horn*

FUNDAMENTALS AND TRADITIONS

Invites thee to the chase, the sport of kings;
Image of war, without its guilt . . . . .

Where are their sorrows, disappointments, wrongs,
Vexations, sickness, cares? All, all, are gone!
And with the panting winds lag far behind.

It is related that Westminster Bridge, in London, was built as the result of enthusiasm for foxhunting, in that the Duke of Grafton, coming down from London to hunt at Croydon, was so annoyed by the irregularity of the ferry that he had a bill passed in 1736 to erect this bridge across the Thames.

Of Sir Robert Walpole, the famous British Prime Minister, and a keen foxhunter, who died in 1745, it is recorded that he gave preference to letters from his huntsman over any matters of state. It is related that Sir Robert brought about the Saturday holiday of Parliament, so that he might hunt the fox at least one day a week. The late Duke of Beaufort, when showing me his wonderful pack at Badminton, in 1922, had to be taken about in a wheel chair, as the result of a bad fall from his coach. He was still so keen on hunting, however, that he followed hounds in a Ford car, even through the gates and across the fields of his marvelous country. In the current year, 1928, we find this enthusiasm reflected on a piece of paper attached to the will of Captain Arthur Marmaduke Whitaker, late Duke of Wellington's regiment, which reads:

Wishes for my wife to carry out at my death: I trust (should it be suggested) that if I die in the hunting season, hounds will not be stopped on my account as I never can understand why people should be made more miserable than necessary.

Lord North, in his ninety-first year, 1927, is a striking example of undying love of the chase. For many years master of foxhounds, he now continues to hunt with his pack of bassets, following in a carriage, and alighting from time to time to gain access to spots where wheels cannot go. The general attitude of Britishers toward sport is again well expressed in Lord North's dedication to his grandchildren of his book entitled, *Hunting*:

I now dedicate this book to you, my dear grandchildren, because I want you to grow up good country gentlemen, doing your duty by your sovereign, your country and your neighbors, rich and poor, and fulfilling all the obligations of your station, and versed in all those pursuits and occupations which make a country life so pleasant and happy. I want you to grow up sportsmen—not, mind you, sporting men—for there is a vast difference between a sportsman and a sporting man.

As in France, so in England have women often been passionately fond of the chase. Queen Elizabeth was as fond of hawking as of following the hounds. It is written that in her seventy-seventh year the Queen was "excellently disposed to hunting, for every second day she is early on horseback, and enjoys the sport long." In the eighteenth century, Lady Salisbury was M. F. H. of the Hertfordshire Hounds, and only gave up this position when she was seventy-eight. Nevertheless, in the early part of the nineteenth century, it does not seem to have been fashionable for women to hunt to any extent, and only toward the middle of that century did their delightful presence in the field become usual, until to-day the women followers of hounds in England sometimes outnumber the men.

Interest in the chase among Frenchmen is sometimes overlooked by their English-speaking brethren, and it is perhaps not generally known that the first pack of hounds maintained especially for foxhunting in France (possibly in any country) was kept by Louis XIII. This pack, which still existed in 1691, was part of the seventy-five couple of scenting hounds and thirty leash of greyhounds following in the suite of the king on all his travels, and was accompanied by terriers. A complete set of digging tools was also carried. Keenness for foxhunting seems to have been not only a royal prerogative, for the compte de Toulouse hunted fox at any time of year, it being recorded that July 1st, 1712, the duc de Berry and the duchesse de Bourgogne went at three o'clock in the morning to take part in one of these hunts. Individual instances of similar enthusiasm for the hunt may be illustrated as follows:

In the reign of Louis XIV, Saint-Simon relates that the duc de la Rochefoucauld, having become almost blind of old age, and no longer being able to ride a horse, hunted in a *calèche.* The archbishop of Lyon, brother of the maréchal de Villeroy, had a superior pack, and although he became blind toward the close of his life, he continued to hunt on horseback between two grooms. Louis XIV hunted until he was a very old man, and on August 9, 1715, at the age of seventy-seven, three weeks before he died, he hunted in a carriage but for the last time. In spite of his natural nonchalance, Louis XV, says the marquis d'Argenson, "worked like a dog for his hounds. At the beginning of the year, he arranged what should be done to the end." He had five or six packs, and it is claimed that His Majesty directed his finances and war orders with much less care than his hunting schedule. It is said that between 1732 (when he first began to hunt) and 1749 his several packs killed three thousand deer.

Ardent enthusiasm for the chase still exists amongst French country gentlemen. In 1927, I had the pleasure of visiting the *doyen* of French masters, M. René Clayeux, at the château des Gouttes, in the department of Allier. Hale and hearty at eighty-two, this splendid old sportsman still acts as his own huntsman in the chase of the roe-deer. When the World War ended, his fine pack which had been his life's work to develop was reduced to one solitary couple. Nevertheless, in spite of his seventy-one years, he again set to work with undiminished enthusiasm, and has built up his present even

FUNDAMENTALS AND TRADITIONS

pack of large black and white hounds. M. Fernand Roy, the famous French race starter, so beloved by the jockeys, a well-known race rider, and sportsman from boyhood, who has hunted many years (especially with Mr. Prince's hounds, at Pau), was still hunting with enthusiasm in his eighty-fourth year (1927).

Not only French men of our day, but French women also, have real enthusiasm for hunting, as witnessed by the aged duchesse d'Uzes, who for many hound generations has been master of her own pack, which hunts the forest of Rambouillet. She still carries on, in spite of wars and vicissitudes. Her kennels, located in an ancient château in the forest region, are most interesting. The walls of the great mediaeval banqueting hall are adorned with hundreds of trophies, bearing mute testimony to the prowess of her hounds.

Americans, too, as well as kings and noblemen, who were really keen on hunting, have ridden in carriages when advanced age or mishaps prevented mounted hunting. Mr. Maupin, the famous Kentucky foxhunter, whose unusual given name was "General George Washington," and who has been called the John Peel of America, died on January 15, 1868, at the home of his sons, in Madison County, where most of his hounds were kept. General Maupin had gone there to hunt, but was so ill that it was found necessary to take him to the field on a mattress in a wagon, that he might hear the cry of the pack which had meant so much to him through life. As he lay there, Dr. Maupin, one of his attendants (and, incidentally, one of his nephews), rode up and asked him how he felt. "Better," replied the old man, with some vigor, "better from listening to that pack than all your medicine can make me."

Allen Potts in his rare book, *Fox Hunting in America* (1912), tells of one American master whose record of more than fifty years in the field is comparable to that of Boothby, John Warde, and others in England:

I remember very distinctly hunting in the Isle of Wight County, Virginia, on February 6, 1905, with Mr. Julius Octavius Thomas, who on that day celebrated his seventy-first birthday, and also celebrated on the same date the fiftieth anniversary of his mastership of hounds. For a half century he had hunted regularly every season in Four Square, his ancestral home, except during the four years of the [Civil] war, and the hounds behind which we rode in 1905 were the descendants of the pack which the gentleman hunted in 1855.... On that day grandsons were riding in the place of their grandfathers of fifty years before ... and the very hunting horns belonged to sportsmen, long since dead, who rode and cheered the hounds in the days when the master of Four Square was but a boy.

A remarkable story of enthusiasm for hounds is recounted by that great Kentucky hound breeder, Samuel L. Wooldridge, of a blind man who had hunted all his life by ear, and had himself driven several hundred miles from the State of Ohio simply that he might be allowed to see through his fingers the famous hound, *Big Stride*, owned by Mr. Wooldridge. When the hound was brought to him, the blind man fell to his knees and most intelligently acquainted himself with every fine point of the hound's conformation. Incidentally, *Big Stride* was worthy of such interest as the best-known hound of his day. On his gravestone appears this inscription: "Opinions die; records live."

Never shall I forget the arrival, one day, at my Huntland kennels, in Loudoun County, Virginia, in 1918, of B. F. Bywaters and Judd Welsh. The combined ages of these grand old Virginia farmer-sportsmen then approximated one hundred and fifty years, and their combined weight was over five hundred pounds. They had bred many of the progenitors of my pack, and on this particular day, being physically unable to ride on horseback, they had come over forty miles of execrable roads, each in his hunting buggy, to see my hounds, which was a rare compliment. In the winter of 1923, when over eighty years of age, Mr. Bywaters had a splendid hunt with his pack, driving in his famous buggy. By good luck, he fell in with his hounds at the crucial moment, and saw them pull down their fox on the slopes of Battle Mountain, in Rappahannock County. Returning triumphantly to his home, followed by his beloved hounds now blissfully content, Mr. Bywaters fell asleep, doubtless with happy dreams, and never awoke again in this Vale of Tears. What more could a true foxhunter desire?

> *And thus Ropero dy'd at Eighty fower*
> *A quick and sudden death, and in the Field.*
> *Could Julius Caesar ere hav wisht for more.*

By the expressed wish of Mr. Bywaters, his pall-bearers were all foxhunters. His old horse, *Pollock*, was buried near him.

As has been indicated, up to the Revolution in France, all great nobles had their private hunts, and this custom existed in Russia until very recent times. As far back as 1260, the German ambassador to the Grand Duke of Novgorod wrote extensively in his reports of hunting dogs. Great pomp and pageantry seems to have been customary in Russia as in most continental hunting. As late as 1903, I visited the establishment of the Grand Duke Nicholas of Russia, which, with its one hundred couple of foxhounds and one hundred leash of *borzoi* (Russian wolfhounds), not to mention one hundred hunt horses, all roans, reminded me of mediaeval hunting. In Russia, by the way, the horses of each nobleman's hunt were all of one color, one master having only piebalds in his hunt, another greys, and so on. The hunting preserves of the Grand Duke Nicholas extended over two hundred thousand acres. The game, which was rigorously protected and fed in winter when necessary, was wolf, fox, and hare. The establishment of the Grand Duke was laid out in "the grand manner"; the ten individual stucco kennels for the *borzoi*, each with a grass court, flanked the dip of a valley aligned with the magnificent hunting lodge of Italian architecture. At the far end of the valley, the foxhound kennels designed in keeping with the lodge, completed the rectangle.

Formerly, no doubt, falconry existed in Russia as elsewhere in Europe, but in 1903 that phase of the sport had disappeared, except among the nomad tribes to the east of the Volga. Speaking of falconry, the term "mews", still used in London to designate the yard-like stables found in fashionable and once-fashionable districts, is derived from the aviaries where in mediaeval times falcons were kept in the moulting season. The term has even reached New York, where we have a "Washington Mews," once stables, now studios.

If the date 1690 is correct for the first pack of hounds kept exclusively for foxhunting in England, as we are told, it can be said (without trepidation) that foxhound packs have existed in America almost as long as they have in the Mother Country. Staghunting with a pack, in the European manner, never has existed in America, and, as there were no large native hare in the East, that sport was necessarily also non-existent.

Throughout America, since early Colonial days, the cry of foxhounds has been heard from the forests of the North to the broad fields of Pennsylvania, Maryland, and Virginia, across the pine-clad, sandy stretches of the Carolinas, and even to the cane brakes of Louisiana. Carrying out the time-honored custom of hounds as courtesy gifts, Lafayette sent several couple of French hounds to George Washington whose diary contains scarcely a page dwelling on his domestic life that has no mention of foxhunting; there are at least two hundred references made to individual hunts, with results recorded, mention of companions, weather, and scenting conditions. His enthusiasm for hunting was so great that even on days of important events in his household he could not be deterred from indulging in his favorite sport, as lines from his diary illustrate.

Often Washington's concern is shown for his pack; he regrets and chafes, because his hounds cannot have better supervision, especially in breeding, for he recognized the points of a good hound, and believed that with proper care he could produce a worthy pack. His periodical absences from home, however, made necessary by his public duties, gave rise to improper care and supervision, hounds got lost or sick, and puppies were poorly trained. Each day, his first thought was whether it was good for hunting. On days selected for the chase, breakfast was served by the light of a candle, the General always breaking his fast with an Indian corn cake and a bowl of milk, "and ere the cock had 'done salutation to the morn,' the whole cavalcade would often have left the house, and the fox frequently be unkenneled before sunrise,"—a picture not unlike the hunting scene in Sir Gawayne and the Green

HOUNDS AND HUNTING

Knight. Even after the Revolution, *pater patriae* lost no opportunity to try for a fox, taking his hounds along with him on any kind of an errand. It warms one's heart to the great gentleman, and one respects him more than ever, to know that Washington was a *real* foxhunter; one whose greatest interest was in hounds and the results of the chase as a game.

He is spoken of, however, as a fine horseman, riding with "ease, elegance, and power," and was always well mounted. His favorite hunter was named *Blueskin*, because of his peculiar blue-grey color. He always said he required but one good quality in a horse,—"to go along." Will Lee, his huntsman (also friend and neighbor), better known in Revolutionary lore as Billy, rode a horse called *Chinkling*, a surprising leaper, and made very much like its rider, low, but sturdy, and of great bone and muscle. Will had but one order, which was to keep with hounds, and mounted on *Chinkling*, a French horn at his back, he would rush at full speed through brake or tangled wood.

Washington's passion for hunting is most aptly illustrated by the two following excerpts from his diary:

1769—September 22: Went a-hunting and killed a bitch fox in an hour. Returned home with an Ague upon me.

September 23: Went hunting again and suppose I killed a fox, but could not find it. Returned with my ague again.

The earliest organized hunt in America, the Gloucester Foxhunting Club, was founded October 29, 1766, by twenty-seven Philadelphia gentlemen, some of whose family names still are prominent in Pennsylvania. The articles of association begin:

We the subscribers, being about to provide and keep a kennel of foxhounds, do mutually agree with each other in manner following, viz:

That each of us do agree to pay into the hands of such persons of the company as shall hereafter be appointed, the sum of five pounds current money, for the purpose aforesaid. . . .

And it is agreed there shall be two hunting days in each week. . . .

The managers shall be enabled to pay James Massey, our present huntsman, any sum they may think necessary for keeping the dogs, and attending the Company as huntsman. . . .

It is agreed, that at the death of every Fox, one of the Company shall carry about a Cap, to collect what the Company may please to give the huntsman.

At any hunt, if the managers, or any of them are present, they shall prevent the Company from crossing the dogs, when they are dragging.

The Company agree to make good all damages that may be done from hunting. . . .

In 1769, the Club prevailed on Mr. Morris to permit his negro man *Natt* (or, as was well known in after times by the name of *old Natty*, by every urchin in town and country), to be enlisted in their service, for the interest

FRENCH KENNELS OF THE XIVth CENTURY.

Ceiling decoration in authentic design and color, painted on wood by Clara Fargo Thomas, 1925. After the MS. of Gaston de Foix.

FRENCH FOXHUNTING SCENE OF THE XIVth CENTURY.

Painted on wood by Clara Fargo Thomas, 1925. After the illuminated MS. of Gaston de Foix, showing scenting hounds of the period.

EARLY VIRGINIA HUNTING SCENE.
From a contemporary frieze discovered in an old Virginia mansion.
By courtesy of Mrs. Chalmers Wood.

FUNDAMENTALS AND TRADITIONS

of the purchase money of his time and for his apparel, and in case of accident, the Company stipulated to indemnify for damages. The first president was Samuel Morris. In 1775, the pack consisted of about sixteen couple of "choice fleet hounds." In 1778, the pack consisted of eleven couple. Even the Revolution did not entirely destroy the organization, for in 1780, it appears that Mr. Morris was owed £3553-15-9½ (apparently in the depreciated currency of the moment). The Club continued to flourish for fifty-two years, and was dissolved in 1818, the dissolution being due, apparently, to the passiveness of the "fashionable, inactive gallants of the present day."

Previous to 1830, there existed in Charlestown, Massachusetts (now part of the City of Boston), a hunt club that annually elected a president, and held many an informal dinner. According to Sawyer's *Old Charlestown*, meets seem to have been arranged the night before, the hunt members appearing the next day, some on horseback and some in carriages. Among these members were Colonel Samuel Jaques, Isaac Mead, Henry Van Voorhis, Colonel Isaac Smith, John Tapley, Robert Lovering, Isaac Larkin, Samuel Jackson, Arnold Cook of Charlestown, and Messrs. Gibson, Thatcher, Bowditch, Washington Munroe, Peter Brigham of Boston, and Moses Whitney of Waltham. The ten to fifteen couple of hounds, which were taken to the meet in couples, were kenneled, up to 1830, by Colonel Jaques, in Charlestown, at his residence on what is now Washington and Richmond Streets. Later they were kept by him at Ten Hills Farm; still later, by John Tapley, at his residence on Spring Hill, Charlestown (now Somerville). The country hunted was from Charlestown Neck, over Powder House Hill (Somerville), Walnut Hill (now College Hill), on to Medford and Woburn. The favorite rendezvous after hunting in this vicinity was the old Black Horse Tavern.

Intriguing accounts of hunting a century ago in other localities by groups of keen foxhunters analogous to the hunt clubs of the present time are available in the files of the American Turf Register. These accounts reveal the fact that these sportsmen reveled in the beauties of nature as they gathered for their early meets; they had a rare appreciation of good hound work; were thoroughly familiar with the technicalities of breeding; cheerfully acknowledged their own mistakes and defeats; and often expressed unique instances of good sportsmanship,—in fact, neither early hours, all-day runs, nor advancing years could dim their ardor. To quote from "A Morning with the Baltimore Pack of Hounds," in the autumn of 1829 (no doubt run over the same ground hunted in recent years by the Green Spring Valley Hunt):

As we passed from the fumes of the town fairly over the hills into the country, we saw the 'king of day' rising in the east, and as with the wand of Midas, turning every cloud he touched into gold, and presenting to the view a scene, that for gorgeousness and brilliant effulgency, I thought I had never before witnessed. I could not suppress the impious wish for the power of Joshua to arrest him in his career, that I might the longer contemplate the magnificent and heavenly prospect; fleeting as it was splendid, and infinitely grand and beautiful; far beyond the poet's imagination, and the painter's art . . . Mr. P., an old huntsman, who seems to have a sort of presentiment where Reynard has chosen his kennel for the day, threw the dogs into another cover—little Bute gave tongue in a water furrow leading to the cover—others came and verified her report, and after a little perplexity the cry became more animated, swelling by degrees, from the solitary note and occasional check, to the warm and full cry, and lastly the exhilarating burst!! . . . It was fifteen minutes that he doubled in a small thick wood, before he could gain distance sufficient to clear his brush in a brake through an open field. The cry during this time was one incessant roar; each huntsman took his stand in the field, watching with breathless eagerness to see him break away. At last he gained distance, and leaving the cover was tally-ho'd in passing through a corn field about a quarter of a mile. The pack soon came rattling on; as he passed it was evident from his open mouth and the sluggish style in which he moved, that we could not count on a gallant run.

Close at his brush the dogs gallantly entered the next cover, where, each striving for the lead, in less than five minutes more a large red fox was run to earth.

It was the first time I had seen this pack, consisting of seven couple of excellent dogs in the finest order and spirits, though I thought too large a proportion were young, appearing to have been entered this season. A gentleman in company told me he was daily expecting two couple of broke dogs from friends in Virginia.

It was evident that their game could not have stood up half an hour longer, but it was supposed that the old rogue had about daylight put a crippled fat canvas-back under his belt. If he did not, I know who did, not many hours after, by the Grace of God and a good friend in Gay Street; the flavor thereof being in nowise injured, by first a bottle of the genuine J. C. and then another of the good old bang-up T— wine; with such in his cellar, who would not gladly fill the office of—Butler.

From the same magazine, for January, 1830, is offered an interesting excerpt of a "beautiful and animated run with Captains Terrett's and Darne's Hounds, within hearing of the Capitol at Washington":

We met at the turnpike gate on the Virginia side, all parties 'true to time.' Twelve couple of hounds were thrown into cover in rear of Whiteback hall. Several young dogs challenged at once, and in a few seconds old Rattler added his note to the cry now swelling into full chorus. A burst followed, and a gallant red fox broke cover with the hounds not far from his brush. He went away over the fields, and through the enclosures to Col. Hunter's, where he doubled short back, running near the river to the causeway; here he was headed by some carts, which compelled him to go up the Sebastian spring to Hoehill, and was again headed at the City road, and again run for Colonel Hunter's, making the same doubles as be-

FUNDAMENTALS AND TRADITIONS

fore. This time he succeeded in crossing the City road and getting away down the wind, passing through the Arlington fields, and the lawn in front of the house, he went to George town ferry, ran through Cooney neck, and made good the Falls hills: but nothing could save him; for after a chase of one hour and twenty-five minutes, he was fairly run into by eleven *couple of dogs.*

In less than an hour after, the same pack unkenneled a grey fox and killed him in fifteen minutes. The field was more numerous than usual, and all were delighted with the morning's sport.—G.

Again, from the same writer in the American Turf Register:

(Christmas night) Capt. T. and D.'s Hounds had a splendid run today—unkenneled a red fox, near the city road, four miles from the river; went away for the George town ferry, doubled to the right at Mason's mill, passed Custis's, the turnpike gate, Hoehill, doubled at Piney hill, went to Colonel Hunter's brick bridge, Whiteback hall, through Arlington fields, Cooney neck, to the Falls hills, where he was run into in handsome style, in one hour and forty-eight minutes, the distance measuring from point to point, or as the crow would fly, is fifteen or eighteen miles.—G.

Of the hunt country and sport in Fairfax County (Virginia), in 1830, we read:

The country is clear and open, with here and there a copse of wood, or pine thicket, and little or no fencing for miles. From the number and respectability of the field of well-mounted horsemen, and the number, beauty, and condition of the hounds, it is evident that foxhunting has lost none of its charms in Fairfax County. Twenty-one horsemen and twenty-one couple of hounds were at the place agreed upon, at the appointed hour. The pack was thrown off west of the Winchester turnpike; unkenneled a red fox in ten minutes, and drove him at a slashing rate to the center of Ravensworth; where, after a quick succession of doubles, over ground stained by sheep, he was run into and killed; giving us a splendid chase of forty-five minutes. The fox was tally'd every five minutes, and the pack was constantly in our view. In less than an hour after the fox harbour cover was drawn, two red foxes were unkenneled. Thirteen couple went away with one, and eight couple with the other; and both sets of dogs killed their fox in fine style, the first in one and one half hours, the second in less than two hours. Before parting for the night, it was agreed to hunt next day; and, accordingly, we had the same field and the same hounds. A red fox was found, and run to earth in little more than an hour; and another killed in one hour and fifty minutes. This chase was like the first—a straight run of some miles, closing with a quick succession of doubles, over pasture grounds, the fox tally'd every five minutes, and the pack constantly in view. Thus ended two days' sport, rarely equalled in the annals of the chase; and wanting nothing but an uniform dress to give it all the splendour of an English fox hunt, and render it worthy of the pen of a Somerville, or a Beckford.

HOUNDS AND HUNTING

The writer will not speak of the welcome which awaits the stranger's arrival in Fairfax County; nor of the ample board and ample bowl — they are in keeping with the good days of lang syne.

Something of the field-trial spirit is reflected in an account of hunting in North Carolina, in 1830, which describes the Smithfield Hunt in a lively manner, its hounds and its sport, winding up with the following rather taunting notice of the Raleigh Hunt declining a challenge sent to it by the gentlemen of Smithfield:

I observe you have occasional accounts from the Raleigh hunt, who, I am gratified to learn, are doing so much for the improvement of their pack; and though I cannot speak in commendation of its merits at present, I think much credit should be awarded to the gentlemen owners for using that better part of valour, discretion, in declining the contest when the glove was thrown them by a formal challenge from that of Smithfield; proposing at the midway house, each party producing ten dogs in two mornings' efforts to manifest a decided superiority in striking, trailing, fleetness, closeness and energy in running; and, in fine, in all the qualities which constitute the excellent and well trained foxhound; but, I trust, with the return of the season, 'new hopes may spring,' and they may be enabled, with the spirit truly characteristic of the generous sportsman, to pick up the glove with the prospect at least of an energetic contest.—M.

It is astounding to realize that in all parts of the United States to-day there are unquestionably hundreds of thousands of hounds hunting varied game. The number of hunts recognized by the Hunts Committee of the National Steeplechase and Hunt Association is sixty-six. Of this number, Pennsylvania has fifteen, Virginia eleven, New York eight, and Massachusetts seven; more than two-thirds hunt fox, three, only, hunt hare, and the balance hunt a drag; foxhound field trial associations number at least one hundred and fifty, and beagle field trial associations, approximately fifty. However, the greater number of hounds in the United States are owned by individual hunters or farmers.

Foxhunting in America is divided into three categories:

First, the farmer-hunter of the North uses a single, slow, deep-voiced hound, his object being to shoot the fox in his runway, which he is able to do, as foxes in the wooded, hilly north country have very definite crossing points which remain unchanged for generations.

Second, the Kentucky, Missouri, Virginia, and Tennessee farmer-hunters, as well as those of numerous other states, own hounds which they hunt in small packs, meeting by appointment, often on foot. In warm weather, they meet on moonlight nights. Their pleasure is found in the racing of their hounds, which they follow largely by ear; hence, their great regard for good cry, coupled with speed. From this class of hunters have sprung the numerous field trial associations. Perhaps the inception of the field trial can be traced to the Grand Circular Foxhunt, announcement of which appeared in the American Turf Register:

The citizens of Jefferson, Berkeley, and Loudoun counties, Virginia, and Washington county, Maryland, are respectfully invited to a Grand Circular Foxhunt, at Whiting's Neck, on Friday, the 1st day of January, 1830. Note: No cur dogs permitted to enter the circle. A full attendance is requested. By order of the Club.

The letter to the editor enclosing this invitation said that 'at least one hundred and fifty foxhounds will be engaged in the chase; and it is said one thousand people will be employed in keeping guard across the narrows of the Neck, three sides of which are bounded by the Potomac.'

The third, and much less numerous class of advocates of foxhunting ride to hounds in the orthodox English manner.

Throughout the world, as a matter of fact, the sport of riding to hounds has spread wherever the impetus derived from Anglo-Norman tradition has been felt. The Roman Campagna is hunted; the hinterland of the Rock of Gibraltar is hunted; the veldts of South Africa are hunted; Australia has its hunting—even far away New Zealand and India have their regularly organized packs; the Shanghai hunt had the unique distinction of being able to hunt the year round, their quarry being deer, otter, civet, fox, badger, wildcat, and hare.

At various times hunting has been attacked as cruel; but, so far as hunting foxes in America is concerned, where earth-stopping is impossible, this seems a doubtful assumption. Personally, I believe the fox enjoys it as much as anyone; at least, if he didn't he could run immediately to his earth or rocky den from which he could not be extracted. But this he rarely does, deliberately keeping up in front of hounds, and on bad scenting days, at least, amusing himself hugely by moving no faster than hounds move, finally, at his leisure repairing to his domicile.

In one instance, for four and a half hours, a fox thus amused himself in front of my hounds (August 17, 1926). His route covered every bad scenting spot he could pick out; he walked on rocks almost continuously for a half mile; he traversed over three miles of stone walls, and in one place walked a rail fence for three hundred yards, retracing his own steps to add to the fun. When he sometimes is killed in front of hounds, he goes out like a sportsman.

The abyss of death means nothing to an animal; instinct alone impels him to run or fight; and the fox in his flight seems rarely worried. Sometimes, he may almost be credited with a sense of humor. Often have I read of foxes having sufficient *sang froid* to kill poultry while being pursued by hounds. Personal friends, also, have assured me of the truth of such tales. For example, the following stories have been recounted to me, the first by Mrs. J. W. E. Adamthwaite, which I give in her own words:

HOUNDS AND HUNTING

Whilst hunting with the Tipperary Hounds in Ireland, in the winter of 1918, I was lucky enough to observe the following incident. Hounds found a fox in a gorse covert about eight miles from Clonmel, and ran him slowly on a bad scent for about twenty minutes, when there was a check. I was standing in a lane near a farmhouse when the hunted fox came down the field toward me, jumped into the lane and out again into the farmyard. He trotted straight through the farmyard where there was a flock of ducks; picking up one of the ducks by the neck, he went on his way, dragging the duck along the ground (not slinging it over his shoulder as it is generally supposed they do). He crossed the fields, and jumped over a stone wall. Meantime, hounds had hit off his line, and as they got closer to him he dropped the duck and made off.

Another instance of this sort was observed by my friend M. Alex Phillipi, when he was a student at the University of Virginia. He wrote as follows:

In the winter of 1925, when hunting near Charlottesville, Virginia, hounds were slowly working the line of a fox in a dusty road. There was a long check. Just then, standing on an eminence, I happened to view the fox in the act of trotting by a flock of geese. He snapped at one, killed it, and dragged it a short distance. At this juncture, hounds began to run, and the fox, dropping the goose, broke into a gallop.

An eye witness, Percy A. Rockefeller, once told me an interesting story of a fox amusing himself in front of a single hound hunting in the snow. There was a frozen crust which held up the fox but not his pursuer, who repeatedly broke through. The chase crossed a clearing in the Adirondack forest where tree stumps were numerous, and the fox would run ahead of the struggling hound, hop onto a stump, where he would calmly sit like a king on his throne, until his frantic pursuer came within a few feet, when he would run on to the next stump, and repeat the performance.

I am not sure, however, that all other animals enjoy being hunted. For example, the following story was told me by Captain A. N. S. Millbanke, a descendant of Lord Byron. While in charge of a district in Kenya Colony, East Africa, he came across a fellow-countryman who kept a pack of beagles with which he hunted various kinds of game, large and small. Eventually, he turned to hunting lions with his pack, as Paul J. Rainey did with American hounds. On one occasion, a lioness found in long grass on the edge of a lake jumped into the water and swam across, in spite of many small crocodiles, followed by the beagles giving tongue in the water. On reaching the farther shore, she stopped to investigate the cause of the rumpus, and the hunter, who had ridden around the shore of the lake, was able to shoot her. It appears that the king of beasts confronted by the startling phenomenon of a pack of hounds is so surprised that he incontinently takes to flight, the yap-yapping at his heels serving only to increase his speed. Perhaps, in time, he also will learn to view the sport of kings with the same appreciation as does the fox.

To-day, more perhaps than ever before, hunting benefits those who are able to enjoy it. In such an age as this, with every influence forcing men to sedentary existence, a sport that encourages one to ride and keep in the open for hours on end is surely of the highest value to health. The qualities that hunting calls for physically, and those it especially develops, are many. I know it has helped me to keep young, strong, and fit, and when the world looked very blue it has still aided me to look at life in a hopeful spirit.

Hunting, almost more than any other form of sport, lends itself to the development of personal qualities, such as patience, consideration for others, courage and initiative, and gives an opportunity for pleasant social intercourse. Less than any other sport is hunting capable of being demoralized by the spirit of professionalism. It never will be possible, for instance, to commercialize hunting by means of gate receipts. Even the horse-coping element must participate actively, in order to do business.

The power that riding to hounds has to make one forget self and the troubles of this life is its greatest asset. Of no other sport has this been so noted in both prose and song.

Virgil appeals to the huntsman in his *Georgics:*

> *En age, segnes,*
> *Rumpe moras; vocat ingenti clamore Cithaeron*
> *Taygetique canes, domitrixque Epidaurus equorum,*
> *Et vox assensu nemorum ingeminata remugit.*

> *Hark, away,*
> *Cast far behind the ling'ring cares of life.*
> *Cithaeron calls aloud, and in full cry*
> *Thy hounds, Taygetus. Epidaurus trains*
> *For us the generous steed. The hunter's shouts*
> *And cheering cries assenting woods return.*

To ride over a beautiful country far from roads and dwellings, to enjoy hilltop views that seldom would otherwise be seen, to observe sky effects from such vantage points, is to enjoy nature as few non-hunting people ever enjoy it. Many are the physical and mental thrills of hunting: the grand cry of hounds, a splendid gallop, the sheer pageantry, the sight of beautiful blood horses, a level pack, and well turned-out men and women. The color, dash, and constantly changing pictures all tend to excite and hold interest as perhaps nothing else can. The appeal of the picturesque in hunting is reflected in all walks of life, and in all sorts of places; in parts of rural America, where no one ever practiced riding to hounds, I have seen the walls of humble

HOUNDS AND HUNTING

homes hung with treasured pictures of the chase as conducted in England, with all its color and delight to the eye.

Anyone who has a love for the picturesque will appreciate the delightful paintings and prints of English and continental hunting; but the following word picture of T. F. Dale of a meet with a first-class English pack is too vivid for me to omit:

The first day that we hunt with the Belvoir will always remain in our memory, so associated is the pack with the history of foxhunting and the foxhound. So many men in the past have looked on this hunt as the very embodiment and type of the best side of our national sport that we feel that a day with the Belvoir is an experience not easily to be forgotten. Suppose then that some Wednesday early in the season we find ourselves at Croxton Park. The day is cloudy, and the wind has a touch of east in it. The remains of the old fishing lodge of the Duke of Rutland are before us, and the pond's steely grey in the subdued misty light of the November morning adds a beauty to the landscape. There is a gathering of all the hardest riders, soldiers, statesmen, men of business, lawyers and farmers, people of every degree of rank and wealth. Then the women are on the best horses that money can buy or judgment select; others are riding less high-bred, but still useful animals; and there are many on foot and quite a cloud of cyclists.

There, too, quietly being walked up and down, is the famous pack, all with a wonderful family likeness in shape and colouring. Clean and bright in their coats, they have the easy grace and motion of perfect shape. Marvelous examples of careful selection they are, combining strength and speed that can tire out and outstrip the best of horses. The Hunt servants are neatly got up in quiet workmanlike manner, and are mounted on horses chosen by one of the best judges in England. A trifle high in flesh for hunt horses perhaps; but when you have said that, you have said all that the keenest critic can find to object to. Every one is full of hope and expectation, for the whole season is before them with its responsibilities of glorious moments, the like of which can be enjoyed only in the hunting-field. The huntsman possibly feels a little anxious, for the whole throng depend on him for their sport; and, as he is judged strictly by results, a bad scenting day, for which he is in no way responsible, may nevertheless lower his reputation. But, after all, he is not much to be pitied, for his work is his pleasure, and he knows as no one else does what those eighteen or twenty couple of hounds can do.

The Master has his cares, for the very popularity of the hunt fills his mind with a continual dread lest some of those reckless youths should take as little thought for his hounds as they do for their own necks. He looks at his watch and nods to the huntsman, who moves quietly off, the pack clustering around his horse and then trotting on in their eagerness as far in front as their respect for the first whipper-in, who leads the way and represents order and discipline, will allow. They know what is before them, and their waving sterns flash white in the anticipation of coming pleasure that fills them.

FUNDAMENTALS AND TRADITIONS

Bescaby Oaks is the first covert to be drawn. The field follow till they are packed in a muddy green lane where they can do little mischief and whence many of them will find it hard to disentangle themselves. But we have edged as near the gate on the right as may be. The leaves are still on the trees, golden, scarlet, and brown, and there is that indescribable scent of hunting in the air that stirs us with the associations of past pleasures of the chase. There is a cheer from the huntsman, a crack of the thong of a whipper-in, then a note from a hound which silences the chatter in the lane and brings everyone to attention. Then arises a tumult of hound voices which sinks into silence and swells out again. The clamour divides and tells us there are two lines, and then a shrill voice sounds from the far side of the covert. Those nearest the gate dash through, up one side and down to the left, half the horses out of hand with excitement; but there is no time to lose for the fox is away, and the Belvoir hounds are already striving forward. With inconceivable rapidity they flit through the undergrowth, and, by the time the first men are through the gate and out of the covert, the whole pack has tumbled out of the wood spread wide for the scent, hit off the line, and are streaming away with a rippling, chiming cry that tells of a scent.

Now, catch hold of your horse by the head and send him along, for even though he has the best blood of the Stud Book in his veins, hounds will beat him for pace. Sit back and let him have plenty of rein at the first hairy fence, for there is probably a ditch as well to clear, and, as he flings the first two fences behind him, there will be more room. The mass of the field are hindering each other at the gate or making for a gap, heedless of the fact that with a good horse the safest and happiest place is in front. But it is the hounds we have come out to see, and the horse is but the means to an end. See, they have overrun the line. The fox, only a cub, feels the pace already and turns down a hedgerow. The hounds never pause nor waver but cast themselves widely and freely to the left, then to the right, and, with scarcely the loss of a moment, they are going as fast as ever. But the pace steadies them, and there is a bit of bad scenting ground where they have to feel for the scent; yet, even though they are hunting closely, they still drive forward, never wasting a moment. There is no dwelling to rejoice over the scent, and though they are not able to race, we shall have to look to it that we do not lose them. The eager puppies and too impetuous leaders are off the line now and again, but the hounds in the middle never lose the scent and recall the others by a timely note. But in the small square covert of thorns the fox, being young and inexperienced, has waited, and that pause has sealed his fate, for this time hounds and fox come out almost together, and it is a race for life for the fox and a steeplechase for the followers for the next two miles till the hounds fairly run into him in the open. A Belvoir burst of twenty minutes of the best! So the day, with perhaps another burst or it may be a long steady hunt, goes on. If you stay to the end, when the hounds turn away for the kennels at the end of the day, you will see that they trot off as gaily as they started in the morning. The Master, the servants, and the much diminished field

HOUNDS AND HUNTING

will have tired out two horses apiece, but courage and condition will apparently leave the hounds as willing and able to hunt when the shadows of the short November twilight put a stop to the sport, as when they left their kennels in the morning.

Now, this pack that you have watched and followed with so much interest and pleasure, is the result of at least a hundred years of selection, judgment and thought. There are fifty or sixty couple in kennels and as many puppies are sent out to walk, of whom not a third will be found worthy of a trial in the pack, and fewer still a permanent place on the hound list. The first definite knowledge we have of the Belvoir hounds is in 1727, in the days of the third Duke of Rutland. His son, the famous Marquis of Granby, spent some of the time he could spare from 'the wars' in hunting, and we know that he improved the pack. The fourth Duke married a Somerset, the beautiful Lady Mary Isabella, whose portrait by Sir Joshua hangs on the walls at Badminton, and from Badminton came two hounds, Champion *and* Topper, *to which many of the famous hounds of Brocklesby and Belvoir can be traced back, through* Songstress.

From 1791 the pack has been hunted by a succession of able huntsmen who remained long at their posts, Newman, Shaw, Goosey, Goodall, Cooper, Gillard and Capell having each hunted the pack in turn from 1791 to the present day.

CHAPTER II.

LIMNERS AND BARDS OF THE CHASE

IT has been remarked that art is the one feature distinguishing mankind from the rest of the animal species, and it would seem that man, hunting for his living long before he developed an individual intelligence, signalized the first awakening of a civilized consciousness by drawing pictures of the animals he chased, or which, in some cases, chased him.

So far as present-day knowledge goes, the first record of any human event is the scene depicted on the fragment of an antler which was found in the rocky shelter at Laugerie Basse, in Auvergne. A primeval hunter, naked save for the long hair which protects his body from the cold, has crept up to a gigantic urus (wild ox, extinct since the time of Caesar), and is seen in the very act of casting a spear at his prey. At any rate, it is fairly certain that soon after the advent of modern man, *homo sapiens*, in Europe, the subject of the chase became an inspiration for his art.

Pictures which represent the earliest period of painting were first discovered in the Altamira cave by a Spanish nobleman, Marcellino de Santuola, of Santander. These are attributed to about 11,500–10,000 B.C., and it is difficult to believe that such wonderful pictures could have been produced at this early stage of human history. This art never has been surpassed in its own field, except perhaps by that of the Greeks—and all this from the Cro-Magnon brain! Some of these drawings, executed in brilliant-colored pigment on the cave walls, are as marvelous in detail as the best animal painter of modern times could produce. The animals have arrows sticking in their bodies. A fresco in a rock-shelter at Alpera, Albacete, Spain, is of early Neolithic times, *circa* 10,000 B.C. It is painted in dark red, and represents a stag hunt, the hunters armed with bows and arrows; the replica of a small animal is thought to be the domesticated dog.

How savage man came to produce such works of art is something of a mystery. Perhaps he was a man of imagination, and, like some modern sportsmen, not averse to illustrating some of his perilous encounters to those gathered round the evening fire; perhaps the first drawing was suggested by a silhouette or shadow of a man or beast thrown on the walls by the light of the flames; the theory has also been advanced that religious motives may

HOUNDS AND HUNTING

have prompted the cave drawings which distinguish this period,—the picture of a bison may have been the expression of a prayer that there might be more bison to hunt for food. In any case, prehistoric man has left us, drawn on the walls of caves and on bones, representations of the aurochs, cave bear, mammoth, fights between reindeer or elk, and pictures of himself in the act of hunting these animals with slings, or with knives of stone or flint; remarkably vivid pictures, too, well drawn and full of life.

> *Once, on a glittering ice-field, ages and ages ago,*
> *Ung, a maker of pictures, fashioned an image of snow.*
> . . . .
> *Later, he pictured an aurochs—later he pictured a bear—*
> *Pictured the sabre-tooth tiger dragging a man to his lair—*
> *Pictured the mountainous mammoth, hairy, abhorrent, alone—*
> *Out of the love that he bore them, scribing them clearly on bone.*

In the Soluteran interlude, 10,000–9,000 B.C., hunting people seem to have been barbaric, keen on the chase but lacking in artistic feelings. They left no trace of animal engraving or sculpture.

In the Magdalenian Epoch, 9,500–6,500 B.C., sculpture appeared in the form of clay models, examples of which are the two figures of bison discovered in the cave of Tuc d'Audoubet, Ariège; in general, the arts of design acquired astonishing development at the hands of a race imbued with a strong aesthetic sense, and their subjects were animals of the chase, such as a combat between two deer, or a hunter chasing a herd of aurochs. The animals were usually depicted in single file, in the style used later by the American Indians in painting buffalo skins. To summarize, art distinguished the Magdalenian epoch in Europe by painting, engraving, sculpture, and carving on or out of stone, bone, and ivory. The early part of this epoch saw the highest pitch in engraving and painting, some in black with much shading; the middle of this epoch saw engraving going out and painting advancing, with a decline of art about six or seven thousand years ago.

Between the comparatively remote cave drawings and the sophisticated tomb pictures of the Egyptians, historical records of art are deficient. We find, however, among the Egyptian relics dating back several thousand years B.C., elaborate pictures of the chase as carried on with hounds, spears, bows and arrows—even the lasso. The Necropolis at Thebes, a comparatively modern foundation of the Eighteenth Dynasty, more than 1350 B.C., shows us bowmen pouring arrows into buffalo and deer. From picture records, gazelle and hare seem to have been especially popular as animals of the chase, and ostriches appear to have been hunted with dogs. In one drawing, we see a hunter returning from the hunt with a couple of hounds, such as are

LIMNERS AND BARDS OF THE CHASE

still used in Arabia, in leash, and a slain deer over his shoulder. Carved on the tomb of King Antef, one of the earliest Thebian sovereigns, still to be seen to the north of Gournah, is a scene depicting the king surrounded by his favorite hounds.[1] The appearance of this pack is interesting, high on the leg, arched in the back, well set up, with short, pendulous ears, but rather disfigured (from our point of view) by curled tails. This sculpture, dating back at least five thousand years, shows a hound of extreme vigor. The inscription indicates the names of these dogs as follows: "Bahuka, Abaker, Pahtes, and Pakaro." Other pictures show dogs similar to modern bassets and mastiffs.

The Egyptians must have been clever hunters, for they seem to have been able to train leopards and cats, the one for gazelle hunting, the other for birds. As in more recent cases, they apparently went to war hunting on their way, for a sculptured plaque, reproduced by M. Leon Heuzy, depicts what seems to be a regiment of Asiatic or African auxiliaries on some sort of military expedition, hunting en route. Of the Egyptians, Plato names six classes, one of which is "hunters." Early tomb pictures show hunting and fishing as favorite pursuits.

On the other side of the Atlantic, in that brilliant prehistoric Mayan civilization of Central America, hunting is depicted in stone carvings; while in the remains left by the Moundbuilders in Tennessee and Ohio are representations of elephants and other animals, as well as copper weapons suitable for the chase.

How much Assyrian and Babylonian civilization derived from the Egyptian is another vexing question; but there is no doubt that hunting was brought to a high state of perfection among this mighty people, who have left us on the walls of temples and palaces many animated and detailed sculptures depicting the pleasures of the chase. Even dresses and furniture were ornamented with similar subjects. In these Semitic kingdoms, as in Egypt, hunting appears in all its magnificence as one of the pleasures of kings and nobility. A bas-relief in the Louvre shows us an Assyrian king shooting lions from his chariot, while dashing forward at full speed. In the same museum, colossal statues found at Khorsabad illustrate royal personages holding tame lions under one arm, while in the other hand they have a stout whip with which to curb undue exuberance on the part of the king of beasts. In the British Museum, a marble bas-relief displays the hounds of the amazing potentate Asshurbanipal, about 700 B.C., straining at the leash by which attendants hold them. These animals seem to be of considerable size and bone.

How passionately the chase appealed to the Assyrians, the Babylonians and the Chaldeans seems to be proved by the fact that their art rises to its highest level in depicting it. Assyrian fables have been found in which the fox and horse are the speakers, and in this period a God of the Chase was recognized,—Nergol. Indeed, love of the chase often seems to go hand in hand with great conquering civilizations.

Thus, we find the Persians in no way behind their neighbors when it comes to Sport. Darius, 550 B.C., was one of the great hunters of antiquity, and had engraved upon his tomb the words:

I loved my friends; I was an excellent horseman, and an excellent hunter; nothing to me was impossible.

Herodotus and Pliny speak of the enormous number of Indian and Assyrian hounds kept by Cyrus, whose maintenance was the duty of four of the principal cities of his empire, which, in consideration of this obligation, were relieved of other taxes. In speaking of these hounds, Pliny states that "they disdained boar and stag to attack only lion and elephant." Under the Assanid Dynasty, hunting was carried on more brilliantly than ever, and the famous cup of King Firoze, now in the Lutnes collection, shows him on horseback, galloping at full speed, shooting bear, stag and lion. There are delightful Persian hunting scenes which have been portrayed down to present times, in one medium or another. The Hittites and the Phoenicians, also, have left pictures of the chase, now preserved in the British Museum, the Louvre and elsewhere.

Possibly the first artistic rendering of woman's entry into the field of hunting appears on the Conversano en Puglia vase, in the National Museum, at Naples, where the Goddess Artemis is shown riding a deer, and carrying two spears. One of the first pictures of women riding astride to the hunt is found on the Androcides vase, where the lady in question, wearing a sort of cap of liberty, and a short tunic, restrains the eager mount upon which she is seated, apparently bareback. With her is another woman on foot, carrying a javelin. The Roman Empress Faustina Augusta had a medal struck which depicted her as Diana, riding a stag side-saddle, in quite modern style.

Plutarch relates that Cratinus, one of Alexander's lieutenants, had a bronze bas-relief executed showing Alexander and his hounds fighting a lion, and himself coming to the rescue. Many amusing methods of lion hunting are depicted by the Greeks, some of which are on the Nasos tomb. There we find several men fighting lions, the former armed with shields. The picture shows the lion just as it has overthrown one of the men, who covers himself so adroitly with his shield that the animal cannot get at him. Another scene depicts a tiger hunt in which a bronze mirror forms the principal element. Men armed with shields and spears have surrounded two tigers; one is already overthrown and surrounded by part of the group; the other, seeking to escape, confronts a mirror and hesitates, thinking it encounters another tiger. The hunter is preparing to spear it. Hunting tigers with a mirror has been celebrated in verse by Claudius. Greek vases show bearded gentlemen returning from the chase with hounds and small game, such as hare and foxes.

Mention must also be made of the Etruscans, who have left us bronze plaques and clay vases adorned with hunting scenes, showing some remarkable breeds of hounds, and including some evidently imported from Egypt. Romancers have it that these hounds were crossed with wolves, lions and tigers, hoping thus to increase their valour and endurance. To say the least, their artists show vigor of imagination in illustrating this manifest fabrication.

There are interesting Pompeian paintings showing stag and boar hunts, in which divine assistance seems to have been needed, as we notice winged personages bearing spears, urging on the hounds.

The Roman Conquest did not diminish the ardour of the Gauls for the chase (mentioned by Caesar), as is shown by an interesting mosaic discovered at Lillebonne, in 1870. Round the central motif showing Apollo pursuing Daphne, are four scenes: the departure for the hunt, in which may be noticed a man leading a tame stag; the hunt itself, with the tame stag as a decoy; another hunting scene, in which three greyhounds and three horsemen traverse the forest full tilt; and, finally, the return and sacrifice to Diana. It is said to date from the second century.

While excavations were under way in Paris, in 1890, fragments of Gallic pottery were uncovered that showed hunting scenes. One of them, in which the hunter faces the boar with a short, heavy spear, suggests modern boar hunting in the Black Forest.

With the fall of the Roman Empire came a period of stagnation in art throughout the West. Not until after the eighth century do we again find hunting as a subject for art coming slowly to the fore, and only in the fifteenth century do we see a sudden and splendid revival with hunting as an important inspiration. From this time on through the eighteenth century, a large percentage of all paintings and tapestries were influenced by the chase.

In the Cotton Library in England, a painting shows a Saxon nobleman of the ninth century with his hounds and an attendant hunting wild boar in the forest.

The famous Bayeaux Tapestry, wrought by Mathilde, wife of William the Conqueror, which hangs to this day in the cathedral of Bayeaux, in Normandy, portrays vividly the principal incidents attending the exploits of her husband. Hounds, horses, and hunting scenes are included.

That women may have hunted during this period is shown by an illustration in a MS. of the Royal Library, dating from the early fourteenth century, in which they appear winding the horn and coursing a stag without any male assistance. Sad to relate, the lady who has just drawn her bow appears to have missed her mark.

HOUNDS AND HUNTING

Perhaps the first, and certainly some of the most exquisite hand-painted miniatures portraying phases of the sport adorn the famous *Livre de Chasse* of Gaston de Foix. This marvelous parchment, now in the Bibliothèque Nationale in Paris, seems to have been perfected originally for one of the royal princes. In 1470, it belonged to Aymar de Poitiers, a connection of the beautiful Diane, who, herself, married a famous sportsman, Louis de Brézé, Seneschal of Normandy. Her father, Jean, having entered into a conspiracy against the king, almost lost his life, and certainly was deprived of his possessions, so that two years after Jean's disgrace we find the book in the possession of Francis I. Left behind in his tent after the battle of Pavia, it passed via a looting Tyrolean *landsknechte* to Bernard of Cles, Bishop of Trent, who presented it to Archduke Ferdinand of Austria, founder of the Ambras collection. After one hundred and twenty-five years, following Turenne's victories in the Netherlands, it somehow became the property of the Marquis de Vigneau, who presented it to Louis XIV. After many wanderings in royal libraries, it reached its final resting-place, in 1848.

It is in this manuscript that we find depicted one of the first foxhunts approximating those of modern times; the pack in full cry, on the very brush of the fox,—the horsemen, I regret to notice, almost riding the hounds down,— and the footmen, somewhat spent, eagerly pointing out Reynard just ahead. There are severl splendid illustrations showing the scenting hound of that day, the feeding and care of sick hounds, and one delightful picture showing Gaston de Foix instructing his huntsmen in the blowing of the horn, which appears to be causing them some suffering.

Three years after the death of Gaston de Foix, in 1394, to be exact, de Fontaines-Guérin completed his book, *Le Trésor de la Vanerie*, in which are some twenty interesting miniatures. The book itself deals mainly with stag hunting which had, by this time, become for the French as national a sport as foxhunting is for the English at present.

The oldest Spanish work on hunting *Libro de la Monteria* was written by Alfonso XI, about 1350, but was not illustrated until 1582. Pictorial representations of hunting, however, were not unknown in Spain several hundred years earlier, as evidenced by the stained-glass windows in the cathedral of Leon, where foxhunting appears. Such portrayal of sports of the field was prevalent in many mediaeval churches, and has been revived in the Sports Bay of the cathedral of St. John the Divine, in New York.

Some of the first sporting prints known were done in Florence in the fifteenth century by an unknown artist of the school of Maso Finiguerra, to whom Italians ascribe the invention of copper engraving. Among other amusing pictures of sport may be mentioned one by Mantegna, the most important of his frescoes in the Castello di Corte, in Mantua, which is supposed to represent a hunting horse and two large mastiffs of Ludovica Gonzaga.

MR. PERCIVAL ROSSEAU'S FAMOUS PAINTING OF HIS OWN HOUNDS KILLING A PANTHER IN TEXAS, 1880. THESE HOUNDS WERE OF FRENCH ORIGIN.

DETAIL OF FRIEZE IN THE PRESENCE CHAMBER, HARDWICK HALL (CIRCA 1597), SHOWING SCENTING HOUNDS OF THE PERIOD.

LIMNERS AND BARDS OF THE CHASE

In Turbervile's *Noble Arte of Venerie*, 1575, which illustrates different phases of the chase, there appears a woodcut which shows Queen Elizabeth being entertained in the midst of a forest scene.

Innumerable tapestries exist which depict hunting in many phases, and while such early mural paintings as remain are in rather a bad state, many Books of Hours and Breviaries contain beautiful illuminations treating of sport, if the person for whom they were destined were known to be a *grand veneur*. A very fine example is *Les Trés Riches Heures de Jean, duc de Berri*, preserved in the Musée Condé, Chantilly, painted about the year 1415, by Pol de Lumbourg and his two brothers. It is diverting to think of such a combination of sport and religion.

An enchanting personage and a great hunter, was the Emperor Maximilian I, 1459–1519. He, indeed, did much to carry on the tradition between mediaeval and modern practices, for he wrote no less than five books on hunting, of which at least two represent his own reminiscences and adventures. Then came the three lesser known but equally important works, *The Secret Book of the Chase, Hunting*, and *Fishing*, the two latter illustrated by Jörg Kölderer. The first pictured use of firearms in the chase is shown in one of these books, where Maximilian is shooting at a chamois with a "fire tube." Maximilian, by the way, really introduced hunting par force into Germany, but it did not become popular there for at least two centuries. About ten years after his death, Maximilian's daughter, the Archduchess Margaret, Regent of the Netherlands, had a series of tapestries executed in Brussels commemorating the *Belles Chases de l'Empereur, Maximilien*. These tapestries, by Van Orley, which now hang in the Louvre, depict some interesting varieties of hounds.

It is impossible not to mention the drawings of Albrecht Dürer, especially one very beautiful picture of St. Hubert, nor the pictures of Lucas Cranach, court painter to three electors of Saxony.

The latter part of the sixteenth century also saw the notable work of Johannes van der Straet (known as Stradanus), who came to Florence, in 1553, at the height of Cosmo de Medici's career, and became designer to the celebrated Azazzia Medicae. The success of his novel sporting designs led him to resign his position and devote himself entirely to such pictures. He went first into partnership with Hieronimus Cock, the best-known engraver in Antwerp, one of the famous family of artists and art publishers. How he got his work from Florence to Antwerp is unknown, but it is certain that he never revisited Flanders, and only occasionally did some of the engravers who worked for him visit Italy. Among his most amusing pictures are those of rabbiting with English small dogs, hare hunting with a trained leopard, and one, especially, showing fox and hare hunting, the men accompanied by hounds, apparently spearing the quarry while at full gallop.

HOUNDS AND HUNTING

The de Guise tapestries, the pictures of Snyders, and the poems of Claude Gauchet and of Noel Conti clearly depict the way hounds and hunting dogs of various kinds were equipped with jackets and spiked collars—a kind of armor against the wild boar at bay.

With a passing glance at the work of Antonio Tempesta, the Florentine etcher, and the illustrations of the famous Coburg *Chronicle* of the early seventeenth century, we come to what are undoubtedly the most interesting English hunting prints of that century, namely, the set entitled, "Severall Wayes of Hunting, Hawking, and Fishing, according to the English manner," invented by Francis Barlow, 1671, etched by W. Hollar.

Because of the great love of sport in Britain, and the excellent market for prints and paintings depicting it, innumerable artists have left us delightful souvenirs, the details of which have influenced the modern generation in many lands to emulate the sporting features of those bygone days. Old English houses are frequently veritable treasure-chests of such works.

John Wootton was one of the earliest and best of the modern English sporting painters, and among his numerous works is a set of eight pictures depicting various incidents of a fox chase. These were painted, probably, about 1735, and are particularly interesting as they indicate the point to which foxhunting had developed at that time. One of them shows a mounted whip with a French horn, and a negro boy wearing a turban, carrying a French horn. An English artist once remarked to me that the most unique thing he noticed about hunting in America was the negro grooms, reminiscent of quaint European paintings.

In speaking of a set of contemporary prints representing hunting scenes in the eighteenth century, Ashton says:

Only gentlemen are represented as being on horseback, the huntsmen having leaping poles. This was better for them than being mounted, for the country was nothing like as cultivated as now, and perfectly undrained; under the conditions, they could go straighter on foot, as with these poles leaps could be taken that no horseman would attempt.

During the latter part of the eighteenth century and the early part of the nineteenth century, there lived a group of artists who produced invaluable paintings, both from the point of artistic merit and as sporting records: Ben Marshall, Stubbs, Alken, Ward, Sartorius, Gilpin, Wolstenholme, Rowlandson, Sir Francis Grant, Sir Edward Landseer. Of all these, the work of Ben Marshall is of the greatest interest to me. His hounds, horses, and men are life like, his color delightful, his technique unsurpassed. In recent years, the production of sporting prints and paintings continues in quantity as well as quality. A. J. Munnings, for example, is rated as a great artist; in fact, the Curator of the Fitzwilliam Museum, Cambridge, once told me that he considered Munnings the leading horse painter of all times. Great American

LIMNERS AND BARDS OF THE CHASE

painters of sporting events are rare. An exception is Percival Rosseau, whose pictures of sporting dogs have the greatest merit. The life-size painting of his own pack, and which caused a sensation in the Salon of 1906, is the most striking picture of hounds I have ever seen, not excepting the best French hunting pictures from the sixteenth through the eighteenth centuries.

Not only in ancient times, but all through the ages, there have been splendid sculptural representations of hunting, such as the wonderful overdoor of the chapel at the château d'Amboise, depicting the vision of St. Hubert. Again, the statue of Diana, the huntress, by Jean Goujon, in the Louvre, is considered the *chef d'œuvre* of that great sixteenth century sculptor.

Coming to the Bards of the Chase, the literature of sport is vast, everincreasing, and full of quaint surprises frequently found in the long-closed volumes of forgotten authors. Xenophon, quoted elsewhere, was most erudite on the subject of hounds, how to hunt them, and the peculiarities of scent. His *Cynegeticos* is a delightful essay on hunting the hare and the boar. He knew in principle as much as we do to-day about hunting, and tells how to breed and train hounds, and gives suitable names for them. Caesar's remarks already have been mentioned, and Virgil's poetry quoted. Through the Dark Ages, while hunting was enjoyed, few detailed accounts were written on the subject, but beginning with the fourteenth century the dawn of modern hunting literature appears.

About 1327, Guyllame Twici, who was grand huntsman to King Edward II of England, wrote a manuscript entitled, *L'Art de Venerie*, of which he said, "Made in his time to teach others." From this manuscript we glean many details about the chase of the hare, stag, boar, and wolf, as well as the hunting customs and manners of the times.

A curious work in French, written before the year 1338, entitled, *Le Roy Modus et la Royne Racio*, is a sort of catechism on hunting. This manuscript, when published in 1486, was the first book dealing exclusively with the chase ever printed in the French language. It covers all known types of hunting, and concludes its dissertations with verses.

The poem of Gace de la Buigne—*Roman des déduits*,—which was begun in 1359 and finished after 1373, in the reign of Charles V, is a complete treatise on venery and falconry, presented in one of those allegorical forms affected in the Middle Ages. King Jean of France, while captive in England with his son, Philippe le Hardi (after the battle of Poictiers), consoled himself by hunting. He ordered his chaplain—Gace de la Buigne, who had accompanied him from France—to commence this poem, wishing his son to be taught the rudiments of hunting, as well as "*Pour eschiuer la pechie doiseuse, et qu'il en fust miel enseigne en meurs, et en vertus.*"

The manuscript, *Livre de Chasse*, by Gaston, compte de Foix, 1387, gives

HOUNDS AND HUNTING

us with much clarity a startling picture of how highly developed hunting had become in his day. He was known as Gaston Phoebus, because this great huntsman and writer, who was one of the Plantagenet family, and lord of two domains in Southern France and Northern Spain, was famous for his physical perfections and flaxen hair. Not only was he a delightful writer, but, personally, an ardent advocate of sport, for he was killed while bear hunting, in the year 1391. His manuscript was written in the French of the period, and contains very explicit data on everything to do with hunting.

The oldest treatise on the chase in the English language is the translation of the de Foix manuscript under the title, *Maystre of Game*, written between the years 1406 and 1413, but with five new chapters dealing with hunting in England. The translator was no less a person than Edward, Second Duke of York, grandson of Edward III. He had been incarcerated for connection with a plot to assassinate the king, and no doubt amused himself not a little while in "durance vile" by dreaming and writing of the sport he loved. The Duke, who probably had hunted in his youth with his kinsman, Gaston de Foix, was immortalized in Shakespeare's *Richard II* as the arch traitor, Duke of Aumarle, previously the Earl of Rutland. In history, this troublemaking Plantagenet gallantly led England's vanguard, dying on the glorious battlefield of Agincourt. The original quaint English of the *Maystre of Game* was given new rendering by Baillie-Grohman, in 1909, thus making this famous manuscript on hunting available to us in book form. It may well be read by anyone who believes that this sophisticated age "knows it all," in order to learn at first hand how extensively the art of venery had been developed five hundred years ago.

In 1486, a lady takes a hand in casting further light on the chase, for the *Boke of St. Albans* is attributed to dame Juliana Berners or Barnes, prioress of Sopwell Nunnery, St. Albans, England. It is compiled from several French tracts, and gives light on hawking as well as hunting, and is especially famous as the first printed book on hunting in English.

Early works on the chase were not entirely confined to technical and instructive treatises, for, in the fourteenth century, Chaucer wrote:

> *Aha, the fox! and after him they ran;*
> *And eke with staves many another man,*
> *Ran Colle our dogge, and Talbot, and Gerlond,*
> *And Malkin with her distaff in her hand.*
> *Ran cow and calf, and eke the veray hogges,*
> *So fered were for berking of the dogges,*
> *And shouting of the men and women eke,*
> *They rounen so, hem thought her hertes broke.*

LIMNERS AND BARDS OF THE CHASE

From Chaucer's time, the literature of hunting in poetry, song, and prose, is considerable, and oftentimes very beautiful—one chances on delightful anonymous bits like the following:

Flying still, and still pursuing,
　See the fox, the hounds, the men,
Cunning cannot save from ruin,
　Free from refuge, wood, or den;

Now they kill him, homeward hie them,
　To a jovial night's repast,
Thus no sorrow e'er comes nigh them,
　Health continues to the last.

Frequently, there appear exhortations to the chase, as in Sir Philip Sidney's *Hunting in Arcadia:*

Kalander entertained them with pleasant discoursing—how well he loved the sport of hunting when he was a young man, that the sun could never prevent him with earliness, nor the moon dissuade him from watching till midnight for the deers feeding. O, said he, you will never live to my age, without you keep yourself in breath with exercise.

Whether Shakespeare ever actually went foxhunting we are not prepared to say; but he must have been very familiar with hunting of some sort, for no one could describe in more apt language certain phases of the chase than did Shakespeare, as the quotations used in this book demonstrate. In *Venus and Adonis* he mentions several kinds of game apparently commonly hunted in his time:

Uncouple at the timorous flying hare,
Or at the fox which lives by subtilty,
Or at the roe which no encounter dare;
Pursue these fearful creatures o'er the downs,
And on thy well-breath'd horse keep with thy hounds.

Somerville's immortal poem, *The Chace*, not only is beautiful, but the subject matter describes various phases of hunting in a manner to enthuse anyone, and, incidentally, the text deals with many technical matters, so that the poem as a whole can be taken as a guide for everything to do with hunting, kennels, hounds, huntsmanship and good sportsmanship. Quotations from this poem were used to adorn the walls of Huntland kennels (described in Chapter VIII) as texts for the proper conduct of the game. Somerville has been quoted in most English books on hunting that have been written since his time, and notably by Beckford, who, in 1781, wrote his *Thoughts on Hunting*.

HOUNDS AND HUNTING

This latter book may be considered the Bible of English hunting. It was written by Peter Beckford in a series of letters to his nephew, who no doubt had been brought up in a hunting *milieu*, and for that reason it may not always be quite clear to the complete layman; but, as a guide to the more sophisticated, and as an incentive to thought and further study, Beckford's observations never have been quite equalled by any one writer. To me it is a beautiful piece of literature, and no wonder, because of Beckford it has been written:

He would bag a fox in Greek, find a hare in Latin, inspect his kennels in Italian, and direct the economy of the stable in exquisite French.

During the last few hundred years, innumerable technical books both in French and English have been written on staghunting, foxhunting, and hare hunting. However, the subject matter of many of them is either personal, or, often, repetition of what has been said before. Few writers in English have dealt with the subject in a really constructive and analytical vein, for most of them have taken for granted certain stereotyped traditions, with little thought as to the reasons for this or that. Notable exceptions to this attitude are, *Foxes, Foxhounds and Fox-Hunting* (Richard Clapham), *Hold Hard! Hounds, please* ("Yoi-over"), also, *Hounds, Gentlemen, please!* (Commander W. B. Forbes, R.N.).

To turn from the highly technical and descriptive works on hunting in its various phases, we find that much has been written in a satirical, romantic, or poetical vein since Somerville's time, the greatest authors not disdaining the subject.

In his creation of "Jorrocks," Robert Smith Surtees gave English literature one of the greatest satirical characters in this or possibly any other language. His set of kindred books, in each of which "Jorrocks" appears, has given hunting people more joy and laughter (and God bless him for so doing!) than any other writer. Surtees was born at Hamsterley Hall, in 1803, and died in 1864. Of his childhood but little is known, except that he was reared in the tradition of sport, three preceding generations in his family, at least, having kept hounds. Surtees became engaged in the practice of law, but did not often allow legal duties to hamper his enjoyment of the chase. Hunting was the life in which he reveled; he traveled much to hunt, and enjoyed the sport hugely. His first book, *The Horseman's Manual*, was published in 1831, and is the only one of his books written under his name. From that date there appeared periodically the well known, *Jorrocks' Jaunts and Jollities, Hillingdon Hall, Handley Cross, Hawbuck Grange, Soapey Sponge's Sporting Tour, Plain or Ringlets*, and *Mr. Facey Romford's Hounds*. These books furnish ample proof of his exceptional powers of observation, and enjoy constantly increasing popularity.

What Robert Browning thought is best stated in his own words:

LIMNERS AND BARDS OF THE CHASE

> *Hunt, fish, shoot,*
>   *Would a man fulfil life's duty.*
> *Not to the bodily frame alone*
>   *Does Sport give strength and beauty.*
>
> . . . .
>
> *Still, tastes are tastes, allow me:*
>   *Allow, too, where's there keenness*
> *For Sport, there's little likelihood*
>   *Of a man's displaying meanness.*

Henry Fielding gives us a merry song as follows:

> *Away they fly to 'scape the rout,*
>   *Their steeds they soundly switch;*
> *Some are thrown in, and some thrown out,*
>   *And some thrown in the ditch.*
>   *Yet a-hunting we will go.*
>
> *Sly Reynard now like lightning flies,*
>   *And sweeps across the vale;*
> *And when the hounds too near he spies,*
>   *He drops his bushy tail.*
>   *Then a-hunting we will go.*
>
> *Ye jovial hunters, in the morn*
>   *Prepare then for the chase;*
> *Rise at the sounding of the horn,*
>   *And health with sport embrace*
>   *When a-hunting we do go.*

Sir Walter Scott, in prose and verse, often gives word pictures of hunting; for example:

> *Up rose the sun o'er moor and mead;*
> *Up with the sun rose Percy Rede;*
> *Brave Keeldar, from his couples free*
>   *Career'd along the lea.*
> *The palfrey sprung with sprightly bound,*
> *As if to match the gamesome hound;*
> *His horn the gallant huntsman wound:*
>   *They were a jovial three!*
>
> *Man, hound, or horse, of higher fame*
> *To wake the wild deer never came,*
> *Since Alnwick's Earl pursued the game*
>   *On Cheviot's rueful day.*

HOUNDS AND HUNTING

William Wordsworth aptly describes enthusiasm for the chase:

> *He all the country could outrun,*
> * Could leave both man and horse behind;*
> *And often, ere the chase was done,*
> * He reeled, and was stone-blind.*
> *And still there's something in the world*
> * At which his heart rejoices;*
> *For when the chiming hounds are out,*
> * He dearly loves their voices.*

Thomas Love Peacock expresses delightfully a huntsman's unchanging keenness for the chase:

> *Though I be now a grey, grey friar,*
> * Yet I was once a hale young knight:*
> *The cry of my dogs was the only choir*
> * In which my spirit did take delight.*
> *Little I recked of matin bell,*
> * But drowned its toil with my clanging horn:*
> *And the only beads I loved to tell*
> * Were the beads of dew on the spangled thorn.*
> *Though changeful time, the hand severe,*
> * Has made me now these joys forego,*
> *Yet my heart bounds when'er I hear*
> * Yoicks! hark away! and tally-ho!*

The Poem of Poems on foxhunting that never fails to stir me is Masefield's *Reynard the Fox*, which has been lauded *ad infinitum* from a literary as well as a hunting viewpoint, and to which I must add my mite of praise. Its masterly descriptions of the fine points of hound work are so perfect, its artistry is so splendid, I never can read more than a few pages of it without having tears come to my eyes with the thrill of excitement and the joy of its beauty.

> *And the hunt came home and the hounds were fed,*
> *They climbed their bench and went to bed,*
> *The horses in stable loved their straw.*
> *'Good-night, my beauties,' said Robin Dawe.*
>
> *Then the moon came quiet and flooded full*
> *Light and beauty on clouds like wool,*
> *On a feasted fox at rest from hunting,*
> *In the beech wood grey where the brocks were grunting.*
>
> *The beech wood grey rose dim in the night*
> *With moonlight fallen in pools of light,*
> *The long dead leaves on the ground were rimed.*
> *A clock struck twelve and the church-bells chimed.*

TYPES OF ANCIENT HUNTING HORNS.

CHAPTER III.

HOUNDS AND HORNS OF YORE

THROUGH countless eons, before any known record of man on this earth, the hound of yore was in the making. The Tertiary Age has left us deposits showing the dog of the *genus canis*, and, incidentally, a horse with three toes. Ten thousand years ago the dog seems to have been the companion of man, as proved by the bone deposits of the Magdalenian Epoch, while the domestication of the dog is mentioned in the earliest known writings, such as the *Vedas*, 1500 B.C., and the *Zend-Avesta*, about 500 B.C.

Since it takes innumerable generations to develop in any animal specialized attributes such as those existing in hounds, it can be surmised that the development of scenting hounds, as we know them to-day, has been going on during many thousands of years. Various zoölogists believe that the jackal (*Canis aureus*) was the tap-root of our innumerable modern breed of dogs. It is remarked elsewhere in this book how the jackal and his wild brethren of to-day speak on the line of hunted game, so, it is not surprising that man has been able to develop cry in his hounds.

In the Egyptian Museum at Berlin, an ancient Egyptian painting depicts tan and white scenting hounds as well as black and tans, also smooth-coated grey-hounds (which some naturalists believe were developed from the jackals of Abyssinia), and terriers with short legs and erect ears.

In Greek mythology, it was Dioscure Castor who first hunted with scenting hounds. In Book XVII of Homer's *Odyssey*, the young hunters follow *Argos*, the white hound of Ulysses, after wild goat, stag, and hare. Nothing escapes this hound, even in the forest, for he excels in following the tracks of game. Homer also compares scenting hounds on a line to Greek and Trojan warriors. Alexander the Great had a hunting dog named *Peritos*, of whom he thought so much that he named after him one of the cities which he built in India. He is also said to have paid Aristotle a large sum for a treatise on hunting.

Xenophon devoted several pages of his book to Cretan and Laconian hounds. Of the latter there were two breeds,—the Castorides and the Alopecides. Xenophon's ideal hound was light, well proportioned, alert, of good voice, with a short head, a high, broad and wrinkled forehead, brilliant black eyes, and a long supple neck, deep chest, thick-set loins, curved hips, straight tail (long and slim), thighs strong, feet round; and they hunted the line well. Arrian describes the Cretan scenting hounds as having rough coats and excellent nose, as well as being fierce, fast, and very clever in rough country; but he also advises his compatriots to import dogs from Gaul. Oppian says that the Greeks used eleven different kinds of hunting dogs, emanating from Greece and nearby countries, as well as dogs brought from great distances including Egypt, Pannonia, Gaul, the Isle of Britain, and India.

The Romans followed closely the Greek practice of importing dogs from the entire then-known world. Gratius tells us much concerning the scenting hounds of his day, mentioning eight different varieties, among them hounds from Sammaria and Persia; and he particularly speaks of the comparative scenting ability of these hounds, including one rough-coated breed. In the first century before Christ, Cicero, in his *de Natura Deorum*, refers to the unbelievable scenting ability of hunting hounds. The poet Claudianus has left us a vivid portrayal of the Roman hunt of the fifth century, in which he describes the goddess Diana advancing with hounds of divers sorts. Rough-coated Cretan hounds apparently still existed from this description. He gives the first mention of the bulldog, as follows:

Magnaque taurorum fracturae colla britannae (*Dogs of Britain ready to break the great necks of the bulls*).

Long before the Roman Conquest, packs of hounds existed in France. It is recorded that one hundred and twenty-two years before Christ, one Biteuth, King of the Arvernes, sent an embassy to the Consul Domitius. The Romans saw with astonishment in the suite of the ambassador a pack of magnificent British and Belgian hounds. Arrian, who declares he wrote his *Treaty on Hunting* to give justice to Gallic hounds, mentions among others, Segusian hounds, emanating from the vicinity of Lyon. These dogs are described as equal to Carian and Cretan hounds for excellence of nose,—but slower,—and of a savage but sad appearance. They had rough coats, were free with their voices, which were of such a lagubrious tone that the Gauls compared them to beggars imploring charity.

A Gallo-Roman monument discovered in the Vosges seems to have been erected to the glory of a dog, *Bellicus*, who is represented as attacking a boar. At the time of Strabo, in the reign of Emperor Augustus, the Gauls brought from Britain hunting and war dogs, which are referred to as important articles of commerce. Charlemagne and his successor, Louis, kept a great variety of hunting dogs, including some from Germany which were considered so remarkable for agility and courage that their reputation reached the Court of the Caliphs at Bagdad, according to the chronicle of Saint-Gall.

HOUNDS AND HORNS OF YORE

During the early mediaeval era, we have little in the way of comparative information on the appearance and ability of scenting hounds; however, the detailed description of all sorts of fourteenth century hunting dogs by Gaston de Foix should be read carefully by any dog fancier, for it mentions, among other numerous breeds, pointing dogs and spaniels, and tells of the manner of their use at this early date. Speaking of scenting hounds, according to the translation of 1416, he says:

The which must hunt all the day, questeying and making great melody in their language and saying great villainy and chiding the beasts that they chase. And therefore I prefer them to all other kinds of hounds, for they have more virtue it seems to me than any other beast. Other kind of hounds there be the which open and jangle when they are uncoupled, as well when they be not in her fues (on their line), and when they be in her fues they questey too much in seeking their chase whatever it be, and if they learn the habit when they are young and are not chastised thereof, they will evermore be noisy and wild, and namely when they seek their chase, for when the chase is found, the hounds cannot questey too much as that they be in the fues (the hounds cannot challenge too loudly when they are on the line). And to rente and make hounds there are many remedies. There be also many kinds of running hounds, some small and big, and the small be called kenets, and these hounds run well to all manner of game, and they (that) serve for all game men call them harriers. And every hound that hath that courage will come to be a harrier by nature with little making.

Gace de la Buigne estimates that in his time, which was early in the fourteenth century, there were in France twenty thousand gentlemen who kept scenting hounds in more or less large numbers.

According to M. le Couteuix and the Baron de Noirmont, at least a dozen different types of scenting hounds existed in France during the several hundred years previous to the French Revolution. Of these, four were known as Royal, in that they were used exclusively in the King's packs: St. Hubert's, the King's White Hounds, the Fawn Hounds of Brittany, and the Grey Hounds of St. Louis. Among the breeds kept by individual nobles appear the following: Hounds of Bresse, Vendean Griffons (rough-coated), Gascon Hounds, Normandy Hounds, Hounds of Saintonge, Poitou Hounds, Céris Hounds, and D'Artois Hounds. In the eighteenth century, a blue tick breed called *Foudras* is mentioned.

From contemporary portraits and bronze figures showing many of these hounds, their general appearance is fairly well known to-day. Of these several breeds, the most renowned is that of St. Hubert, that patron saint of hunting whose story is told in Chapter One. It is possible that this very ancient breed, the exact origin of which is absolutely lost in the mists of antiquity, is the same famous Belgian breed mentioned by the Latin poet, Silius Italicus:

[41]

HOUNDS AND HUNTING

Ut canis occultos agitat cum Belgicus apros
Errores qui ferae solers per devia, mersa
Nare legit, tacitoque premens vestigia rostro.
(*Thus, a Belgian hound follows the hidden boar and*
Cleverly unravels the track of the beast,
Nose to the ground,
Silently tying to the trail.)

This is how the perfect tufter (*limier*) seeks out his quarry. These hounds, known in the twelfth century as Flanders Hounds, then existed in two colors, —white, and black and tan, according to Vlit in *Venatio Novantiqua*. Charles IX of France (1550–1611), in his comments on hunting, speaks of these hounds as too slow for stag hunting but excellent as tufters, in which capacity the black and tans sent annually to the king by the monks of St. Hubert were used with great success until 1789, according to d'Yauville. The probable descendants of these hounds to-day are known in England and America as bloodhounds, having preserved their characteristics through the ages.

Although most British scenting hounds doubtless trace their ancestry back to importations by the Norman Conquerors, and in spite of the age-long antipathy of Frenchmen and Englishmen for each other, the French frequently imported hounds from Great Britain. Whether it was because the French nobility were such keen enthusiasts that they imported for the purpose of comparison, or whether the English hounds were particularly well adapted for certain purposes, or were more carefully bred, is not quite clear.

From the beginning of the seventeenth century, importations into France became frequent. In 1602, Henry IV received from James VI of Scotland several packs of scenting hounds for which horses and mules were sent in exchange. In 1605, the same king wrote to the Prince of Wales, son of King James, "My nephew,—when my son is able to write, he will thank you for the pack of hounds which you have sent him."

In his book, *Meute et venérie pour lièvre*, Ligniville speaks of a very fine pack of eighty harriers sent by the King of England to the Duke of Lorraine, about 1600. A detailed description of his own black and white hounds is given with comments on their manner of hunting and their faults. Of special note is a bitch *Jouelle* (Jewel), presented to Ligniville by M. le milord Hée (Lord Hay), "of the same breed brought by the English king from Scotland at the time of his coronation." Also, a dog, *Toller*, emanating from the pack of the Prince of Wales, which the chief huntsman of Lorraine caused to be brought from England by special messenger.

According to Ligniville, Yorkshire hounds, and hounds from the North were superior to French hounds (perhaps he referred to Northern beagles, or "cat" beagles). To test his belief, he hunted his hounds against those of a M. de Camp-Rémy, who had brought a pack of fifteen couple of very superior hounds to Lorraine to vanquish him. This is probably the first pack field trial on record. French archives show that Louis XIII had among his hunts a pack of Scotch hounds for hunting hare, which was kept intact down to the time of Louis XVI.

Another quaint record (1642) tells how the prince de Marsillac sent French wines to England in exchange for hounds and horses. About this time, according to the Bulletin of the French Historical Society, it is recorded that a certain young sportsman named Beaulieu Picard went to visit his father-in-law, having with him a pack of English scenting hounds that he had won from an Englishman on a wager as to who had the fastest horse.

All this data proves how keen and erudite the ancients were on the subject of hounds, and how much trouble they took in order to improve their packs. They were so keen they were even inspired to poetry—what modern sportsman could attempt to emulate Jacques Savary, who in 1655 published a poem in Latin lauding English hounds for hare hunting? He highly prefers them to French hounds *which are more beautiful but less docile, less valiant, more apt to bother sheep. The English hound is ugly, but not riotous. He withstands cold better; some English hounds even have better voice than French hounds—the latter cry; the former roar.*

> *. . . . turpis sed criminis expers*
> *Anglus, forma placet galli, temeraria mens est.*
> *. . . . tantum latratibus ora*
> *Pandunt galligenae, latrat, sed mugit et anglus.*

This last statement is of interest, in view of the tendency to muteness of modern English hounds. As to the "roaring" of English hounds, the statement probably applied to Southern hounds, as Savary records that the Northern hounds had thin voices.

Although, according to Oppian, the Greeks imported large dogs from Britain, including Irish wolfhounds, little is known of hounds in the British Islands until after the Conquest by the Normans, who were fanatical huntsmen. It is odd that some of the hounds which they probably took to Britain (such as bloodhounds) should still exist there, although now practically extinct on the continent.

The English bloodhound is, from its appearance, unquestionably the descendant of the black and tan hounds of St. Hubert, as already mentioned; but the earliest distinctly English breed was the Talbot, the name originating from the ancient family of that name. This breed had many characteristics of the bloodhound in appearance and style of hunting; but its colors,—

HOUNDS AND HUNTING

white, black and tan, red and fawn,—according to French authority, indicate that its origin was derived from the crossing of the white breed of St. Hubert, the black and tan St. Hubert, and the Fawn hounds of Brittany. These ancient colorations, and in some measure the voice, still reproduce themselves with utmost precision in the Old Virginia hounds, although the conformation and manner of hunting is entirely different from the Talbots, who may be, nevertheless, their remote ancestors. Another characteristic in common is that of the rat tail. Numerous writings and many pictures fix very definitely the characteristics of the Talbots and their more or less direct descendants, the Southern hounds, which breed is undeniably described by Shakespeare:

> *My hounds are bred out of the Spartan kind*
> *So flew'd, so sanded, and their heads are hung*
> *With ears that sweep away the morning dew,*
> *Crook-kneed'd, and dew-lap'd, like Thessalian bulls;*
> *Slow in pursuit, but match'd in mouth like bells,*
> *Each under each.*
>
> Midsummer Night's Dream.

According to several writers, there was one variety of the Southern hound that was very exaggerated in characteristics, which made it almost grotesque in appearance, a grotesqueness that was further accentuated by the custom of docking the stern quite short.

In the seventeenth century, the slow Southern hounds began to lose popularity in favor of the fleet Northern hounds. These hounds originated, according to various authorities, by a cross between the Talbot and Scotch deerhound. Salnove, Sélincourt, and d'Yauville agree that it was this sort of hound that was so extensively imported into France, as mentioned previously. Stonehenge and Richardson state that from such hounds, again crossed with greyhounds and large terriers, the modern English foxhound originated.

The cross of the long dog and the terrier has left its mark in short ears, a voice sparingly used and lacking the bell-like tone of the ancient hounds. The Frenchman, Savary, in his Latin poem already mentioned, describes them as "slender, active, like strong greyhounds, curved of flank, long of muzzle, pointed of ear, cat-footed, all nerves, and very fast. They have a 'clair' voice, and hunt with drive to kill." D'Yauville describes them as standing from 20 to 23 inches.

In very early times, it is probable that the Talbot and its variations were used promiscuously on all sorts of game, although hare hunting was undoubtedly the most popular in the sixteenth and seventeenth centuries. Among the Norman conquerors, stag hunting had been the pursuit *par excellence*, and

1. WHITE HOUNDS OF THE KING (HENRY II), BY JEAN GOUJON, XVI*th* CENTURY.

2. HOUNDS OF THE GLOUCESTER FOX HUNTING CLUB, THE FIRST AMERICAN HUNT CLUB. FROM A CONTEMPORARY DRAWING, CIRCA 1800.

3. BALTAZAR, FRENCH HOUND, BY DESPORTES, CIRCA 1700.

4. HOUNDS BRED BY PETER BECKFORD.
From painting by Sartorius.

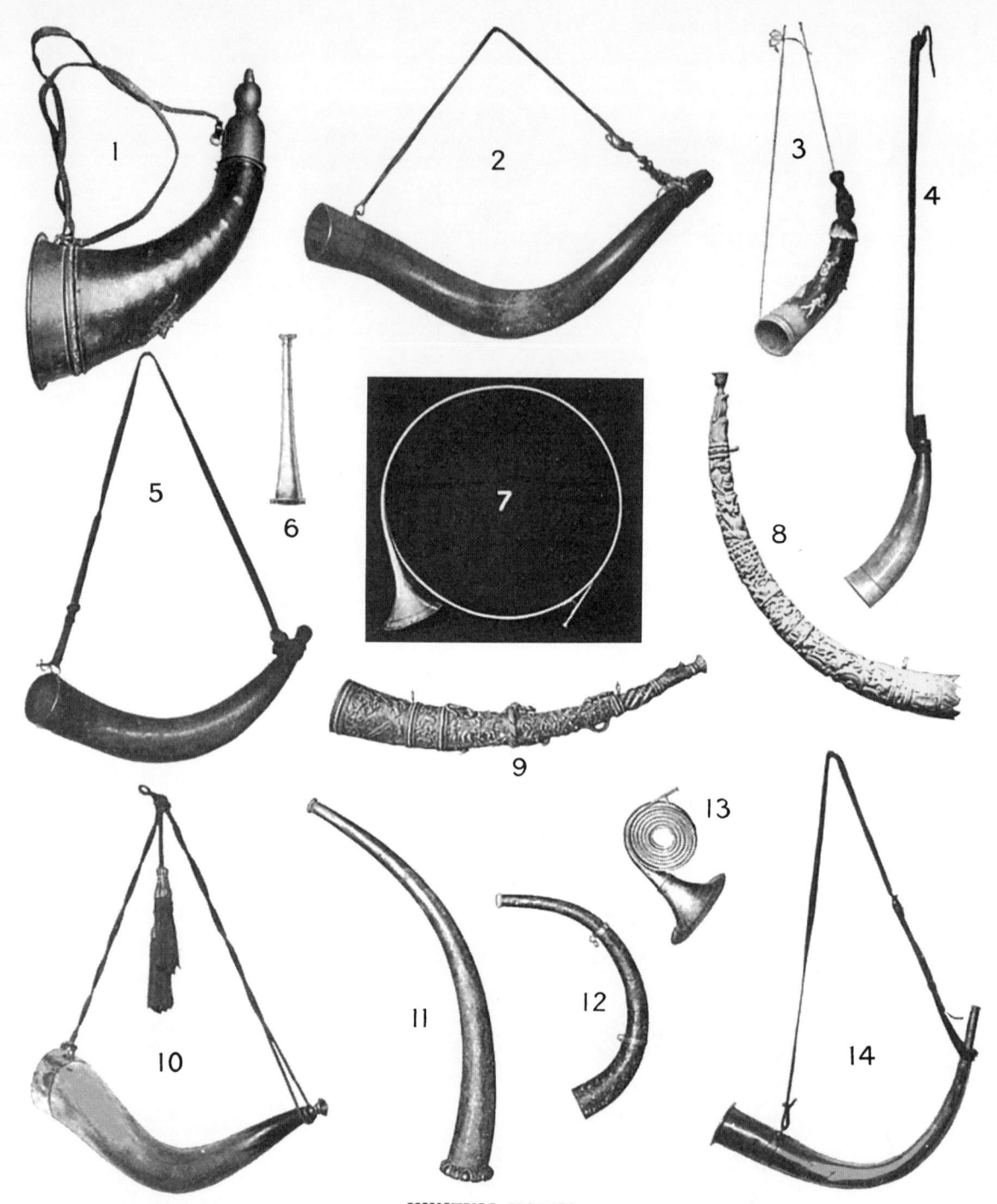

HUNTING HORNS.

1. Late nineteenth century *Trompe de Lorraine*—bell, 5¾ inches.
2. Horn of "Uncle" Bob Eastham of Rappahannock County, Virginia, engraved with foxhunting scenes. 25 inches.
3. Horn from Texas carved with negro head and hunting scenes. 11 inches.
4. North Carolina horn. 11 inches.
5. and 10. Virginia horns.
6. Silver horn presented to the author by Lord Lonsdale. This type is now universally used in Britain. 10 inches.
7. Eighteenth century French horn, 3 feet 4½ inches across; bell 6½ inches.
8. French Oliphant of the seventeenth century, 3 feet 3½ inches long.
9. French horn of the seventeenth century—silver. 1 foot 1½ inches long.
11. Seventeenth century *cors de chasse*, or Huchets; wood covered with thin leather, small end tipped with ivory, bell—4¼ inches—finished with ivory band, 3 feet 3¼ inches.
12. Postilion or huntsman's horn, wood tipped with ivory—Seventeenth century.
13. Hunting horn circa 1760, circular, 5 double turns. 1 foot 3 inches.
14. Brass horn brought from Russia by the author.

the kings of England maintained the Royal Buckhounds down to the time of Queen Victoria; to this day, the hounds hunting deer by royal privilege in the New Forest are known as buckhounds. In the seventeenth century, a Frenchman describes the Royal Buckhounds as resembling the White hounds of the French king, and standing 24–25 inches. Perhaps a description as accurate as any is Somerville's delightful portrait:

> . . . . *his wide-op'ning nose*
> *Upward he curls, and his large sloe-black eyes*
> *Melt in soft blandishments and humble joy:*
> *His glossy skin, or yellow-pied, or blue,*
> *In lights or shades by Nature's pencil drawn,*
> *Reflects the various tints; his ears and legs,*
> *Fleckt here and there, in gay enamell'd pride*
> *Rival the speckled pard; his rush-grown tail*
> *O'er his broad back bends in an ample arch;*
> *On shoulders clean, upright and firm he stands;*
> *His round cat foot, straight hams, and wide-spread thighs,*
> *And his low-dropping chest, confess his speed,*
> *His strength, his wind, or on the steepy hill,*
> *Or far extended plain; in ev'ry part*
> *So well proportion'd, that the nicer skill*
> *Of Phidias himself can't blame thy choice.*
> *Of such compose thy pack.*

As previously mentioned, rough-coated hounds existed on the Isle of Crete in the dawn of history. In France, rough-coated (griffons) hounds have existed since pre-Roman times; and from these it is believed that the rough-coated Welsh hounds originated, brought from France to Wales seven hundred, or more, years ago by the sporting abbot of a monastery. It would seem that Welsh hounds have changed little in hundreds of years, for all the characteristics of the mediaeval hounds still exist in them, such as splendid cry and the trait of tying to the line.

For many, many years, small hounds for hare hunting have been known as beagles. In 1686, according to the *Gentleman's Recreation*, Blome wrote of three varieties then existent,—Southern beagles (resembling dwarf Southern hounds), Northern beagles (sometimes called "cat" beagles), and Little beagles. Southern beagles were renowned for their very melodious cry. In the seventeenth century, they were very much sought after in France, according to Ligniville, Sélincourt, and Savary. They stood not more than eighteen inches, were black and white in color, and were bred especially for voice and careful manner of hunting. In the eighteenth century, they became known as harriers. Little beagles rarely reached a height of fourteen inches. They were the veritable bantams of all hounds. Richardson claims to have seen one measuring only seven inches, and Vlit refers to some so tiny that he saw three attack a hare in its form which escaped in spite of them.

Sélincourt claims that in his time it was the fashion to dock Little beagles very short, which disgusted him greatly, because one of the chief characteristics of scenting hounds, the feathering of the stern, was necessarily absent. Queen Elizabeth's famous pack of "singing" beagles were so known because of their delightful cry. They were so small that any one of them could be put in one of the gauntlet gloves then worn, and it is said to have been common practice to transport a whole pack of such beagles in saddle panniers.

In the past few centuries, hounds and hunting methods have changed very materially, but the token of the huntsman, the horn, still remains the one requisite of his office as in days of yore. It is the one means, other than his voice, that a huntsman has of keeping a pack together, and making them as well as followers of hounds understand his whereabouts and what is transpiring.

The mediaeval type of hunting horn, made from the horn of some animal, is still in general use in America, strange to say, although in Europe it began to disappear several hundred years ago.

The tip of this earliest type of hunting horn was fashioned into a cupped mouth-piece, while the sonorous and melodious sound produced was influenced by the length of the conical tube and circumference of its flaring bell. All sorts of animal horns were used, including that of the ibex, but those of domestic cattle were the most common. Thousands of these are still in use in rural America, and are employed not only for hunting, but are blown by the farmers' wives to call the men from the fields. In Arkansas, conch shell horns are used even at the present time, and one that I know of in Virginia can be heard for a remarkable distance.

When first used by the Romans as a signal, the note of the *cornu* (literally meaning, the horn of an animal) was called *classicum*. Although the Greeks, Romans, and Gauls were in the habit of using horns in war service, we have no proof that they used horns in hunting. Apparently, the Greeks used a straight horn, called a *salpinx*, for army signals and religious ceremonies, and the Latins used the *tuba*, blown by *tubicen*, as signal for attack and retreat in war and games. It is certain that the Franks and other Germanic people from early times employed hunting horns; one definite proof exists in an ancient Latin manuscript, which mentions Clotaire II calling his hounds:

Tunc cornu curvo, plenis buccis anheliter, latratus canum acuit.

Some very ancient horns still exist, and in the treasury of the cathedral of Aix-la-Chapelle is still preserved the ivory horn of Charlemagne. This horn is said to have been made from the tusk of the elephant "Aboul-Abbas" which was sent to the emperor as a gift by the Caliph Haroun al Raschad.

French romance and history frequently eulogizes the horn, as in the vivid account of Roland's "dread horn of Fontarabia," named after an ancient town in Gascogny. In the battle of Roncesvalles, when fatally wounded, Roland blew on this *oliphant*, the third blast breaking the horn in two. Over the din of battle the blast was heard as if it had been a voice from the other world; birds fell dead at the sound, and the whole Saracen army drew back in terror; Charlemagne hearing it at St. Jean Pied de Port, thirty leagues distant, wished to go to Roland's aid, but the traitor Ganelon deterred him, saying that without doubt his nephew was only hunting in the mountains. Cervantes says that this horn was of gold and ivory, and of massive size, larger than a massive beam.

The premature death of Charles IX was attributed by many of his contemporaries to his passion for blowing the horn. One of those to entertain this belief was Louis XIII, who began hunting at the age of seven, and prided himself on his ability to blow his horn all day without being inconvenienced. A famous English horn of the eleventh century, known as the Borstall horn, is two feet and four inches long on the convex bend, the inside diameter of the bell measuring three inches. According to tradition, Edward the Confessor presented this horn to one Nigel as a trophy for killing an immense wild boar, and by this horn as token, he and his heirs held lands of the English crown.

In the Middle Ages, a number of women were experts on the horn. Of Madame de Beaujeu it was written:

> *A sa belle bouche elle a mise*
> *Sa trompe, dont moult bien s'aydoit.*

In an old French poem, the duc de Belin is described as departing for the hunt, a wonderful horn hanging from his shoulder:

> Pend *à son col un cor d'ivoire chier*
> *De neuf viroles de fin or bien loiés (lié)*
> La guiche *en fut d'un vert paile prisié.*

Animal horns were used in France down to the eighteenth century. They were frequently furnished with mouth-pieces and bands of more or less precious metal; some horns were provided with a stopper that they might be used for drinking purposes.

Horns of metal appeared in France in the fifteenth century, semi-circular in form, resembling the primitive type made from horns of animals. Those used by princes and great lords were often of gold and silver, frequently engraved and decorated, or studded with precious stones. Such a horn, made of brass, I brought from Russia, in 1903, where they were then in common use.

The little trumpets coiled in the center, which appear in the pictures by Rubens, were doubtless of metal, but were not in vogue until the end of the sixteenth century. In the imperial Russian collection of arms there was a beautiful gold-plated silver trumpet ornamented with fleurs-de-lis, said to have belonged to Henry II of France.

Maricourt speaks of the trumpet of the king having a mouth-piece of gold. The best "trompes" were entirely of silver. French authors do not seem to know of what material the English horns were made, which were so very highly esteemed in France in the fifteenth century. Louis XI did not appear to have been surprised when he received one of them in exchange for a splendid gilded bowl presented by him to the Count of Warwick, on his departure from Rouen, in 1467. Another French reference to English horns appears in the accounts of the ducs d'Orléans preserved at Blois:

. . . . *cxvii francs pour cause de xxiii cors de chasse envoyés d'Angleterre.*

The record further shows that such English horns were often suspended by means of silken cords enriched with gold and silver threads.

In spite of the growing popularity of metal horns, the use of animal horns seems to have survived in France, at least, until 1700. The use of metal horns evidently was increasing all over Europe, for, writing of Denmark, in 1694, Lord Molesworth mentions huntsmen "having their great brass hunting horns about their necks."

Metal horns have had varied shapes, and Maricourt says that at one time there were trumpets which had five or six coils, but they were given up because of the difficulty in blowing them. A picture by Van der Meulen painted about 1670, shows the first circular horn similar to the French horn now in use, but much smaller, and suspended from a cord. These little circular horns were succeeded in the early eighteenth century by the large horns having one and one-half turns, called after Dampierre, the huntsman who first used them. In the pictures of d'Oudry, all the huntsmen carried such horns, which were made of silver for royalty and chief huntsmen.

In the reign of Louis XVI, the French horn was modified so as to have two and one-half turns, as being less clumsy, and this is the style of the French horn to-day. In England, it is known as the Compassed horn, as it possesses a compass, or range, of twelve notes, from C below the line in the treble clef to G above the line. From the shape of ancient horns, it is quite evident, as in the case of modern English horns, that it was possible to blow but one note, the different calls being distinguished by long or short blasts and the interval between them, a single note being designated as a "mot."

From the thirteenth century, there were many recognized calls on the horn, one French author naming up to the number of thirty-six calls, including fanfares. Fourteen calls indicating the progress of the hunt may be tabulated as follows:

Cournures de chemin,
" *d'ésemblé,*
" *de quête,*
" *de chasse,*
" *de vue,*
" *de mescroy,*
" *de requêté,*

Cournures d'eauve,
" *de relais,*
" *d'ayde,*
" *de prise,*
" *de retraite,*
" *d'appel de chiens,*
" *d'appel de gens.*

Never have I heard of any animal horn being used for hunting in modern England, but it is certain this type was used there even after 1700, and horns of various shapes, similar to the several French models previously mentioned, were sometimes used even in the eighteenth century. Since then, however, in Britain, the straight horn has become the vogue. Early English straight metal horns were often from eighteen to twenty-four inches in length, but have gradually been reduced until to-day they measure from nine to twelve inches. The quality of the note is regulated by the length and diameter of the tube—the shorter the horn, the higher the note. These horns are generally made of copper, German silver, or solid silver throughout, perhaps of combinations of these metals. It is said that horns of this shape have also been made of boxwood; and for those who cannot blow the horn with facility, a reed horn has been invented, containing a metal tongue, which requires no skill to blow, but produces only a sound like a child's toy.

The straight metal horn is unquestionably easier to handle and quicker to use, say, when hounds are gone away, than the cow horn, but there have been many discussions in America as to which horn can be heard best by both hounds and field in blind, hilly, heavily wooded country. Character of sound is very important under such circumstances, important to a degree incomprehensible to one whose hunting has been confined to England. For some time, I have been convinced that the metallic note of the metal horn can be the better heard in contrast with the soughing of wind in woodlands. In a pine tree country like North Carolina, the soft note of the cow horn can easily be confused when at a distance with the sound of wind in the tree tops, but on a still night, the mellow note of this horn travels a long distance and is impressive to hear. The penetrating sound from a metal horn is eulogised in the following account clipped from a New York newspaper during the World War:

A Victoria Cross has been awarded to Colonel John Vaughan Campbell of the Coldstream Guards for a gallant feat on the Somme battlefield. He rallied his men at a critical moment, led them through a very heavy barrage of fire, and was one of the first to enter the enemy trench.

HOUNDS AND HUNTING

The Colonel led his men with a revolver in one hand and a foxhunter's silver horn in the other, and the hunter's horn seems to have had a wonderful effect on the British Tommies . . . .

It was a silver horn presented to him by the non-commissioned officers and men of the First Battalion when he left to join the Third Battalion. He found that the clear ringing notes of the horn were more easily heard, and on the battlefield there was no mistaking it.

In the extraordinarily difficult situation, the horn was probably the only thing that would have rallied the men so quickly. In the inevitable break-up of a formation during an attack, men get lost, and the sound of many whistles being blown by the officers must be sometimes confusing. Early in the war the Germans tried to confuse the British soldiers by imitating bugle calls, and the bugle is not now used to the extent that it was then. But the huntsman's horn was a new thing to the Germans. It startled them and brought dismay to their ranks, and they ran like foxes with the hounds in hot pursuit.

CHAPTER IV.

PRESENT DAY HOUNDS

FEW people realize that there are, perhaps, several hundred thousand hounds hunting foxes and wolves in all parts of the United States. There are thousands of other hounds used for mountain lion, bear, and deer; beagles and "rabbit dogs" run into tens of thousands; and as for coon dogs,—frequently a cross between a hound and something else, with some of them running mute and some giving cry,—their number is legion. Perhaps this estimate is conservative, in view of the fact that the Dog World recently estimated the total number of hounds of all sorts in this country as 1,500,000.

These hounds are usually owned by individual farmers or hunters. They are retained for their hunting qualities and voice, little heed being given to color or shape. In different parts of the country, such hounds vary materially in characteristics, and as their ancestry is mixed, they are difficult to breed true to type. However, they can hunt their game day or night, winter or summer, as they are adapted to the hunting peculiarities of this continent in a way that no other hounds are.

In spite of the vast number of individual hound owners, there are comparatively few large packs of true American hounds of any kind. In referring to "packs," is meant where seventeen to twenty couple are hunted together and carefully drafted for evenness of running ability.

Many people refer to "American hounds" as if there were only one type with uniform hunting characteristics. Actually, there are several distinctly different strains, varying widely in color, conformation, and style of hunting. There are few accurate records which throw light on the actual origin of these various strains of hounds, but certainly France, England, and Ireland assisted.

The first mention we have of hound importations to America appears in a diary of one of De Soto's retainers. In describing the embarkation for America, 1539, he writes: *Now it is the noble Governor, De Soto, with his train of six hundred knights in doublets and cassocks of silk, and his priests and splendid vestments, with his Portuguese in shining armor, his horses, hounds, and hogs, all ready for a triumphal procession to kingdoms of gold and ivory.*

HOUNDS AND HUNTING

It is further mentioned that the hounds were utilized to hunt Indians instead of foxes and hare.

While De Soto's importation may have been the original one, the first record which is of any practical value to us is that of a seventeenth century importation to Maryland, the story of which is very interesting.

The cavalier, Robert Brooke, the first known master of foxhounds in America, was born in London, June 3, 1602, the son of Thomas Brooke (member of Parliament, 1604–1611). In 1650, Robert Brooke sailed for the Crown colony in America in his own ship, taking with him his family, a large retinue of servants—forty persons in all, and his pack of hounds. He landed June 29 at Della Brooke, twenty miles from the mouth of the Patuxtent in what is now Calvert County. It was due to this importation that the family of Brooke hounds, which was so famous in Maryland for over two hundred years, originated. These hounds have had material influence as the tap-root of several strains of American hounds, as may be seen by reference to the letters and records of Messrs. Trigg, Maupin, Wade, and Walker; also, reference to the files of the American Turf Register and other sporting magazines from 1794 to 1864, reveals the fame of these hounds at that period.

Until a few years ago, Charles F. Brooke, of Brooke Grove, near Sandy Springs, Maryland, hunted a pack descended directly from the first importation, as had all of his ancestors before him, the strain remaining in the same family ownership for nearly three hundred years—which is, indeed, unique in America. As late as 1915, several couple of these hounds, which were of a light tan color, were in my pack.

Apparently the first mention of hounds in Virginia occurs in the court records of Northampton County in 1691, mentioned in Dr. Philip Alexander Bruce's *Social Life of Virginia in the Seventeenth Century*. Mike Dixon was called before a magistrate upon a complaint that he kept a pack of "dogs," which attacked passersby. Mike pleaded that his pack of "dogs" was necessary to the safety of the colonists in that they destroyed "foxes, wolves and other varmint." It seems that the justice agreed with Mike, and that the road was moved back so that the hounds might be undisturbed.

As the colonies developed, the number of hounds increased; from the time the first pioneers set their faces westward until the last covered wagon was dragged by struggling oxen over the Oregon trail, horses and hounds were important members of each outfit. The first Englishman (except, possibly, Indian captives) to cross the Alleghanies and explore the Cumberland River with its important gateway to the West, and the first Englishman to set foot on the soil of Kentucky, was Dr. Thomas Walker, scholar, sportsman, and explorer, of Castle Hill, Albemarle County, Virginia, who imported hounds from England in 1742.

In 1749, he started westward with his horses, guns, and hounds. On the

PRESENT DAY HOUNDS

evening of March 29, while still in Virginia, he recorded in his journal: "Our Dogs were very uneasie during the Night." The next day the record continues: "We kept down Reedy Creek, and discovered the tracks of about twenty Indians. . . . We suppose they made our Dogs so restless last night." On the date of April 7, the following entry appears: "We rode eight miles over broken land. It snowed most of the day. In the evening our Dogs caught a large he-bear, which, before we could come up to shoot him, had wounded a Dog of mine so that he could not travel, and we carried him on horseback until he recovered." So it was, that even before Daniel Boone, this gentleman sportsman, with the wounded foxhound strapped upon one of his horses, and a small pack of Virginia hounds following, passed through the wilderness of Cumberland Gap, which he named. On April 26, he had arrived in what is now Kentucky, and wrote: "A bear broke one of my Dog's forelegs." The actual number of hounds in this expedition is not recorded; however, no less than three couple belonged to Dr. Walker, his companions evidently owning others; for it is mentioned that in the hunting of a large elk, "he killed Ambrose Powell's Dog in the Chase, and we named the run Tumbler's Creek, the Dog being of that name." This creek was the headwater of what is now known as the Kentucky River, much to the regret of later sportsmen who would prefer to have had the sporting dog *Tumbler* immortalized.

Four months and seven days later, when Dr. Walker again saw the red brick of Castle Hill, under the hot noon sun of July 16, he had killed for food thirteen buffalo, eight elk, fifty-three bear, twenty deer, and about one hundred and fifty turkey, in addition to "small game."

George Washington, who had kept hounds from his youth (and whose Mount Vernon estate was only a few score of miles from that of Dr. Walker), was, with British officers and residents of New York, a subscriber to an importation from England, in 1770, of hounds, horses and servants. John Evers was master of this pack, which was kept at Hempstead, Long Island.

Washington evidently exchanged hunting stories as well as war stories with that gallant personage, the Marquis de la Fayette, as a result of which he was enabled to record in his diary:

1785—Aug. 24. Rec'd 7 hounds sent me from France by the Marqs. de la Fayette by the way of New York, viz., 3 Dogs and 4 Bitches.

Nov. 29. Went out after breakfast with my hounds from France and 2 which were lent me yesterday. Found a fox which was run tolerably well by 2 Fr. bitches and one of Mason's Dogs. The other French Dogs showed little disposition to follow, and with a 2nd Dog of Mason's got upon another fox which was followed slow and indifferently by some and not at all by the rest until scent became cold, so cold that it could not be followed at all.

Dec. 1. Three or four of the French hounds discovered no greater disposition for Hunting today than they did on Tuesday last.

HOUNDS AND HUNTING

Dec. 5. My French hounds performed better today and have offered hopes of their performing well when they come to be a little more used to Hunting and understand more fully the kind of game they are intended to run.

These hounds are described by Mr. Custis as being of great size; their voices are referred to as being "like the bells of Moscow"; their dispositions necessitated their being carefully confined.

The origin of the hounds owned by the Gloucester Foxhunting Club mentioned elsewhere as the first organized hunt in America, is not definitely known, but it may be assumed that they were English, because in 1808 it is recorded that Mr. Davies and Mr. Ross, of Philadelphia, made an importation of the "best English foxhounds" for this hunt. From a contemporary drawing, it appears that these were light, active hounds, closely resembling English hounds of the period. Some were spotted, some were black and tan, and in the Gloucester Foxhunting Club records special mention is made of a fine red bitch, *Music*. Frequent reference is made to cry, which is in one case referred to as a "bellow."

The Baltimore Hunt Club, which was organized in 1818 and became most famous, seems to have been alive to the necessity of the best of hounds, and made many importations from England. As late as 1830, a newspaper record announces the arrival of "one foxhound bitch, the leader of Lord Doneghal's pack, with five pups by his crack dog; the hound and the pups for the Baltimore Hunt and all sent in by Mr. Adair." About 1825, it is said that the British ambassador imported a pack from England to be used in the vicinity of Washington.

The origin of the hounds belonging to the hunt club of Charlestown, Massachusetts, previous to 1830, is not clear, but it must be surmised that they emanated from Great Britain.

Little by little the ownership of hounds by all sorts and conditions of people continued to spread throughout the United States. A unique instance indicating the widespread interest in hounds appears in the following notice of public sale, or vendue, in Kentucky:

Having sold my farm and I am leaving for Oregon Territory by ox team, will offer on March 1, 1849, all my personal property. [Then follows a long list of everything for sale from spinning wheels to slaves. The latter, it is stipulated, must be sold "all together to same party."] . . . *and six heads of foxhounds, all soft mouth except one.* . . . *My home is two miles south of Versailles, Kentucky, on the McCanns ferry pike. Sale begins at 8 o'clock A.M. Plenty to drink and eat. I. L. Moss.*

French hounds were imported to Louisiana, probably in the seventeenth century, by an early ancestor in America of Mr. Percival Rosseau, the famous limner of sporting dogs, whose delightful paintings of my foxhounds are

BLOODHOUND.
Excellent nose but not shaped for speed.
Champion Ledburn *Beau Brummel*.

FELL HOUND OF CUMBERLAND.
Symmetrically made for rough country. *Kiskin*, champion Eskdale and Ennerdale Hunt Show.

PENNSYLVANIA HOUND.
Excellent nose and cry.

BIG STRIDE.
S. L. Wooldridge's famous field trial Walker hound.

SIR EDWARD CURRIE'S CROSS-BRED
WELSH BITCH, *Hefty*.
Imported and photographed by the author, 1922.
These hounds have excellent nose and cry.

ROUGH-COATED WELSH.
Excellent nose and cry. *Conqueror*, res. champion Welsh National Hound Show.

TAUNTON VALE HARRIER.
An active small hound. Photo by author, 1922.

FRENCH STAGHOUND
Notable for size.

TYPES OF MODERN HOUNDS.

TYPICAL FRENCH STAGHOUNDS OF THE DUCHESSE D'UZES' HUNT.

THE AXE VALE HARRIERS OF DEVONSHIRE.
A light-colored pack of old fashioned blood lines. Photo by author, 1921.

KERRY BEAGLES FROM MR. RYAN'S SCARTEEN PACK IMPORTED IN 1927 BY
MRS. W. GOADBY LOEW, MASTER OF THE HARFORD HUNT OF MARYLAND.

PRESENT DAY HOUNDS

reproduced in this book. This family had received from Louis XIV a large land grant in that territory, and for many generations they lived in the manner of *grands seigneurs*, enjoying among other things the pleasures of hunting bear and panther in the cane brakes. Their hounds were of the Normandy breed, *Franc Comptoise*. They were big, with high occiputs, long-eared, rat-tailed, and were known locally as *Porcelaines*, because of their white and tan markings.

The family fortune having become depleted by the Civil War, Mr. Rosseau as a very young man migrated to Texas to enter the cattle business. Although he experienced there many thrilling adventures, the marks of which he still bears in the form of bullet wounds, his inherent love of the chase came to the fore when he realized that this new country was a game paradise. Fortunately, the breed of ancestral hounds still existed, and there remained behind kind friends who selected six couple of these hounds and placed them in collars and chains, in October, 1878, in charge of the captain of a Mississippi River packet, at Point Coupé Parish, Louisiana. Thus, they were taken to St. Louis, a distance of two thousand miles by river; then entrained for Denver, at which place they were transferred to the narrow-gauge railroad for Pueblo, Southern Colorado. Being met at Pueblo by the owner, these hounds were taken on foot with his camp and cattle outfit another five hundred miles south to the Panhandle country of Texas, a total distance of nearly four thousand miles. This country was just then being opened up, and there Mr. Rosseau had a permanent winter camp on the headwaters of the Salt Fork of the Brazos River, in the brakes of the staked plains.

It was from this winter camp that he hunted panther with these hounds and their descendants, for a number of years. The country thereabouts was full of game, in fact, deer were so numerous that they caused much trouble until hounds were thoroughly broken by being ridden down and lashed with the cow whip. When Mr. Rosseau left Texas, he gave his entire pack of over thirty couple to various ranchmen, and he believes their descendants are still hunting in that vicinity. This pack was unquestionably the first pack of scenting hounds in that part of the South-West.

Mr. Rosseau painted a remarkable picture of thirty-one of his hounds, life size, which hung in the Paris Salon, in 1906, depicting his pack killing a panther, or mountain lion. It was thought by French critics that the painting was fanciful, until a letter was shown from Theodore Roosevelt, saying that the event portrayed was most realistic.

An Irish importation of 1830 was largely responsible for the tap-root of the Henry, Birdsong, and Trigg strains. Walker hounds have English crosses as late as seventy years ago.

Whatever may have been the exact source of the several varieties, the understanding of what these varied sorts of hounds can do, how they do it, and how they can be improved for specific purposes, is of constructive interest to us to-day.

Certain strains of hounds in America have been bred for many generations with the primary object in view of winning field trials (at which they are very successful) rather than for pack work. The requirements for field trials are not entirely those desirable for a pack which is to be followed by riders in the orthodox English manner of foxhunting. Extreme individuality is the trait sought for field trial work, and my experience teaches that such hounds possess that for which they have been bred,—speed, drive, and very wide ranging manner of hunting. For pack work, however, they are prone to be over-anxious at a check, and, compared to some hounds, they sometimes lack nose and cry. Speed! Speed!! Speed!!! has been the watchword, and characteristics undesirable in a pack are occasionally overlooked in them as individuals. Field trial hounds, in common with many others, are not free from certain faults characteristic of any hounds bred for speed, such as, skirting and deliberately running mute when in the lead so as to get away with their fox alone; again, they may sometimes be mouthy,—that is, they will run amuck, when there is no line, in their keen desire to lead. When scenting is good, they very successfully account for foxes; but, in my belief and observation, under difficult conditions they are hardly as consistent in their work as a good pack of steady Virginia hounds, which with their supernose are able to stick to a failing scent to the Nth degree.

Foxhound field trials in the United States are held all over the country by strong organizations, in a spirit of good fellowship. The keen competition and progress which they have engendered have done much to excite interest in careful breeding and vast improvement in hounds along the lines desired.

In Britain, especially in Northern England, hound races known as "trail" competitions are the only events analogous to the American hound field trials, and occur at such affairs as the Ullswater Sports. This typical country gathering, held near Lowther Castle, the seat of Lord Lonsdale, in Cumberland (where the author was a guest in 1920), is one of the multifarious interests sponsored by this greatest of sportsmen. Games, competitive events of all kinds, including the hound "trail," are held. In such races, a drag is laid on the hillsides of bowl-like valleys; at a given signal, hounds are slipped and race away. Every move of every hound can be seen over the course of six or seven miles. An American competition of this sort of which I know has, in recent years, occurred under the auspices of the Millwood Hunt, near Framingham, Massachusetts.

In a very rough or wooded country, where it is impracticable to follow very fast hounds, I believe Pennsylvania or Maryland hounds are excellent. They have fine cry and pack beautifully. Unfortunately, they are sometimes mouthy, speaking on almost any kind of a line; individuals dwell badly, and

PRESENT DAY HOUNDS

are often faulty in conformation, frequently having splayed-feet, swaybacks, crooked front legs, and cow-hocks. Nevertheless, when they find a fox they run him well, and their excellent nose and cry in some respects counterbalance other weak points. One of their characteristic colors is blue tick, but black and white hounds and black and tans are not infrequent.

Excellent hounds have always been bred in Virginia, and the old-fashioned Virginia hound as bred by a few intelligent men in the Rappahannock section of Northern Virginia for many a decade, is a hound which seems to be able to consistently reproduce its characteristics where animals are of the pure strain.

After many years of experience, the author has become convinced that the most efficient pack hound in the world to hunt a fox is this Old Virginia foxhound. Anyone can become foolishly sentimental over a breed of animals; however, I have continued to breed this strain of hounds not on account of sentiment or romance, but because, after searching throughout Europe and America to discover hounds excelling them for pack hunting under difficult conditions of scenting and rough country, I have failed to do so.

Such hounds may be considered deficient if they cannot regularly hunt hard at least three days a week, or more than this if required. They must have sufficient determination and stamina never to stop trying as long as their fox remains above ground or there is a vestige of a line left. A pack of such hounds must be able to account for foxes in the roughest woodland and hill country in July heat (as my pack is required to do), sound of foot, and sufficiently agile to negotiate the steepest of rocky cliffs in the North, as well as have enough nose and drive to kill red foxes in sandy Carolina. This pack must hunt with dash and style, carrying great head, negotiating burnt-over tracts, and pressing tirelessly for hours, if necessary, through briers, cane, half-frozen swamp water, as if there were nothing to stop them, and, gallantly killing their fox, come home with their sterns up, a pack in fact as well as in name. In a grass country, these hounds must be able to outpace, under good conditions, the best of thoroughbred horses.

To summarize: such hounds have ability based on the following essentials,—

Nose—that the hound may follow the line of a fox and show sport under almost any difficult American conditions.

Maximum cry—by which a pack may be heard in undulating American country of large woodlands.

Drive, stamina, and determination to get forward and stay at it.

Mentality—that adapts itself to pack hunting and control by a huntsman.

The strain of hounds from which my pack is descended has been owned from father to son for numerous generations of Virginia land owners. They have never been known by a name more definite than the "old family" of hounds. I believe, although I have not been able to corroborate my theory, that these hounds are in some measure the descendants of importations from the most fashionable British packs of the late eighteenth and early nineteenth centuries. The basis of my belief rests on the fact that the antebellum Virginia landed gentry were descended from the class of Britishers who were keenest on riding to hounds, and who always bred and owned the best of hounds and horses. In history and in fiction, one constantly sees references to the hunting proclivities of the Virginians. The entries already cited from the diary of George Washington relative to his hounds further illustrate this point.

An interesting bit of evidence of the Virginian enthusiasm for hounds and horses in early days is a painted frieze taken from an old Virginia house. This frieze is now the property of Mr. and Mrs. Chalmers Wood, of New York, and depicts the members of a large family starting for the hunt. They are mounted on blood-like horses, the young cavaliers looking very gallant, and the young women with tricorne hats and flowing skirts extremely pretty on their side-saddles. Unfortunately, the part of this frieze which depicted hounds was destroyed through some accident; so, from this source we have no knowledge of the type at this period. Unquestionably, many of the landed proprietors of Virginia kept in close connection with their English cousins, frequently visiting England for sport and travel until the outbreak of the Civil War.

The last and most convincing evidence which I have to offer that the true stamp of the Old Virginia foxhound is to-day similar to the great British hounds of the late eighteenth and early nineteenth centuries, is that of contemporary English portraits.

The British hound as shown in the picture by Sartorius (*circa* 1780) of Peter Beckford's pack, seems to have been an animal suggesting in bone, conformation, and color this Virginia foxhound of the present time. Other hounds of this stamp were depicted by Marshall, Davis, Pollard, Alken, Wolstenholme, Basil Dighton, Ferneley, and J. F. Herring. From 1810 to 1840 was the greatest day in English hunting. It was before the advent of the railroad, and at a time when most English gentlemen were country bred. They understood the difference between riding to hunt and hunting to ride. It was before the days when hound shows and fashion had helped to destroy in English hounds the cry which once must have been theirs, and the nose which the old records of the day indicate was considered so essential.

During the many decades that have elapsed since the famous packs of Hugo Meynell and "Squire" Osbaldeston were in their prime, the English foxhound has very materially changed, certainly in color and conformation, and unquestionably in cry and nose. In the matter of conformation, a careful study of the portrait of Osbaldeston's *Furrier* will perhaps illustrate this contention.

PRESENT DAY HOUNDS

The traits that interest a typical Virginia hound owner of to-day are, precisely, nose and cry. Therefore, in spite of probable excellent working characteristics in early importations, there may even have been improvement in working ability for local conditions during the past hundred years. It should be remembered that hounds in Virginia have been bred for their racing ability in accounting for foxes, and for cry, also that the present day hounds are the "survival of the fittest" along these lines.

There must have been innumerable unrecorded importations, the influence of which it is impossible to trace. The facts concerning one importation, however, the known effect of which is widespread, are as follows:

About 1830, Bolton Jackson, of Maryland, imported two hounds from Ireland, *Mountain* and *Muse*. These hounds were presented to Captain Sterret Ridgley, who gave them to Governor Ogle of Maryland. He, in turn, gave *Mountain* (then known as *Old Mountain*) to Captain Charles Carroll, of Carrollton, who presented him to Dr. Buchanan of Sharpsburg, from whom, in 1840, Dr. T. Y. Henry, of Virginia, got *Captain*, bred by Dr. Buchanan, (probably in 1838), who was a direct descendant of imported *Mountain* and *Muse*. Dr. Henry, who was a grandson of Patrick Henry, hunted and bred from *Captain* and his descendants for several years in Virginia, where they became famous as the Irish hounds.

Probably the true Virginia foxhounds of the present time are descended in part from this blood, although the exact records are unobtainable on account of the upheaval caused by the Civil War. At least, the hounds bred by Dr. Henry tally in description with the Virginia foxhounds, the best blood of which I have assembled and breed to-day, with the hope that it may be preserved for the use of the future sportsmen of this country.

In a pedigree chart corrected in the sixties by George L. F. Birdsong, a number of descendants of Dr. Henry's *Captain* are charted as follows:

Name	*Whelped*	*Breeder*	*Color*	*Height*
Trooper	1842	Dr. Henry	Black and tan	24 inches
Willis	1842	Dr. Henry	Black and tan	26 inches
Fleet	1844	Birdsong	Red	
Ruth	1846	Dr. Henry	Black, white tips	20 inches
Virginia	1846	Dr. Henry	White, black tips	20 inches
Capt. May	1848	Birdsong	Red tipt and white	
Ringgold	1851	Birdsong	White and black	Very tall
Hodo	1853	Birdsong	Black, white tipt	26 inches
Butter	1854	Dr. Bidler	Red, white tipt	
Dallas	1858	D. W. Womble	Red, white tipt	
Longstreet	1860	Birdsong	Red, white tipt	24 inches
Venus	——	J. Garret	Black and tan	

HOUNDS AND HUNTING

The same chart indicates that Ellio Yuille, of Charlotte County, Virginia, about 1840, imported from Great Britain a dog hound named *Streaker*. This hound was designated on the old pedigree as a full beagle, which doubtless meant Kerry beagle, as his descendants are described as large hounds—reds and blacks, and blacks and tans, measuring up to 24 inches high. The Irish hounds also helped to produce the Birdsong (later called July) hounds of Georgia, and the Trigg hounds of Kentucky, as already mentioned.

The story as told by Haiden C. Trigg is as follows:

In the early forties, Dr. T. Y. Henry . . . presented George L. F. Birdsong, of Thomaston, Georgia, with a pair of puppies from his pack of hounds, which at that time had made an enviable reputation in Virginia. Mr. Birdsong sent a wagon overland (more than five hundred miles), there being no railroad at that time, for the dogs. They proved to be superior to any dogs he had owned up to that time. In 1844, or 1845, Dr. Henry being threatened with that dreaded disease, consumption, was ordered South by his physician. He started, traveling leisurely by wagon, accompanied by a party of friends, carrying his fine kennel of hounds with him, stopping at different points, putting in the time hunting and fishing as it suited their fancy. Mr. Birdsong, being informed of his movements, intercepted Dr. Henry en route, spending some days with him.

On reaching Florida, the deer being plentiful, Dr. Henry's dogs frequently ran them, when they would always take to the bayous and lagoons. When swimming after the game the dogs would be killed by alligators that infested these waters. Dr. Henry soon realized that his much-prized pack would be exterminated if something was not done. He wrote the facts to his friend, Mr. Birdsong, telling him that he might have the remnant of his famous pack if he would come after them. Mr. Birdsong, while sympathizing with his friend in his misfortune, was glad of an opportunity to secure these much coveted dogs, and at once started for them.

The famous Trigg hounds of Kentucky descended from the Irish hounds in the following manner:

In 1860, Haiden C. Trigg, an enthusiastic hound breeder (whose sporting *nom de plume* was "Full Cry"), began acquiring hounds from George L. F. Birdsong, of Georgia. Among these hounds were several by Mr. Birdsong's famous *Longstreet* (1860), descendant in the sixth generation from Dr. Henry's *Captain* (1838) on the sire's side, and in the fifth generation from the same dog on the dam's side. *Longstreet's* pedigree shows five crosses of *Captain*.

The Birdsong, or July, hounds of Georgia were derived from the descendants of the Irish hounds of Dr. Henry, and a dog named *July* obtained from one Gosnell, of Maryland, in 1861, and imported to Georgia by Miles G. Harris. Mr. Trigg indicated that Mr. Birdsong was satisfied that *July* traced

PRESENT DAY HOUNDS

back to *Captain* (1838) and the original Henry Irish hounds. Of the origin of Maupin and Walker hounds, Mr. Trigg says:

In the early fifties, General Maupin and his friends imported many dogs from South Carolina, Virginia, and Maryland, sparing no expense to improve their stock. In 1857, they imported from England, I think, three dogs, Fox, Rifle, *and* Marth. *About this time, General Maupin got from East Tennessee the dog,* Tennessee Lead, *which he, Maupin, thought the best dog he ever owned. The cross of the English dogs, and especially the 'Lead' cross on their previous importations produced a dog which has justly become famous, and was known as the* Maupin dog. *This strain has been preserved and bred with great care by W. S. Walker & Brothers, of Garrard County, Kentucky, and are known to-day as the Walker dogs.*

Some fifteen years ago, the American adherents of English hounds of the Peterborough stamp usually believed that such hounds were equal to other hounds in working qualities; but experience seems to have qualified this belief even to the most dyed-in-the-wool English show hound advocates. To-day, all sorts of expedients are being tried by masters in the United States who admire the appearance of English hounds to compromise between efficiency and the fashionable English standard of appearance. They are trying all kinds of crosses between the various stamps of American hounds (let us say, Kentucky, Virginia, Pennsylvania) and various sorts of English bitches, —Stud Book, Fell, Sir Edward Curre's modified Welsh, even English harriers, and the reverse of all these crosses. Of course, the result is chaotic, not necessarily in the first generation, but, obviously, under the Mendelian law there can be no definite predominant characteristic consistently reproduced in a large percentage of the descendants.

Because the Peterborough show type is the hound that most often appears in illustrations, and is the hound exclusively used in fashionable English hunt countries, Americans frequently overlook the fact that, in addition, among the hundreds of packs in Britain to-day, there are several types of hounds not bred to the show standard. Incidentally, this show type has been most often exported, although it is probably the least useful of all British types for overseas conditions. It represents, however, a marvelous feat of breeding, if an artificial standard of conformation rather than working qualities is the objective sought.

To explain: more than a hundred years ago, hound packs of Great Britain had already arrived at a surprising state of perfection. This is indicated by innumerable paintings. Hound breeding was fostered by the best type of English gentlemen who had plenty of resources and high ideals of what a pack should be. Packs had been handed down from father to son, in many instances, through several generations, and, thus, continuity in breeding policy resulted. From being more or less the natural pursuit of the country squire, hunting became the most fashionable of all British amusements, and with this zeal for hunting came a craze for perfection of its every detail from a spectacular point of view. In 1911, there were nearly four hundred packs in Great Britain and Ireland, not counting foot harriers, beagles, and otter hounds.

The first hound show was held at Redcar, in 1859, and since then exhibitions have, little by little, augmented interest in the show points of hounds, regardless of their working ability, until the show type English foxhound has become marvelously uniform in a certain standard of conformation most pleasing to the eye that is accustomed to such a standard. However, while this "perfection to please the eye" has gone on, certain qualities have been neglected, notably, nose and cry. Its cry is now deficient, and its nose is regarded by many as the most inefficient in any breed of scenting hounds.

In following out the theory that a stout, strong hound was necessary, the mania for bone and substance has gone so far that it has developed an animal unable to get about with agility, by reason of its very weightiness, at least in rough countries. Although a horse must carry weight on its back, while a hound carries none, no one would think of such a thing as attempting to ride a cart horse with enormous weight of bone and muscle at speed over a rough country. This very weight, useful to throw against the collar in pulling a heavy load, creates its own handicap where flexibility of action is a requisite. A well made blood horse standing 16 hands, 2 inches, with no superfluous weight to carry, has a heart, presumably, just as large as his cart-horse cousin of the same height; but the superfluous weight of the cart horse must in itself incapacitate that animal from any sustained action at speed.

In the same way, a well made hound standing, say, 23 inches, symmetrically put together anatomically, with sufficient bone on which to hang muscle, must have an advantage over a hound of equal height that carries weight of bone and muscle more than essential for strength. In other words, where there is superfluous bone, the unnecessary weight which the hound has to carry must be nothing but a handicap. If one were to systematically breed race horses for more bone than necessary to carry essential muscle, it would hardly be considered among the racing fraternity as ordinary common sense.

When the eighteenth century writers on English foxhounds mentioned "cat feet," they must have meant reasonably well-knit, tightly-made, strong, yet flexible feet as opposed to the splay-footed hound; but it is hardly possible that they ever dreamed of the exaggerated cat-footed hound of 1928—feet with toes so short that they are like stumps, rising into pasterns so straight and rigid that the result is a foreleg which must jar the shoulders every time the hound puts his feet to the ground, at least on hard going.

For evenness of type, color, and racial characteristics, Peterborough

PRESENT DAY HOUNDS

judgments have through many years developed something very interesting to look at; but, is it a foxhound any more than the modern show fox terrier is a fox terrier in the original sense? So definitely has this modern show type been fixed in the eye of the fashionable English hunting world that a present day master of a fashionable hunt would no more think of having in his pack a hound that deviates from the accepted standard, regardless of its ability, than he would think of appearing at the opening meet of the season in mufti. It simple "is not done."

The British are the greatest breeders of live stock the world has ever seen or probably ever will see. They breed their mares to the winner of the Derby; they breed their greyhound bitches to the Winner of the Waterloo Cup; and yet they often breed their foxhound bitches to the Winner of the Peterborough Show, which winner is judged by the artificial standards mentioned above without regard to what this same animal can do in accounting for foxes, or whether he has cry or nose. The singular part of it is that the best hound in his work that ever lived but not conforming to Peterborough-winner qualifications, would be comparatively worthless at the famous English hound auction sales.

Shortly after the war, I visited one of the smart English packs, and was shown a very beautiful lot of hounds, uniform in size, color, and characteristics, a lovely even lot to look at. After enjoying the spectacle and taking many photographs, I talked at considerable length with the huntsman, who was a rather unusually intelligent man, and the master, a man of striking personality. I explained to them that, because in America I hunted a bad scenting country of large woodlands, nose and cry were of vast importance to me, and I would be glad if they would point out the very best hunting hounds in the pack. The huntsman kindly brought out on the flags three rather undersized and comparatively light-boned bitches not strictly conforming in color or otherwise to the rest of the pack, and which I had not previously been shown. These bitches, he said, because of post-war shortness of hounds, had been purchased from a provincial pack, but were the best hounds in their work in the kennel. I was immediately interested, and inquired if he had bred from them. "O, no, sir, wouldn't think of doing such a thing—it would quite degenerate the pack, sir," said he. "But," I inquired, "did you not say they were the best hounds in their work?" "O, yes, sir, but one could not think of breeding from them, sir, it wouldn't do, sir, to have a pack that looked like them."

Shortly after this incident, I had the pleasure of hunting for one whole day over a very beautiful country with this pack. I remember distinctly that four foxes were viewed away. Conditions looked good to me. It had rained all the day before, and yet all four foxes were lost within three fields of where hounds had been put on the line—hounds palpably lacked the requisite scenting ability to carry on. Whatever the huntsman and the master thought, it was evident that nose and hunting qualities are valuable requisites in any country, even England. Fashion and custom are, indeed, ruthless despots.

The preceding comment on English hounds from a working point of view is important purely to give an idea of their degree of usefulness in America, and, that I may not appear to be prejudiced, the following extracts from an editorial article in The Foxhound (monthly magazine formerly published in London) for July, 1911, are offered:

Let us take the opinion on this subject of one who may be said to be the pioneer of Hound Shows, Mr. Thomas Parrington, who was the organizer of what was practically the first meeting of its kind in the year 1859, at Redcar. Moreover, it was by his instrumentality . . . that the Annual Peterborough Meeting was instituted. . . .

In reply to our enquiry, his answer is that he thinks 'the hounds of the present day, as exhibited on the flags, are superior in conformation to those shown from forty to fifty years ago; but as to endurance, nose, tongue and courage, I think they are inferior.' . . .

If we accept Mr. Parrington's statement that nose and tongue in the modern foxhound do not compare favorably with the same senses as exhibited by his ancestor of the past, to what circumstances are we to attribute the deterioration in these respects?

The answer, we believe is to be found in the fact that by concentrating attention on the qualifications in breeding hounds which produce perfection in conformation we have somewhat overlooked these important factors to success in the hunting field . . . excessive development in one particular must act detrimentally upon the others. Thus, if the head is to be bred to a certain shape, care should be taken that the formation in no way interferes with the proper exercise of the vocal cords or the olfactory nerves.

Are we sure that these matters are receiving proper attention? Or are they being lost sight of in the general anxiety to breed to the standard type only?

We hold the opinion that the tendency of the present day is to secure type at all costs . . .

If 'Nimrod' is in any way correct in his computations, we have here fairly conclusive proof that the average pace of hounds now is not so great as that of seventy years ago. . . . It was supposed (in 'Nimrod's' opinion) 'to occupy the strictest attention of a sportsman for the space of ten years in order to form a complete pack of foxhounds, and this was accomplished only by observing the following rules:

'First, the country may have something to do with it; a closer hunting and more patient hound being required for some soils than others.

'Form or shape must also be minutely attended to . . . But the chief requi-

PRESENT DAY HOUNDS

site in a hound, either fox or hare, is what is called nose, *or the faculty of smelling, without excellence in which, form is of little avail.'*

In The Foxhound, November, 1910, the following ideas are expressed:

To ask ourselves the question, 'Is the present fashionable exclusive type of foxhound conducive to the best results in sport and economy in every variety of country?' We use the word 'exclusive' advisedly. For the result of the past half century of hound breeding has been (principally owing to the enormous importance placed upon the shows) that one standard of type, and one only, has been set up; no doubt excellently suited to the country for which it was originally intended, but in our opinion, and as we shall endeavor to prove absolutely unfitted for sport in hunting countries of a different nature. Nevertheless, it is the standard, and consequently it is the aim of the majority of the Masters to attain to it.

It is a fact, accepted as incontrovertible, that each variety of hunting requires its particular type of horse. . . . Why then is the same truth not applicable to the hound, which is expected to cover the same varied courses?

As we see it, this state of affairs is productive of two ill effects, namely, (1) a tendency to the production of a type of hound ill-suited to a great many hunting countries; and (2) the increased cost of maintenance of a pack.

We think we shall be expressing a general opinion when we say that a hound of good constitution should be able to hunt five days a fortnight without suffering any ill effects from its exertions. Moreover, that such a hound should be a 'runner up' until its eighth or ninth year, living hard, doing well and keeping in good condition up to the end of the season.

Now we maintain that there are but few packs in Great Britain the members of which are capable of going out three days a fortnight without a considerable amount of 'culling,' and 'the culled' are chiefly to be found amongst those which are the most fashionably bred with the fleshy cat-like feet of modern requirements.

It is argued by those who support the exclusive breeding of the fashionable type of hound that they are bred with a view to an ever-increasing capacity for pace. Is this so? Consider the records of pace over given distances in the latter half of the eighteenth and early part of the nineteenth centuries. It is a matter for much question if the fashionable hound of the present day can equal, and much less surpass, such performances as that, for instance, of the Hon. J. Smith-Barry's Blue Cap *in the ever famous match over the Beacon course at Newmarket; and it is certain that a comparison of the staying powers of the two—the past and the present—would result unfavorably to the latter.*

Referring to hounds for comparatively rough country, such as Radnorshire and West Hereford, The Foxhound continues:

The banks are very steep, and in places precipitous. The scent is catchy, and the general characteristics entirely different. Here hounds require to be of tireless energy, persevering over a difficult line, rather than racing on a breast-high scent, as in the pastures of Warwickshire.

HOUNDS AND HUNTING

Therefore, a big hound is quite out of place, 23 inches being the ideal height. He must possess good neck and shoulders, a short back with well-sprung ribs, good loins and powerful quarters. All these are necessary factors for the best results. Big bone and overshort pasterns should be avoided, whereas a slightly lengthened foot, not flat, or spread, is desirable, and lasts longer over the rough countries. Of somewhat light frame generally, above all he should be really well-balanced and possess as much quality as possible. Such a hound in his own country would accomplish as much, or more, work than would a Warwickshire [fashionable type] *hound, and with less fatigue to himself.*

Referring to the Fells of Cumberland and Westmorland:

The foxes are for the most part found on the ledges of the mountains whose sides vary from 45° to 70°, and are sometimes even more steeply inclined; with a surface formed of rock or loose shale, they graduate into slippery grass slopes at the base. Hounds therefore hunt the 'drag' slowly up until they find.

For this country the hound which has proved the most useful is one of light frame all round, hare-footed entirely, exceptionally well let-down and developed in hind quarters, with good neck and shoulders and loin, ribs carried well back, long in pastern, and withal shallow in make. Great scenting powers and endless endurance are needful, with a considerable amount of pace. Financial considerations here necessitate small packs. Individual hounds must therefore 'come out' more frequently and remain longer in the kennel as 'runners up' in the field. Owing to the rough conditions under which they live, they are able to accomplish both these ends where the fashionably bred hounds would fail by reason of the more artificial surroundings.

Experience in the Fell districts has shown that the 'cat-foot' cannot endure the work of this country; that shortened pasterns do not minimize the jar sufficiently, no matter how good the shoulders are; and further, that a hound over $22\frac{1}{2}$ inches in height is severely handicapped when turning and twisting on the steep mountain sides. He is in consequence generally 'left'; and in descending or ascending he is equally behindhand if he possesses anything like the standard in bone or conformation of frame.

Now imagine a Warwickshire hound in such a country! He would be absolutely unable to cope with the conditions or to live with the native-bred hounds. If such an experiment were attempted, we venture to say that two, or at most three, seasons would be the limit of his powers of usefulness.

Comparing the utility of the show-type hound, this magazine says:

The fashionable hound 'would probably come out' four days a fortnight, and continue to be a runner-up until his fifth or sixth season . . .

The Radnorshire and West Hereford hound (a pack not bred strictly to show standard) could do his five days a fortnight if required; his duration of utility would be at least a year longer. The number of hunting days of the Ullswater (Fell) representative is four days per week *(he has done six days) . . .*

MR. THOMAS' *Flier*, '26

"A hound that carries as little superfluous weight as the thoroughbred horse, yet has sufficient bone on which to hang ample muscle." In tale male through eighteen generations, this hound traces to *Mountain*, imported from Ireland in 1830. *From an etching by Bert Cobb, 1928.*

Mr. Thomas' *Frantic*, '20

"Such hounds have strength and substance without lumber—they are well moulded and knit to stand wear and tear, nor yet so large or over-boned as to be unable to negotiate timber, woven wire fences, or walk the top of rails. The outward energy seems to denote the nervous energy within." *From an etching by Bert Cobb,* 1928.

PRESENT DAY HOUNDS

Once more we ask, do these conditions show a satisfactory state of affairs, and is it not time that more encouragement be held out to those desirous to breed for sport in their own country?

Bryden speaks highly of Fell hounds, and is very definite in his statement that the fashionable hound of England has decidedly deteriorated in qualities of nose and cry, within his knowledge. Mr. Bryden speaks from a wealth of experience, having hunted, since 1868, with no less than sixty-four packs.

A few Fell hounds have been imported to America, and it is said they have good cry and have hunted well here, as compared to their more fashionable English cousins which lack their working qualities. Fell hounds have never been influenced by fashion. Ability to hunt and kill foxes in the mountainous Fells of Cumberland has retained in these hounds strength, agility, and cry, and has prevented the advent of purely fashionable characteristics, such as, excessive bone and over-straightness; they closely resemble many American hounds which have been bred for working qualities only. A very comprehensive exposé on the subject of Fell hounds, with carefully analyzed reasons for their excellence is Richard Clapham's, *Foxes, Foxhounds, and Foxhunting*.

Other British hounds which have done fairly well in America, some of which I imported in 1920, are those of Sir Edward Curre, who hunts the Welsh hills adjoining Chepstow. This pack is the best example of "hounds bred for country" of which I know.

Sir Edward, whose guest I was fortunate enough to be for some days, and with whose pack I had the pleasure of hunting, in 1922, recounted to me a most interesting story of how his pack through a quarter of a century had been bred up to meet the requirements of his country. These, in his mind, included,—*nose*, that hounds may hunt out their own line unaided in the hills, where it is impossible to ride straight after hounds; *cry*, that they may be heard when out of sight; and *color*, that they may be seen in the distance. His original hounds were largely rough-coated Welsh, which he said were inclined to dwell much, and tied to the line too hard to suit his mind; but, desiring to take advantage of the excellent nose and cry of the pure Welsh hound, he had crossed them with light-colored hounds of Peterborough-type, breeding to develop a suitable pack for his particular purposes. Sir Edward certainly has perfected a pack that is different from any other in existence. It has excellent working qualities compared to Peterborough-type hounds, as evinced by the fact that these hounds of Welsh blood do most of the work in one or two packs in America which are otherwise composed of English Stud Book hounds. His pack to-day is a splendid one to look at,— nearly pure white in color; very few of the hounds have broken coats; their feet are closely knit; they have wonderful loins, and are splendidly muscled, but perhaps carry too much weight to negotiate the roughest going to the best advantage.

Among present day British hounds, which should be of interest to Americans on account of their comparatively good nose and tongue,—are several packs designated as harriers. Several of these packs also hunt fox. For many generations they have been especially bred for working qualities, the show fashion not having affected their characteristics. They are of old-fashioned light coloration, badger pies, hare pies, and whites predominating; they are free from lumber and superfluous bone, and, on account of having color of high visibility as well as working qualities and cry, should be more useful in America than fashionable Stud Book hounds. Notable examples of these harriers are, the Axe Vale, of Seaton in Devonshire; the Cotley, of Chard in Somerset; the Quarme, of Exford, Somerset; and the Taunton Vale, kenneling near Taunton. The two former packs hunt both hare and fox, and trace their lineage (as do the Quarme) to the ancient light-colored staghounds which hunted the wild red deer of Exmoor in the early part of the nineteenth century.

English Stud Book harriers, of which there are many smart-looking packs, are modeled closely in conformation on fashionable foxhound lines, in fact, many of them are actually small foxhounds. Unquestionably, they have better nose than their larger prototypes, but their cry is deficient, which makes them unsuited for best results in America.

The Millbrook (New York) country is the only location in America where European hare and red and grey foxes are all hunted. A very smart harrier pack, originally bought in toto from Henry Hawkins, Everdon Hall, Daventry, England, was hunted and bred in the Millbrook country for about ten years, and there was always much rejoicing when these harriers found a fox, as it was commonly agreed they could hunt a fox better than the English Stud Book foxhounds which then also hunted the same country. Oakleigh Thorne, master of the Millbrook, very kindly presented me with this harrier pack when my Virginia hounds began hunting the Millbrook country, in 1922; and hounds of both sorts were hunted together for the purpose of comparison, but the harriers were found deficient for my purposes. Experiments in cross-breeding both ways were disastrous failures, the results being misfits of the worst description—probably the outcross was too violent.

Most recognized packs of hounds in Ireland are of the Peterborough stamp, but there are many scratch packs, usually trencher-fed, and innumerable individual hounds (used largely for hare hunting) which are of the old-fashioned sort. In many a village the weekly ringing of the church bell for Mass is also the signal for hounds to gather from their several mid-week abodes for the Sunday afternoon hunt. I shall never forget the description given me by the Reverend Father D—— of how during the "throubles" one

PRESENT DAY HOUNDS

Sunday, in 1920, while he was saying the Mass, he heard noises without the church, and saw his stable boy nip out. A fierce fight ensued to save some of the hounds from being stolen by wandering "republican blagyards," and great was the regret of His Reverence that he himself could not have been in the fracas.

In County Cork and County Kerry, one can see hounds in almost any village, and many an adventure they have when they perchance get into the wrong bailiwick. There remains fixed in my memory an incident wherein I saved a life in the person of a black and tan hound pup, who, having attempted to purloin a leg of mutton from a butcher's shop in Ennis, was set upon by the butcher's terriers. The pup retreated, giving bellows of terror like the siren of an ocean liner. With retreat finally cut off by more terriers, a battle royal followed, until my stout walking stick was put to good service.

According to many, the best pack to hunt a fox in Ireland to-day is the Scarteen "Kerry" beagles. For two hundred years or more, this private pack has been handed down in the Ryan family, of Knocklong, in Limerick. Their progenitors are thought to have been brought originally from France, perhaps by returning "soldiers of fortune." Hunted by that famous sportsman, John F. Ryan, the Master of Scarteen, these hounds are still rated as harriers, although it is many years since they hunted the hare. Noted for nose, pace, and cry, they are nearly always black and tan without white, although occasionally one is seen similar in color to red Virginia hounds; and they have been carefully bred for performance, fashion and fancy having been ignored. They have all the physical attributes essential to activity, pace, and stamina, with no superficial lumber to carry, closely-knit feet, natural-shaped pasterns, not so straight as to lack spring, good shoulders, backs, loins, and thighs. The one characteristic open to criticism is their tendency to light-colored eyes.

Mr. Ryan's country is one of the very best in Ireland, not only for hunting foxes but for breeding horses. *Galtee More* and *Ard Patrick*, winners of the Derby, respectively, in 1897 and 1902, were foaled not two miles from Scarteen; and almost at their paddock gate was formerly a covert made entirely of sticks which always yielded a fox.

Most Britishers and Americans do not realize how much hunting there is in France to-day. In spite of the World War, there are many private packs and innumerable individual hounds. The latter are used singly for wild boar and hare shooting. In Central France (Auvergne), one may see in any small town many hounds just as one does in County Clare or County Kerry, in Ireland. In this part of France some of the hounds are rough, or broken coated, and are no doubt descendants of the hounds mentioned by Arrian.

French hounds vary from rough-coated "griffons courants" to miniature smooth and rough "bassets." These hounds differ according to the individual use or fancy of the several maîtres d'equipage. The variations are no doubt partially due to the diversified character of French terrain and the different sorts of game hunted. The following are among the best known varieties which still remain more or less pure, but which of necessity have been crossed through the years with other French hounds, and in some cases with English hounds: Hounds of Gascony, Hounds of Saintonge, Vendean Hounds (rough and smooth-coated), Hounds of Haute-Poitou, and d'Artois Hounds.

Since most French hunting is in woodlands, it can be understood that cry in French hounds is very important as well as nose, as hounds must of necessity depend upon themselves and not upon the huntsman. Although there are hound shows in France, no attempt is made towards standardization as in England, since French masters are not prone to be affected by fashion, but remain individualistic in their views, and believe firmly in hounds suited to their divers needs. There are many hounds that still maintain characteristics of olden days, especially with regard to the long ear, high occiput, large size, and hunting traits already mentioned, such as were imported to America, about 1923, by Charles E. Mather, master of the Brandywine Hunt of Pennsylvania.

Masters in France are so keen on the hunting efficiency of hounds that informal pack trials were held in the winter of 1927, under the direction of M. Michel Beauchamp, of Vaumas, Allier. The several packs hunted roe-deer on alternate days, in order to test their respective hunting merits.

The hounds of the duchesse d'Uzes, which hunt stag in the forest of Rambouillet, are well made, white, tan and black, about 26 inches high. The black and white hounds of M. Michel Beauchamp, and those of his neighbor, that famous old sportsman, M. René Clayeux, are also very large. They are splendid to look at, the dog hounds standing up to 27 inches, and the bitches only a little less. There seems to be less difference in size between French dogs and bitches than between English hounds of different sexes.

Considering that these packs were decimated during the World War, their evenness of size and type is remarkable. They have excellent feet of the greyhound sort, and are very deep in the ribs, have plenty of bone, and are well put together without exaggerated characteristics. These hounds and their kennels are kept in beautiful condition, which is not true of all packs in France, or in America. Both these packs hunt roe-deer—I believe them to have excellent nose and cry. The hounds of M. Beauchamp are said to be the best "chiens du change" in France. By this is meant, that once they have well settled on the line of a given roe-deer, they will not change even though the hunted animal should go through an entire herd of its fellows. I was assured that this attribute is largely hereditary, in the same sense that the trait of "pointing" is hereditary in bird dogs. Of course, training is also involved; but not having personally observed the method employed, I shall not attempt to describe it: yet, if the New Forest foxhounds can be largely kept steady from rioting on deer, and the New Forest buck hounds can be kept steady from fox, then the characteristic of "chiens du change" can be comprehended.

The individualistic view of French masters that hounds should be bred for country, seems to me only common sense, as conditions vary in all localities. It must be repeated that what is incomprehensibly difficult in America may be quite easy in England, or *vice versa*. Such differences are attributable to varied causes, such as scenting conditions, characteristics of hounds, ability to frequently blood hounds on a given quarry; or the facility of being able to rate hounds on a given "riot," which in turn is dependent on terrain and ability of the hunt staff to keep in touch with the pack,—so difficult in a blind, rough country.

Among modern hounds, the beagle takes an important place, not only because in recent years it has been developed in hunting efficiency and smartness of conformation, but because, in following beagles, especially on foot, one may learn more about the principles of hunting and the wiles of quarry than in any other way. In 1927, The Field records sixty-two packs of beagles in Britain; but there are, unquestionably, many other small packs. In the United States, beagles are very popular not only for hunting various sorts of hare, which are shot in front of one or two hounds used for such shooting, but there are a dozen, or more, well organized packs having regular meets, and turning out in smart livery. In some instances, these hounds are followed on horses, but *pedibus cum jambis* is the most common means of keeping up with them. The quarry is usually the so-called cotton-tail rabbit (*Lepus sylvaticus*), and in Virginia, at least, the cotton-tail runs extremely well, giving hunts that for points and distance satisfy the average American follower on foot.

The National Beagle Club is only one of many American associations holding beagle field trials, which have done much to excite interest and improve the breed. The field trials of this association are held on a preserve near Aldie, Virginia (which the author suggested for their purchase), some fifteen years ago. Classes are included for single hounds, couples, two couples of 13- and 15-inch hounds, and packs of five couples. In these trials, the judges are mounted, that every move of the quarry and hounds over the rolling hills of the preserve can be seen, thus insuring accurate notation of the ability of each individual hound: such inaccuracies as are bound to occur in judging American foxhound trials where hounds cannot be closely watched are obviated. Trials of similar character are not unknown in France. In 1927, such a trial was held under the patronage of M. Hubert Devaulx de Chambord, chateau de Chambord, Tretau, department of Allier.

In France, basset hounds of ancient origin (rough and smooth coated), are used for shooting as beagles are used in America, and, I believe, *dachshunde* are in Germany; in fact, the basset must be closely related to the dachshund as it is similar in conformation. Bassets are fair-sized hounds, weighing from 35 to 45 pounds, with short, crooked legs. They have excellent cry. In England, there are several packs of bassets; in America, there is but one good-sized pack. My observation in England of these hounds is that they are less accurate in their hunting ability than beagles, and are inclined to be mouthy. In field trial competition with good beagles they would probably be defeated.

The otter hound, of which there are no packs in America, is a rough-coated breed of big hounds, very similar in appearance to the true Welsh hound and perhaps closely related. There are several packs in Britain, which give excellent sport after the wily otter along the many streams in summer months.

CHAPTER V.

ATTRIBUTES OF A GOOD HOUND

A REALLY fine working hound is unquestionably an extraordinary animal, probably the most unusual of all domestic animals. He must have prodigious endurance, the best nose of all sporting dogs, cry, speed, strength, agility, brains, acquired experience, and be under the mounted huntsman's control where proper pack work is *de rigueur*. No other domestic animal used for sport is called upon for all the qualities that must be found in a good hound.

In speaking of a "good hound" in modern parlance, confusion is apt to arise as to what is really meant,—hunting ability or arbitrary standards of conformation pleasing to one point of view, while, perhaps, displeasing to another.

Conklin said, "can we ever get rid of *wishful thinking?*" This very "wishful thinking" is ofttimes applied to hounds which are considered perfect in every respect, simply because they meet fashionable standards of superficial appearance. In 1770, Wesley said, "Passion and prejudice govern the world—under the name of Reason." Nothing was ever more true than this saying, as applied to hounds.

To advocate one type or color, and to decry all others through blind ignorance of their ability is a near-religion to some breeders.

Everything is more or less comparative in this world, and this truism seems most applicable to hounds. In the minds of many people there is, unfortunately, no very definite standard of excellence by which to judge hounds in the field. In England, there is an accepted show standard, but even there the standard of hunting excellence is often ill-defined. In horse racing there exists the winning post test; but the hunting ability of hounds frequently remains a matter of opinion on the part of someone whose knowledge may be too localized for purposes of comparison. For instance, the average American huntsman may never have seen an efficient large pack: the average Englishman has perhaps never heard really good cry nor seen unusually fine hound work under difficult conditions of terrain and scenting. It may be well to con-

HOUNDS AND HUNTING

sider that what is a useful hound for one country and purpose is not necessarily the best hound for another.

> *On the straightest of legs and roundest of feet,*
> *With ribs like a frigate his timbers to meet,*
> *With a fashion and fling and a form so complete,*
> *That to see him dance over the flags is a treat.*

However, Whyte Melville in these delightful lines has not mentioned qualities which must be carefully looked for in selecting a hound for excellence in his work,—ability to account for his quarry by means of his nose, unusual physical and mental powers, excellence of voice and the proper use of it, so that we may follow him when in woodlands. If a hound has inefficient nose or insufficient experience to use it, or has little voice, or uses what he has falsely, he can hardly be of much use to us in America.

The wish being "father to the thought" has caused keen argument in all countries since time began as to what is a good hound. Let Shakespeare be a witness:

> *Lord*—Huntsman, I charge thee, tender well my hounds:
> Brach Merriman, the poor cur is embossed;
> And couple Clouder with the deep-mouth'd Brach.
> Saw'st thou not, boy, how Silver made it good
> At the hedge corner, in the coldest fault?
> I would not lose the dog for twenty pound.
>
> *First Huntsman*—
> Why, Belman is as good as he, my Lord;
> He cried upon it at the merest loss,
> And twice to-day pick'd out the dullest scent;
> Trust me, I take him for the better dog.
>
> *Lord*—Thou art a fool; if Echo was as fleet
> I would esteem him worth a dozen such.
>
> Taming of the Shrew.

In America, in general, hounds have been bred for their ability to meet local hunting conditions and perhaps too little for other characteristics. These local conditions, varied and difficult to overcome, have, however, led to the development of remarkable hounds—remarkable not for looks but in achievement.

In certain sections,—notably Virginia, Kentucky, and Tennessee,—where the custom of racing hounds for love or lucre obtains, the selection of the fittest during many generations has fostered and developed the best

ATTRIBUTES OF A GOOD HOUND

hound, probably, in the world, in its ability to find, work a cold line, hunt at speed, and account for foxes. Under the difficult local conditions of scent and going, such hounds are able, if necessary, to "stay" for hours, negotiating the roughest possible terrain, often including rocky cliffs, burned forests, sandy wastes, ploughed fields, brush and briers; fording brooks, swimming rivers; and able to follow scent in hot September and snowy January, in dusty roads and frozen fields, with speed and drive. This may seem fine romance to some people, nevertheless those who have hunted in America can testify to the accuracy of the contention that these conditions are not exceptional but are the general rule.

The type of hound that can do all this carries as little superfluous weight as the high-class thoroughbred or trotting horse, yet has sufficient bone on which to hang ample muscle. Such hounds have strength and substance without lumber—they are well moulded and knit to stand wear and tear. In no sense are they weedy, nor yet so large, over-boned or clumsy as to be unable to negotiate timber or woven wire fences, or walk the top of rails and stone walls. The natural foxlike feet of such hounds, similar in their strength and spring to those of the greyhound, are singularly able to withstand lameness. As in the thoroughbred horse, the outward quality seems to denote the nervous energy within. The appearance of such hounds is well illustrated by the etchings facing pages 66 and 67.

It must be obvious that it is relatively simple to portray fine hounds, but quite the reverse to consistently breed them; hence, it may be well to analyze some of the problems involved.

In the remarks elsewhere in this chapter on developing a good pack, it is stated that very few young hounds enter my "old" pack until they are eighteen months to two years old. Assuming that it takes two years before a young hound begins to show precise indications of its abilities, there must be two years of waiting for proof of the breeder's wisdom, in the case of each hound. Therefore, theoretically speaking, only five generations of line-breeding can be produced in ten years. In actual practice, one produces much less: in other words, it takes at least a decade to satisfactorily prove any theory of breeding.

Is it wise to imagine that one can arbitrarily produce any theoretically ideal hound in a generation or two by crossing X and Y? Would it not be better to decide what requirements are needed in the pack, and then attempt to ascertain what existing strain of hounds *already* possesses the maximum of such qualities and can most consistently reproduce the same? Possibly, in time, such hounds may eventually be improved toward the end in view. Two or three years spent in really ardent investigation of the merits of various strains and their power to uniformly reproduce specific requirements, will save time and money, provided it is carried on analytically, dispassionately, and from a world-wide point of view. Empiric experimentation, on the other hand, affords but little guarantee of ultimate success.

To further complicate the matter, breeding is not an exact science, for there are so many unknown and fluctuating factors with which to contend. As a matter of fact, circumstances beyond the control of any one man, especially in volatile America, usually make breeding experiments of little avail, for the reason that so few exact proofs of results are quickly obtainable.

It is suggested, if nose, determination, and cry are desired in a pack, one should select a definite strain of hounds known positively to possess a maximum of such qualities and the ability to reproduce them. This done, assuming that one can reproduce a large number of young hounds per annum equal or superior in ability to their parents, and still have more hounds than are needed, then, and then only, draft for color and other non-essential points to suit the fancy. Do not think, if you desire first, last, and all the time certain qualities,—say, A, B, and C,—that there can be produced something else in addition (say, Y) by magic or by crossing with some strain that has mediocre ABC qualities, but maximum Y qualities. It is mathematically obvious that the only way to retain the ABC qualities, and still add the Y quality is by judicious mating *within* the given strain, and perhaps occasional diluted-out crosses having the Y quality as well as the ABC qualities. It should be remembered that untold patience is all-essential to insure results.

Because it has cost me endless time and effort to learn what has just been written, the suggestion is humbly offered that the above deductions cannot be overemphasized.

To sum up, it can hardly be repeated too often that one must have in mind a standard of perfection. It is also essential that one should select breeding hounds *known* to have been proved by comparison to such a standard, and *know* that their progenitors have a like dependable history. These points should be seriously recognized and remembered.

In breeding, one should never, absolutely never, breed a hound *only* because he or she is a good individual; one should be cognizant of *all the characteristics of the ancestry*. A pedigree a mile long is useless if it cannot be translated; one must be able to definitely and accurately interpret the quality of the ancestors. If the breeder, or someone in whose opinion absolute confidence may be placed, does not know and highly approve from every angle the working ability of a hound's progenitors, he should not breed the brute, but "let George do it," if he so wishes. The one who knows will win.

Oh, worthiness of nature, breed of greatness,
Cowards father cowards, and base things sire the base.
                                                                Cymbeline.

To help the novice recognize the vital requirements in a good hound, I

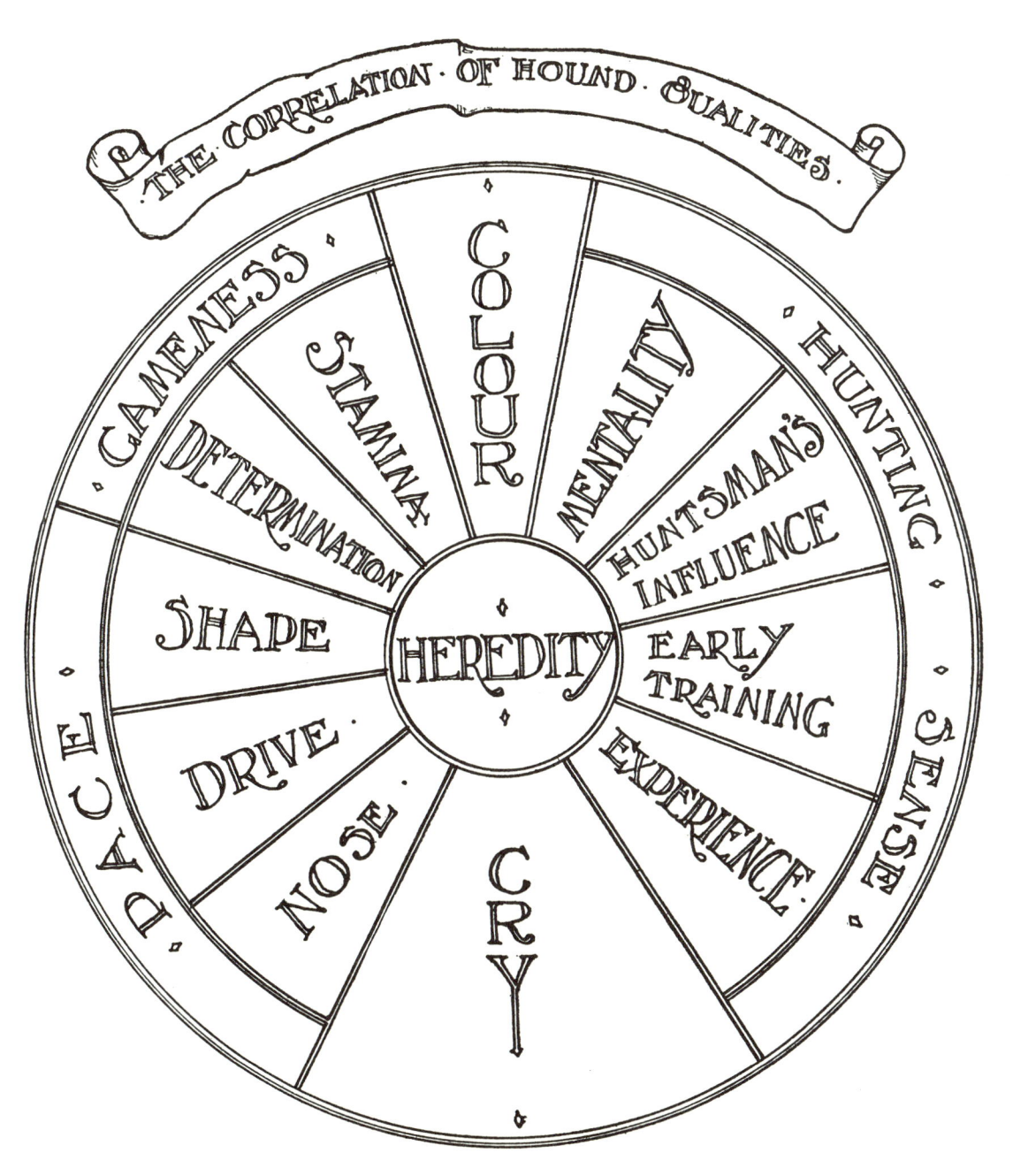

THIS DIAGRAM IN THE SEMBLANCE OF A WHEEL SHOULD BE STUDIED WITH THE THOUGHT THAT HEREDITY (THE HUB) CARRIES QUALITIES (THE SPOKES), AND THAT CERTAIN QUALITIES COLLECTIVELY (E.G., NOSE, DRIVE AND SHAPE) SUSTAIN THEIR SEGMENT OF THE RIM (PACE).

EXAMPLES OF NATURAL AND ARTIFICIALLY-SHAPED FEET.

The difference is marked between the pads shaped by nature of those prodigious runners, the fox and the wolf, and the pads shaped by fashion of the modern English Show Foxhound. (1) Red Fox; (2) Grey Fox; (3) Coyote; (4) Wolf; (5) Virginia Foxhound; (6) Peterborough type Foxhound, showing round foot and tendency to toe in; (7) Artificial shape of overstraight, exaggerated, cat-footed hound; (8) Toe down—frequently found in hounds with feet shaped as in Fig. 6.

ATTRIBUTES OF A GOOD HOUND

shall attempt to analyze the relation of certain traits and how to reproduce them. If the diagram on page 76 is studied, some idea may be gleaned of the attributes of a good hound for use in America. To analyze the physical and mental attributes intelligently is no easy task; nevertheless, I shall take them up in order.

HEREDITY, it must be remembered, is the fundamental basis of innate characteristics. To illustrate, pointers and setters have the characteristic trait of pointing. Hounds have the characteristic traits of running a line and speaking on that line.

PACE depends on three qualities,—*nose*, *drive* (volition to get forward), and *shape* (symmetry giving physical power).

As one cannot reproduce the maximum possible pace in hounds under all scenting conditions without the above three qualities properly combined, *ipso facto*, it seems only reasonable to start breeding operations with hounds that are known to have all three qualities in the fullest possible degree. If slow hounds are desired which cannot go fast under any conditions, breed to the improperly made ones—speed is with these mechanically impossible, even if they have good nose. If the objective is hounds that can go fast only when scent is good and otherwise do little, breed to shape and drive, and forget nose.

Nose (or scenting ability) and the experience to use it correctly is all-essential, because in nine days out of ten, nose is the all-important requisite in accounting for foxes, while the tenth day may be an occasion when conditions are such that any dog can run a fox. For most occasions the best-nosed hound in the world is none too good; even before the Christian Era, this fact was recognized, for Xenophon wrote, "And vowing a part of the spoils to Apollo and Diana the Huntress, he should let loose that of his dogs which has the finest nose."

In America, during certain seasons, it sometimes does not rain for weeks, and, as scent in a large measure depends on moisture, it is hopeless to attempt to account for foxes under these conditions, except with hounds having the best of nose, and with the experience to use it to the greatest advantage. Other hounds, it may be repeated, are comparatively useless, and, assuming they find a fox, or one is found for them, they are usually unable to run its line under these unfavorable conditions for more than a few fields to a loss. To bother to keep a stable of hunt horses, to bother to breed, feed, train and hunt hounds, in fact, to go out with anything but hounds that can run a line under almost any conditions, seems the height of folly. Would it not appear that a pack of hounds that cannot account for a fox nine days out of ten must be inefficient? Indeed, no diversion should be made from steadfast insistence on the best nose in hounds, for such hounds more surely account for foxes in heat or cold, drought or wind. Regardless of conditions, one should not accept excuses for any pack that cannot throughout a given season kill or mark to ground a large percentage of all foxes found.

Scenting ability varies greatly in all dogs. The greyhound, for example, which for ages has been used for sight hunting only, is much less efficient as to nose than the foxhound. In lesser degree the various types of "scenting hounds" have varying ability.

Of these, perhaps the bloodhound has the keenest nose, but, because of its shape and volition, it is not suited for foxhunting—it lacks speed.

The modern fashionable English foxhound has symmetrical form, based on artificial show standards, and splendid drive, but, in the opinion of many people, the least efficient nose of any scenting hound. Such characteristics make it difficult for English hounds to account for foxes under American conditions. This is rapidly becoming realized in this country, so that at the present time there are few packs of English hounds in America to which it has not been found expedient to add some better-nosed hounds.

As well as shape, full well he knows
To kill their fox, they must have nose.

As outlined in Chapter IV, even English critics believe that nose in English foxhounds has been discounted in breeding, while shape, color, and drive have been considered the main issues. The moral is, first of all to *breed for nose*, starting with hounds which have the very best, as well as proper shape and drive to account for foxes against almost any odds.

In England, it is customary to blame the weather for poor sport, by the popular remark, "There is no scent to-day." Would it not be better to pay more attention to the scenting ability of hounds and less to the weather, on the ground than man controls hound breeding and *le bon Dieu* controls the weather? Why not breed hounds for nose, and abandon vain efforts where Jupiter Pluvius is concerned?

In connection with the subject of nose, there exists an all-important phenomenon that should be carefully considered. What is there, in the gift of scenting ability that enables a hound to decide instantly which way the quarry went, and prevents him in any stage of the hunt from heeling the line? A thoroughly good and experienced hound will never err in this respect, which asset is a super-requirement in each individual of a first-class pack. For a lone hound to make an error is one thing, but, where a pack is concerned, one individual making an error may lead the entire pack astray, and lose the fox and lose the day. To illustrate this point, an excerpt is given from an account of a hunt which appeared in Horse and Hound, January 21, 1928:

There was a big field all waiting for a hunt in the open . . . a call was made on the way at the newly-laid drain belonging to Mr. Champion, and mirabile dictu, *out went an old dog-fox. Unfortunately, on hounds being brought up they*

ATTRIBUTES OF A GOOD HOUND

ran heelway, and it was not until half way through the ensuing hunt that most of the pack got together, and even then there were four couple who never got to head.

In England, it seems not unusual for hounds to run heel. There are probably three reasons for this,—typical English hounds, on account of local conditions, are more manhandled than is physically possible in topographically rough America, and, therefore, such hounds have less opportunity of being dependent upon themselves for accuracy; often English hounds are brought to a view halloo under great excitement, accompanied by the galloping of horses, and thereby may flash the wrong way; again, they may, when brought to an halloo, catch the body scent of a fox floating in the breeze, and in their eagerness run heel with the scent in the air.

In comparison, it is marvelous to see a thoroughly good pack of Virginia hounds unravel a complicated line where any error might cause a complete loss. In North Carolina, grey foxes will often run straight away some distance, and then dart into a swamp and start doubling, sometimes foiling their own line several times in a few minutes in the most complicated manner; and yet hounds seldom seem to doubt for an instant which line is one minute old and which line is two minutes old. It is all a mystery to me, and very wonderful. This ability in a thoroughly experienced hound of not heeling the line is frequently seen to the best advantage in beagle field trials in America, where every movement of the hound and quarry can be viewed. The American hare is, perhaps, even more clever in foiling his own line than the European hare, and splendid is the ability of good hounds not to be outwitted by Puss, while useless is the pack hound that will practice this fault.

Finally, it should not be forgotten that the first axiom in connection with speed or hunting pace is,—no hound can run a line correctly faster than he can smell it; or, to say it briefly, no good hound is faster than his nose. If a hound in a pack consistently runs faster than he can smell the line, he is shirking his proper share of the work by unfairly trying to take advantage of the honest hounds that are doing the real work of hunting the line. In field trials, hounds sometimes attempt to run faster than their nose, and will, in consequence, overrun badly. For perfect pack requirements, such overrunning is inexcusable, in that it will cause the loss of many a fox, especially under difficult conditions, and inevitably ruin many a hunting day. This fault is nothing new in hounds, for Shakespeare says in *Henry VIII*:

> . . . . *We may outrun*
> *By violent swiftness, that which we run at,*
> *But lose by overrunning.*

Do not think for a moment that I advocate the pottering sort of hound that has a good nose but prefers smelling the line to getting forward on it. He is as faulty in his way as his poor-nosed cousin. A hound that dwells on a line, "boohooing" repeatedly in the same spot and thus losing precious time, is certainly not a type to be admired. Drive, or the volition to get forward, is what such potterers lack.

Drive is a trait developed notably in modern foxhounds. It may be summed up as a predominating desire to reach the objective. The bloodhound, for instance, bred for centuries to very careful, slow work on a leash, is more interested in the line than in the quarry. The good foxhound is interested in the line primarily as a means of attaining the quarry. To illustrate further, the bloodhound will tie to the line regardless of extraneous affairs, as if his nose were glued to it, whereas the good foxhound, hearing the cry of his fellows ahead, will instantly leave the line to get forward to them. The best hound in his work is one whose qualities of nose and drive are well balanced.

Shape. To have pace, a hound must be symmetrical in conformation, otherwise speed becomes mechanically impossible. There are hounds in America which have the best of nose, but are so badly put together, so unsymmetrical, that they simply cannot run fast, even if they have drive. Sway-backed, cow-hocked, duck-footed, such hounds are hampered by unsurmountable physical disabilities.

Eliminating color, there are many points of view as to what a good foxhound should look like. Unfortunately, in this connection we are apt to simultaneously consider the form and the fashion to which we are accustomed. The fallacy of this attitude can perhaps best be exposed by comparative illustration. If we acknowledge that among the greatest long distance runners in the world are the thoroughbred horse, the wolf, and the fox, we will have something mutually understandable with which to begin. They are all symmetrical, so may we not take such symmetrical standards of shape as a guide for our ideas of what a well-shaped hound should be? They all have sufficient bone on which to hang muscle, but not so much as to find it a burden; they all have shoulders and pastern joints that are not so straight as to give any jar, and legs that swing like pendulums. In the case of the wolf, and the fox, the products of the survival of the fittest, the feet are strong and closely knit, but sufficiently flexible, and with toes sufficiently developed to give spring to their movements and make it impossible, from their very flexibility, for lameness to develop even in the roughest going imaginable. Who ever heard of a fox or wolf lame from natural causes?

By the premises, can there be virtue in any artificial standard of shape in a hound that does not lend itself to the utmost physical ease in action? It would seem that the nose to smell, the volition and experience to go, and the mechanically correct workability of the body is all one should hope for.

If a breeder goes in for a certain color, an unnatural bulk calling for surplus weight of bone, flesh, and muscle to be carried, exaggerated ideals of soi-disant straightness that tend to tottering pasterns and stump-like feet

ATTRIBUTES OF A GOOD HOUND

and toes, and then expects the perfectly balanced working machine, is he not hoping for more than Nature can supply?

I strongly advocate efficiency of the working senses within a body mechanically perfect; but this perfection in shape must be based on a standard of results such as exists in the thoroughbred horse, the product of the winning post test, and not such as is influenced by the changing fashion of the show ring. It is really quite illogical to judge working efficiency by the artificial standards of ring judges—for fat cattle, yes, and possibly draft horses and show dogs, but certainly not for foxhounds. Stress laid on prize awards and Sunday comparisons in kennel has been the ruin of many a working pack of hounds. No one admires more than I true beauty of form, evenness of size, color, uniformity of type and all the little niceties of a well-ordered pack; but, when efficiency is overlooked and strictly artificial show-ring standards supplant it, has not the time come to call a halt and appeal to reason?

HUNTING SENSE depends on mentality, early training, experience and huntsman's influence. For any particular quarry hunting sense is often, I believe, an inherent characteristic in hounds of varied sorts. A beagle prefers to hunt hare, it would seem, bird dogs point naturally, and, so a foxhound seems to have natural aptitude for the pursuit of Uncle Remus. A hound having plenty of hunting sense seems to know just where and how to act in an emergency; so, it is from such that it seems wise to reproduce. The fact of having the right *mentality* makes for innate sagacity, but even when this trait is transmitted from parent to offspring, it can be largely influenced by *early training* with chastisement for wrong doing.

Experience is, of course, vastly important, and is properly acquired only by much hunting from puppyhood with steady old hounds who never teach bad tricks. Experience teaches among other things that over-anxiousness does not pay. A hound's mentality may be affected by the *huntsman's influence;* for example, if constantly interfered with by a huntsman when attempting to work out a line, he will soon lose volition to do it for himself.

It should be remembered, therefore, that a naturally good hound may be spoiled by a bad huntsman, or bad company. One should weigh his training, as well as his breeding, when taking the mentality of a foxhound into consideration. The mere fact that a hound has good pace, nose, or cry, is no criterion that he can or will use them to the best advantage.

GAMENESS depends upon *determination* and *stamina,*—characteristics on which great stress should be laid. Determination means will, and stamina stands for endurance (physical strength to go on). A hound that has not both determination and stamina cannot be game. Together these two attributes endow the animal with gameness; no hound that lacks this trait should ever be bred, regardless of what other good points it may have. There are hounds that are good one day and bad another. Their faultiness in this respect should not be excused: they are not "game," and the chances are that they will transmit their weakness if bred. Would anyone breed to a race horse that was not "game"? Why do so in a hound?

In 1921, the First Chase Futurity was held at Crab Orchard, Kentucky. It was intended to last three days, but was run for five days. Two days before the field trials, *Scout*, a hound of the Trigg strain, belonging to Robert Rodes, was caught in a steel trap. In spite of the devoted efforts of J. S. Kirby, who handled the hound at the trials, and the assistance of two ladies who worked with him all night in a vain attempt to relieve the injury, the hound was lame when taken to the trials. (Incidentally, the two ladies were daughters of Haiden C. Trigg, who had bred the ancestors of this hound.) *Scout** ran practically on three legs for five continuous days of hard running, finally winning the event by manifestly superior work over all other hounds in everything from cold trailing to speed. This is the most extraordinary case on record, to the best of my knowledge, of gameness in a hound.

Determination is all-important in a great hound. Nose, symmetry, drive, together produce pace, but without determination few foxes can be accounted for. There must be physical ability to try, try, try, regardless of conditions while there is a vestige of line left—the stamina, the heart, and the will never to give up. With apologies to Kipling:

To force the heart and nerve and sinew
To serve their turn long after they are gone.

Determination is not to be confused with drive. To quote Lord Charles Bentinck, D.S.O.,

A hound may be the hardest of drivers, and yet do a great deal of harm out hunting. One that through pure light-heartedness or jealousy races on without having the scent is apt to carry the other hounds along with him, they thinking that by the way he is going ahead he must have the line, and thus the fox is lost.

If several hounds in the pack are addicted to this habit, the number of foxes killed is likely to be small. This sort of thing, when hounds dash wildly on with their heads in the air, is entirely different from the way a good pack, when it comes to a check, flings itself, making its own cast, every hound's nose down and every hound searching for the scent.

An excellent example of determination occurred in the case of the beagle bitch Field Champion Piedmont *Floretta*, '24, belonging to Frank D. Stuart and myself. This strongly made 13-inch hound, weighing seventeen pounds, is by Field and Bench Champion Piedmont *Captor*, out of Piedmont *Flora*, she by Champion Piedmont *Forger*, out of Champion *Julietta*.

On September 28, 1926, she won the 13-inch class at the Adirondack Club

* A son of *Scout* won the All-Age Stake in the National Foxhunters Association Trials in 1928 at Charlottesville, Va.

ATTRIBUTES OF A GOOD HOUND

meet, held in rough, mountainous country, running continuously for three hours on Canadian hare, known as "snowshoe rabbits." Three days later, she was started in the championship class, all ages and sizes up to fifteen inches. There were twelve starters, of which *Floretta* was the only hound under thirteen inches. This test was for five hours of hunting; scent was good, and for four hours and forty minutes this little bitch led the field. Suddenly her cry was missed, and the judge found her paralyzed in the hind legs, but still determined and trying to get forward on her front legs. In spite of her performance, the prize had to be given to another hound. Four days later, she was entered in the 13-inch class at the Northern Hare Club meet which she won against fifteen starters. In two hours she caught two Canadian hare, said to be the only instance of such performance on record.

Rival, '24, son of *Ruth*, '17 (she, perhaps the best foxhound bitch ever owned by the author), when at the point of death with pneumonia, in October, 1927, hearing hounds being drafted for hunting, staggered to his feet in determination to go with the pack. Finding no other means of egress from his hospital room, he jumped out of a window, the sill of which was three feet from the floor, and fell twenty feet to the ground below.

Many years ago, that keen sportsman, Mason Houghland, while visiting in the small town of Hallsville, Kentucky, heard hounds running through the streets one moonlight night. Hurrying to the house door, he espied a fox fleeing for his life, closely pursued by a pack, which was led at some distance by a famous local hound named *Lead*. So closely pressed was the quarry that he jumped over a parapet at the street end, dropping sixty feet to the base of a cliff. *Lead* sprang to the top of the parapet, hesitated but a moment, apparently realizing the consequences, then leaped into space after the fox.

Stamina is the physical ability to carry out determination, and is, of course, to be considered as most essential in breeding. Few people realize how far a hound travels in an ordinary hunting day; but any American observer will agree that the distance will be twice as far as that of the mounted huntsman,—in some rough countries several times as far. Assuming that the pack hunts six hours, and the huntsman's horse travels at an average pace of five miles, or a total of thirty miles, hounds will have covered from sixty to seventy miles.

A substantiated story has been given me from Oklahoma which is a marvelous example of "determination plus stamina equals gameness":

One Sunday morning, in December, 1924, nine couple of hounds hunted by P. B. Lowrance, of Ponca City, Oklahoma, found a wolf just north of Fairfax, in the Osage Indian nation. The chase swept northwards across a country of big pastures; three riders,—Lowrance, Sid Delleplaine (a Cherokee Indian), and a cowboy,—followed for eighteen miles, until their spent horses prevented going further. Late that same evening, these hounds killed

HOUNDS AND HUNTING

the wolf in a farmer's barnyard fifty miles northwest of Hunnewell, Kansas, approximately one hundred and twenty-five miles air line from where they found. Six couples were at the kill. The farmer noted the address of their owner on their collars, and telephoned Mr. Lowrance, who went on the following Tuesday after his hounds, picking up a missing couple en route.

CRY is the method that one hound has of telling another what is going on. In woodlands or rough country, cry is very important, for without it other hounds cannot possibly know what is transpiring, nor can followers of hounds know where the pack is. Hounds know what their fellows are saying, and an observant huntsman can usually tell by the quality of the sound, and by observing the attitude of the steadiest hounds, what the cry indicates.

Young foxhounds may riot, giving tongue with enthusiasm on hare. In such cases, not only is the pitch of the cry different, but it usually begins staccato. The huntsman can easily detect the false ring in the note. As for old hounds, they will usually raise their heads, pricking their ears as much as a hound can, but paying little attention to the excitement, as though they were thinking, "Go to it, boys and girls, I used to enjoy that once myself."

Let any one hound in a pack speak once on the line of a fox, every individual in the pack within hearing will instantly be on the *qui vive*, often stop, cock their heads to listen, and at a second challenge be off like the wind to join in the fray. Hounds on a cold line of a fox will give quite a different quality of note from that given on a fresh line. The one seems lower in scale, with the notes longer in duration; as hounds work the line toward the fox's kennel, the volume of cry increases in tempo, and rises in key and volume until, when the fox is "up," as they say in the South, the sound of a grand pack of Virginia hounds in full cry may be likened by music lovers to a great orchestra at crescendo in the second movement of Beethoven's Ninth Symphony. The only difference is that the hounds give a blood curdling twang to their performance which the musicians do not have.

English show type hounds of the present day supposedly speak little when in *full cry*, hence, for the modern Englishman the expression is a misnomer. Even Masefield says:

> . . . . . *the pack* . . .
> *Running like racers nearly mute* . . .
> *Then they were coming, mute but swift* . . .
> *The hungry hounds too tense for crying.*

With Virginia hounds the case is reversed. The faster they go the more tongue they give, and the only time under such conditions that the cry seems to falter at all is when hounds are ascending a steep incline in warm weather. Full cry *is* full cry with such a pack, and gives stimulus enough to tempt the novice to jump a stone house if it were in his way. If the thrill oc-

ATTRIBUTES OF A GOOD HOUND

casioned in most minds by really good cry in hounds is very remarkable to man, what must it be to hounds!

It is thus, of course, the most essential means of keeping a pack working together and in coöperation, especially in rough country of bad visibility. No man-made sound will make hounds run so eagerly on the line of their quarry as the cry of fellow hounds. Incidentally, to stay anywhere near a pack of Virginia foxhounds under reasonable conditions demands a first-class blood horse, which hardly seems to sustain the English contention that great cry and pace do not go together. From my knowledge that fast American hounds give maximum cry at speed, it is difficult for me to understand why English hounds at speed do not give at least as much cry as their acknowledged weak voices will permit.

Cry, to be retained, must be bred for. It is, in my belief, an artificial, man-made development in hounds, since it exists only in rudimentary form in other dogs, foxes, and wolves, which are said sometimes to give cry when hunting their game. My friend, Captain F. N. Miller, who so successfully managed Meadow Brook polo, and who spent many years in India, assures me that jackals hunt at night in large packs, often led by a hyena, and invariably, when running their quarry, give a rudimentary cry (or yap) similar to a pack of hounds, although less melodious. Coyotes in Western America, in running jack rabbits (*Lepus campestris*) give cry which may be described as a sort of "yip."

During the Middle Ages, as hunting was done largely in forests, cry was all-essential, was unquestionably bred for, and even the quality of it was much stressed. In Shakespeare's time, it seems to have been fashionable to have packs of hounds drafted to musical scale:

> *My hounds are bred out of the Spartan kind,*
> *So flew'd, so sanded, and their heads are hung*
> *With ears that sweep away the morning dew;*
> *Crook-knee'd, and dew lap'd, like Thessalian bulls;*
> *Slow in pursuit, but match'd in mouth like bells,*
> *Each under each. A cry more tuneable*
> *Was never halloo'd to, nor cheer'd with horn.*
>
> Midsummer Night's Dream.

> *. . . . was with Hercules and Cadmus once,*
> *When in a wood of Crete they bay'd the bear*
> *With hounds of Sparta; never did I hear*
> *Such gallant chiding; for, besides the groves,*
> *The skies, the fountains, every region near*
> *Seem'd all one mutual cry; I never heard*
> *So musical a discord, such sweet thunder.*
>
> Midsummer Night's Dream.

HOUNDS AND HUNTING

*Thy hounds shall make the welkin answer them
And fetch shrill echoes from the hollow earth.*
Taming of the Shrew.

*Whilst the babbling echo mocks the hounds
Replying shrilly to the well-tun'd horns,
As if a double hunt were heard at once,
Let us sit down and mark their yelping noise.*
Titus Andronicus.

Quoting from *Hunting in Arcadia*, Sir Philip Sidney, 1590:

Their cry being composed of so well-sorted mouths, that any man would perceive therein some kind of proportion, but the skilful woodmen did find a music.

A book printed in 1675, called, *Country Contentments*, or *The Husbandman's Recreations*, by Gervase Markham, contains the following:

If you would have your kennel for sweetness of cry, then you must compound it of some large dogs that have deep, solemn mouths, and are swift in spending, which must, as it were, bear the base in the consort; then a double number of roaring, and loud-ringing mouths, which must bear the counter-tenor; then some hollow, plain, sweet mouths, which must bear the mean or middle part; and so with these three parts of music, you shall make your cry perfect: and herein you shall observe, that these hounds mixed, do run just and even together, and do not hang loose off from one another, which is the vilest sight that may be . . . .

In the Spectator, 1711, "A Hunting Scene with Sir Roger," we find this apt comment on cry:

Sir Roger being at present too old for foxhunting, to keep himself in action, has disposed of his beagles and got a pack of stop-hounds. What these want in speed, he endeavors to make amends for by the deepness of their mouths and the variety of their notes which are suited in such manner to each other, that the whole cry makes up a deep concert. He is so nice in this particular, that a gentleman having made him a present of a very fine hound the other day, the knight returned it by the servant with a great many expressions of civility; but desired him to tell his master, that the dog he had sent was indeed a most excellent base, but that at present he only wanted a counter-tenor.

Good cry evidently continued to exist in some English hounds down to the early nineteenth century, for, in describing a hunt of 1811 with the Gloucester Foxhunting Club, near Philadelphia, the cry of hounds bred from the best imported English foxhounds is described as "deep-toned music, harmonious to the huntsman's listening ear."

If my theory of artificial development of cry in hounds is correct, it must also be correct to assume that it will disappear unless systematically bred for. Inversely cry may be bred out, a particular illustration of which fact is shown in the following account by "The Druid":

ATTRIBUTES OF A GOOD HOUND

About 1800, Sir Thomas Mostyn, who hunted Oxfordshire, seldom saw any hounds except his own, and had a great dread of tongue. He had in his pack a bitch named Lady *who was nearly mute,—a draft from Lord Lonsdale,—from whom sprang most of his pack. She bred them nearly mute, and he continued to breed from her blood almost entirely . . . They would go hopping on a scent two or three fields together without speaking, so that a person who was not accustomed to them would hardly know whether they were on scent or not. They could not hold the line, solely from want of tongue.*

The muteness of the modern fashionable hound of England is due, in my opinion, to the small stress laid upon the value of cry, with the result that it has largely disappeared. In consequence, many who hunt with modern show standard English hounds have never experienced the thrill such as comes from hearing good cry emanating from a pack of eighteen to twenty couple of Virginia hounds. Assuredly English packs formerly had it, for, as we have seen, the old writers mention the music of hounds; but, to-day, the smart-looking packs bred along show lines have no thrilling "music" left in their voices. What a wonderful stimulus is grand cry in a pack, and how useful! In most American countries, followers of hounds must depend on cry to know the whereabouts of the pack, and without it they would, consequently, have little pleasure. On windy days, even in a fairly open country, if hounds of deficient cry go down wind or over the crest of a hill, even though they be only a half-mile distant, it is usually impossible to hear them. In most British countries of small covers, followers are less dependent on cry; the line taken by hounds can rarely be lost, especially as the hundreds of riders make a tail like a kite, the pack taking the position of the kite.

COLOR is not of material importance. No good hound can be a bad color; but in practice, as affected by fashion or fancy, many a good hound is passed by for a bad one because of color. If winning race horses are not valued for color, there is no good reason why hounds should be. A hound of a color that is of high visibility in the country hunted, such as white hounds on a green hillside, or black and tan hounds on a snow-covered landscape, is ideal; but any moving object is visible against any colored background if not too distant; so, color for visibility is not all-important.

A symmetrical pack of uniform color and size is a splendid sight to look at, whatever the color may be. There is surely strength to that argument; but, to reject a great hound for color, or not to breed him for that reason, is quite absurd if the objective is accounting for foxes under any and all conditions.

Some strains of hounds have a tendency to certain colorations. So, assuming that you have a good strain of black and tan hounds, splendid in their work and conformation, do not, I pray,—just to suit a whim,—suddenly attempt to produce a white pack to the detriment of other qualities.

HOUNDS AND HUNTING

To breed to color, disregarding other useful attributes is a great handicap. In America, at least under our difficult climatic conditions,—a short season at best, where every day counts so much,—hounds should be bred for working qualities to the exclusion of fads. Only when pack perfection in other respects exists is it time to breed or draft for color, all other comparisons being equal.

There is a natural and very useful trait in hounds which is so remarkable that it is almost uncanny, and that is the homing instinct. This sense is so well known to the initiated that they are seldom surprised by its display, but examples may be useful for the edification of the layman.

There are foxhunters in America who generally run their hounds at night. Some of these men live in towns, and take their hounds out in the country to a spot where a fox may be found. The hounds range away by themselves, pick up the line of a fox, and, maybe, run it for many hours. The hunter often moves about on foot in his attempt to keep within hearing distance of his hounds. If hounds run out of hearing, the hunter will perhaps light a fire, beside which he will sit while listening through the stillness of the night for the cry of his hounds on the returning line of the fox. A hound may possibly run his fox to ground some miles away from where he found, but, in any case, he will (unless interfered with) invariably return to where he left his master. In his master's absence he will await him there for hours, or track his footsteps.

An interesting story of homing quality appeared in the American Turf Register, in 1829,—an owner of foxhounds who lived in Fairfax County, Virginia, presented to a friend in Baltimore an old hound named *Merkin*. This hound was embarked on a steamboat at Alexandria, and finally arrived in Baltimore via the Potomac River and Chesapeake Bay. In a few days he was left at liberty, and, apparently not liking his new quarters, he promptly vacated. In a short time he appeared at his original master's kennel in Fairfax County, a distance of fifty or sixty miles overland through an entirely strange country.

Numerous accounts in the American sporting press tell of hounds that having been taken on trains hundreds of miles to field trials, became lost at the trials, and have shortly found their way back to their homes. In one account, the hound must have crossed the Mississippi and Ohio Rivers in some unaccountable manner.

A story appeared in The Chase, in 1926, of a young hound that had been taken from Charlotte to Georgetown, North Carolina, on a hunting expedition. While hunting, he became lost, and his master having had to leave for home, the hound found his way back over the road, which he had never before traversed except in a car, a distance of one hundred and seventy-five miles.

SQUIRE OSBALDESTON'S FAMOUS FOXHOUND SIRE, FURRIER,
Descendant from Mr. Meynell's pack. After the painting by Ferneley, 1825.

MEYNELL WAVERLEY, '09,
Champion dog hound at Peterborough, 1911; imported in 1914 by Mr. A. Henry Higginson,
M.F.H. of the Middlesex, and President of the Masters of Foxhounds Association of America.
From a painting by Cuthbert Bradley, reproduced by courtesy of Mr. Higginson.

ATTRIBUTES OF A GOOD HOUND

The Chase recently printed another remarkable example of homing instinct, in which a hound owned by M. S. Simpson, of New Madison, Ohio, was sold and taken by train November 20, 1927, to Minot, North Dakota. On December 12 this valiant hound, emaciated and footsore, appeared at his original home, having traveled an approximate distance of twelve hundred miles. Finding no one at home, he traced Mrs. Simpson to the local school house, where she was instructing her class. Mrs. Simpson hearing a familiar baying, went to the schoolyard to investigate, and was overwhelmed by the hound's demonstrations of affection.

By using comparisons, an attempt has been made to portray a *good* hound. Now, sad but true, we must take up our *chronique scandaleuse*, for some hounds have vices, on account of which they should never be bred nor retained. Often, vices in hounds arise from jealousy of their fellows, as among men and women, and hounds so addicted are, of course, valueless in a pack, for they will often do things of a dishonest character in company which they would not be able to do in running the line of a fox alone.

Frequently, a young hound having a tendency to some particular vice can be cured of it by severe chastisement at the right moment. Inversely, if an inexperienced or dishonest huntsman persistently encourages a hound to do wrong, that hound may be ruined forever. Many *are* so ruined by bad huntsmanship, as outlined in Chapter VI.

In certain countries, there are often smooth cattle paths or rides on which a hound can easily run, as opposed to the rough going elsewhere. Oftentimes, foxes use such paths, leaving traces of their night wanderings. A young hound coming suddenly on such a spot will perhaps become excited and wildly run the path, giving false cry as he goes. If he can fool his huntsman into encouraging him in such falseness, he will soon be ruined; but, if properly chastised, his youthful enthusiasm may be constrained. One or two unsteady hounds that will falsely run paths may spoil almost any hunt, and may soon ruin an otherwise good pack.

Occasional unsteadiness may be caused by temporary lack of work in any hound; but often faultiness becomes chronic in hounds that have been allowed to run riot in bad company when young.

Any young hound that will *hunt* the line of a dog, or heel a line, should be broken of this fault, or drafted at once, for he is worse than useless. There is no excuse for an old hound addicted to such a vice.

A fast hound with weak cry is a nuisance, because he may, at a check in woodlands or rough hilly country, get away alone without being heard by the balance of the pack or by the hunt staff. A hound that will deliberately run mute, in order to steal away from the balance of the pack, is inexcusable.

Occasionally, as a hound grows old and feels his powers failing, he will acquire such tricks through jealousy. Vices due to jealousy or unusual intelligence are very interesting to observe, but are impossible to cure, and, hence, it is a great disappointment when an otherwise good hound acquires them.

Speaking of jealousy, many years ago I owned a splendid-looking two-season hound which for speed and general ability dominated the pack in the field. The following season, the pack was considerably improved by the acquisition of the famous *Virgie*, '14, *Gertie*, '14, and *Music*, '15, and our young hero of the previous year found himself outdone. He proved himself a bad sportsman, and actually, when outpaced on two occasions, deliberately returned alone to kennels. He became sullenly jealous, one day attacked the huntsman, and in consequence was drafted. His heart was apparently broken by defeat.

In 1925, I had at Millbrook a really great hound, *Ripper*, then in his fourth season. He had good cry, but was several times observed that year deliberately running mute a whole field ahead of the pack. He was, of course, also drafted.

Skirting is almost the worst fault a pack hound can have. It is a form of jealousy. Such hounds are usually impossible to break of this vice. They will frequently run parallel to the pack at some distance from it, not following the line at all, but wildly gambling on picking up the scent ahead of the balance of the hounds in case the fox suddenly turns. Hounds bred for field trial work seem particularly addicted to this habit.

Once, the author owned an extraordinarily good foxhound who never had skirted in hunting red foxes in Virginia; but, in 1919, when hunting in North Carolina, this hound apparently learned that by keeping outside the small swamps frequented by grey foxes, he could often waylay the fox as it was driven out by the balance of the pack. It proved useless to try to break him of this trick.

Dwelling on a line when other hounds have gone away, or giving cry when harking to a pack from any distance, are faults which may possibly be corrected in a young hound by an observant whipper-in who does his work properly.

Now, that I have listed the merits and demerits of a good foxhound, let me again inquire, if it takes two years of time, not to mention the cost, to raise and train a young hound to a stage where its good and bad qualities can be detected, is it worth while to reproduce from anything but the most perfect? To recognize perfection in arriving at a standard of merit, one must be sure of his own knowledge as a judge, and that his knowledge is free from prejudice. To know how to apply the general principles of breeding in this very complex animal, the foxhound, when it comes to the virtues of line-breeding, in-breeding, etc., one should make a complete study of the subject as written by the great authorities on the several breeds of livestock. Having acquired a general knowledge of the experiences of great breeders, one soon will be convinced that nothing can be done without a thorough understanding of the heritage of the animals to be reproduced, because each one of them in some measure influences even remote descendants. No one would think of breeding thoroughbred mares, dairy cows, or even heavy laying hens to a sire of unknown heritage; and, yet, in America at least, it is being done with foxhounds. What great folly and how pathetic is this attitude when hunting ability is desired.

It is difficult to understand why men will be careless in hound breeding while being particular in other lines of breeding. I know an American who breeds thoroughbred horses, has the best of blood, and thinks blood lines all-important, yet last year he bred twenty foxhound bitches to a dog belonging to a friend of mine simply because he liked the looks of the dog. He had never seen the dog hunt, and nobody knew how he was bred.

I have another American in mind who breeds foxhounds, selecting largely for color, and I'll wager that he has no knowledge of any of his hounds' progenitors, their ability, or their appearance back two generations. Another American imported a hound from England at a long price from which to breed working foxhounds. This imported dog never had seen a fox. He had won a prize as a puppy, and then had his leg broken. He had enormous bone, and that fact was apparently all that was considered.

An appeal is made, herewith, never to follow the irrational examples just cited, nor yet to be affected by the mania for breeding to a smart-looking hound, if that is his only virtue, even though his pedigree is long.

Certain comments have already been made to the effect that out-crosses must be indulged in with infinite care. Mendel, in 1853, laid down his now well-accepted principle of the impossibility of breeding a cross true to its own type, on account of its innate tendency to split up into its original pure or uncrossed forms.

At one time, I was in a great hurry to add certain attributes of conformation to my pack, and searched the world for possible out-crosses. Having found a type of hound that had most of the outward characteristics desired, and possessed of fair nose and quality of cry, I did some cross-breeding both ways; that is, using my Virginia hounds as sires, and *vice versa*. My experiments came to very unsatisfactory results, as I might have known had I thoroughly absorbed the teachings of Mendel. While I was flirting on the side with this expensive experiment, several years passed. During this time, my own line-breeding system showed splendid results in improving the appearance and hunting qualities of the pack, and its ability to breed true, in consequence of which I became convinced that a continuous policy of line-breeding, with very diluted out-crosses, if any, is the only policy that gives reasonable assurance of desired results. This method may not be spectacular, but it is sure.

Breed improvement, commonly called line-breeding, means the restriction of matings to individuals of one line of descent. Its object is to get the best out of a given race, and to better that race if possible.

The chief danger in line-breeding is that of selection by paper pedigree—forgetting, or being ignorant of the attributes of the individual. Elimination in line-breeding is just as important as in any other system, and a line-bred pedigree is valuable or worthless in direct ratio to the individuals that made it. No other system of breeding has ever secured the results that line-breeding has; but, to secure results in this manner, personal knowledge of each hound and strict adherence to individual selection is all-essential. Line breeding carried to its limits involves the inter-breeding of hounds closely related. This is termed "in-breeding," and this system has produced some of the greatest animals in all breeds, but is dangerous unless the utmost attention is paid to individual weaknesses.

On the whole, the breeder's problem is to obtain the strongest aggregation of hounds properly balanced as to conformation, superior as to performance, and which will be able to transmit their qualities by virtue of homogeneous hereditary characteristics. When all is said and done, there is nothing like actual observation of the results of using one line of blood in combination with another, and the proven virtues of certain sires and dams as producers. Their value is incalculable.

It is hoped that the attributes of a good hound have been made clear. Multiplying that perfect hunting machine by sixty, the result will be a useful pack, able to turn out eighteen to twenty couple three times a week. The extra hounds will be needed, because there always will be a certain number that are cut, lamed, or otherwise laid up. Such a pack will have no hounds under eighteen months old, and rarely any over six years of age. In other words, every four years an entirely new pack of hunting hounds will have to be provided, a renewal that will require the utmost thought and attention.

In England, since early times, great stress has been laid on pack perfection. Buckingham bred a very even running pack for James I, as is testified to by a personal letter of appreciation for "so fyne a kennell of young howndes. All of thaime runne together in a lumpe both at sente and veue." In 1614, Buckingham again wrote, and this time to Lord Rochester offering him the "best pack of howndes that ever ran upon English ground." Before 1700, at Belvoir, at Badminton, and at Brocklesby, packs existed which have continued down to the present time. The Quorn hunt was for one hundred years under the control of but two masters. This is a great thing for a pack of hounds, especially when the last master has been intimate with the system

ATTRIBUTES OF A GOOD HOUND

of his predecessor from boyhood. Fortunately, such was the case with this particular hunt, when Hugo Meynell, in 1753, succeeded Thomas Boothby, who had begun his mastership in 1697. Many other enthusiasts, such as "Squire" Osbaldeston and the ancestors of the present Lord Lonsdale, did much to lay stress on the perfection of packs, so that they had already reached a high standard of excellence in the early nineteenth century.

Great Britain and Ireland are, even to-day, the only two countries where there are any number of beautiful looking level packs of uniform type. They are the product of a definite breeding policy exercised through many generations, as has just been cited. Continuity of breeding policy and intelligent management by educated gentlemen has made all this possible. In America, we must try to achieve equally good results, but modified for our purposes and conditions of hunting. The first essential of pack excellence with us must be levelness in hunting ability of the highest order.

An ideal pack must be composed entirely of great individual hounds,—say, seventeen to twenty couple,—perfectly matched for speed and ability, hunting with the utmost unanimity. There must not be a single individual in the pack as a "filler-in," or for appearance only. In his work, each hound must be the *best*. He must have individuality, yet be subject to control. Often, I have been asked what was my best hound. My reply always is, "I cannot answer. They must all be good." Of course, some hounds are better than others for different phases of the chase. Some hounds are good *strike* hounds, i.e., they will find the first traces of a cold fox line with more keenness than others.

A fourteenth century poem illustrates how such a clever hound may *find* by smelling each leaf and grass blade for "ends of scent," and thereby become the means to the end of a fine hunt:

> *The Mass is sung to end, the pages wait*
> *The guests' arrival, and upon them pressed*
> *The sops in goblets, while to the main gate*
> *The serving men bring courses of the best,*
> *For all that troop is to the hunting dressed;*
> *Brisk is the earth with frost on stock and stone,*
> *And the great steeds impatient of arrest,*
> *And as with joy departed is each one,*
> *Out of his cloud-rack ruddy rose the mighty sun.*
> *When they had ridden to the greenwood side*
> *The hounds of their long leashes free they cast;*
> *A traverse way athwart the wood they ride,*
> *And through the horns they blow a rousing blast.*
> *A little hound that by a thorn-bush passed*

HOUNDS AND HUNTING

> *Shrilly gives tongue, his fellows answer back,*
> *The huntsmen cheer, the rabble fall in fast,*
> *Hounds swift and lithe follow the fox's track*
> *As forth by many a difficult grove he leads the pack.*

Some hounds will be at their best after the fox is up; some will stick to an almost hopelessly cold line with greater interest than others. All must have their good points—none too fast, none too slow, all coördinating.

> *Keen on the scent*
> *At fault none losing heart! but all at work!*
> *None leaving his task to another! answering*
> *The watchful huntsman's caution, check or cheer*
> *As steed his rider's rein. Away they go!*
> *How close they keep together! What a pack!*
> *Nor turn nor ditch nor stream divides them—as*
> *They move with one intelligence, act, will!*

When working a line, a good pack must carry a good head. For example, from left wing to right wing, according to circumstances, the distance should be one hundred yards, more or less. On one occasion in North Carolina, my pack was working a very cold line. So good was their coördination and mutual trust that the twenty couple advanced across a burnt-over bog at a walking pace like a skirmish line of soldiers; now one spoke here, now one there, on the meandering trail of the fox.

To carry a wide head at speed is good; for a pack to carry head on a cold line is splendid. A pack that tails out, because of unequal physical ability or age is certainly not satisfactory, and, of course, no pack should include individuals with any of the vices that have been mentioned.

A "lot" of hounds is one thing, a *pack* of hounds quite another. It is frequently the case in America that a "lot" of hounds is called a pack; but such an improper appellation should not be tolerated. When young and old, fast and slow, true and faulty hounds are taken out, it is inevitable that the huntsman will come home more or less houndless, and the sport he gives will naturally be indifferent.

> *But above all take heed, nor mix thy hounds*
> *Of different kinds; discordant sounds shall grate*
> *Thy ears offended, and a lagging line*
> *Of babbling curs disgrace thy broken pack.*

On the contrary, there is satisfaction indeed in hunting a pack selected to work like a machine,—hounds that can be hunted wide or close, under such perfect control when seeking for their fox that the huntsman can almost feel each one of them, as if on the end of a silken thread.

Many years ago, in attempting to organize pack trials under the auspices of the American Foxhound Club, I made the following suggestion for the guidance of judges in selecting the best pack to show sport to followers of hounds:

Special consideration of the pack's qualities may be made in
* A—Striking or finding.*
* B—Trailing or hunting a cold line.*
* C—Hunting with drive.*
* D—Speed and evenness of running as a pack.*
* E—Gameness.*
* F—Cry.*
* G—Accounting for foxes.*
* H—Levelness of conformation, size, and color of pack.*
* I—Manners of pack, obedience to voice and horn.*
* J—General condition after hunting.*

Now, that the qualifications of a great pack have been defined, it is time to enlarge on the difficulty of assembling and keeping such a pack up to its full strength. The expense and work involved is vast, and, frankly, it takes almost a fanatic to make a success of it. In England, to assemble a fairly good pack of hounds is largely a matter of price, there are so many homogeneous packs from which to select, and their blood lines are so well known; moreover, one often can buy a complete kennel of long-standing excellence; but, in America, English hounds are rarely satisfactory in accounting for foxes, and I have never heard of a good pack of American hounds being for sale *in toto*. Hence, to create a high-class pack of any stamp of American hounds is no easy matter. Time, money, and great enthusiasm are all-essential.

Each year some new hunt is contemplated, and I am approached for hounds. One must be excused for being somewhat caustic when, on September 15th, Mr. X inquires how he can acquire some good hounds to hunt his new country on September 25th—they must hunt well, be good looking, thoroughly pack broken, and cost next to nothing. He usually explains that his fellow enthusiasts have some nice horses which have cost from $1,500 to $3,000 each, and "some hounds" are needed immediately.

All this would be funny if it were not sad. At a meet one morning, a new and ardent sportsman inquired with vigor if a good day's sport was to be expected. My reply was to the effect that it would be disappointing if the day were bad—thinking to myself that I had been fifteen years preparing for it, had gradually and carefully selected and bred perhaps two thousand hounds to create and maintain the pack he was to hunt with that morning, and that

HOUNDS AND HUNTING

I would be unwilling to acknowledge what it had all cost. A conception of the meaning of these unspoken facts might have set him thinking a bit, and made him less careless about riding on hounds—an offense he actually committed.

In the chapter on Present Day Hounds, the origin and characteristics of my pack of Virginia hounds has been enlarged upon, but it may be well to explain here the rather unusual method of producing that pack and keeping it up to utmost efficiency.

Many racing men maintain a racing stable and a breeding stud. This is my practice with hounds. I maintain an "old" pack, which for some years hunted nine months a year, moving like a racing stable with the seasons,—from June to November hunting in the Millbrook country, New York; from November to March in the Overhills country, North Carolina. This pack left North Carolina in March, 1927, and hunted until May 21st at Montauk Point, Long Island, New York, thus completing a season in which hounds hunted in twelve months going out one hundred and twelve days.

This "old" pack rarely has a hound in it under eighteen months of age, or one older than five seasons. It is recruited from my breeding and training pack, which for years was kenneled in a rough hill country near Paris, Fauquier County, Virginia. New kennels were built at Hunting Hill, near Sperryville, Rappahannock County, Virginia, in 1927. Here the older hounds are bred; here certain of the old pack are returned for the breeding season, and here the young hounds are entered. This system was inaugurated in a small way, in 1912, and has gradually developed until, in 1926, the huntsman of my breeding pack, Charles W. Carver, walked one hundred and two couple of puppies. The puppies are all ear marked with tattoo ink, and walked with farmers living on isolated farms scattered over several counties. These farmers usually have a few steady old hounds of their own, and the puppies often begin hunting fox when six to seven months old. Thus, they are well versed in fox lore when at twelve to fourteen months of age they are entered with the breeding pack.

My system of training young hounds in a pack by themselves, guided by a nucleus of steady old hounds, was established as a means to the end of utmost efficiency. Since I inaugurated this system, I have discovered that it apparently was the system of Beckford; and it also was the practice of Meynell, "the father of modern English fox hunting," from 1753 to 1790. Of his practice it has been written:

His Old Pack consisted of three years old and upwards, and no two years old was admitted, except a very high opinion was entertained of his virtues and abilities.

The Young Hounds were hunted twice a week, as much in woodlands as possible, and in the most unpopular Coverts. The Young Pack had always a

ATTRIBUTES OF A GOOD HOUND

few couple of steady Old Hounds with them. The Old Pack hunted the best country. When any bad faults were discovered, they were immediately drafted, for fear of contamination.

Skirting, over-running the scent, and babbling, were the greatest faults.

Perfections consisted of true guiders, in hard running, and close, patient hunters, in a cold scent, together with stoutness.

Mr. Meynell's Hounds were criticised by himself and his friends in the most minute manner. Every Hound had his peculiar talents, and was sure to have a fair opportunity of displaying them. Some had the remarkable faculty of finding a fox, which they would do almost invariably, notwithstanding twenty or thirty couple were out in the same covert. Some had the propensity to hunt the doubles and short turns. Some were inclined to be hard runners. Some had a remarkable faculty of hunting the Drag of a Fox, which they would do very late in the day. And sometimes the hardest runners were the best hunters; and fortunate was the year when such excellences prevailed.

Mr. Meynell prided himself on the steadiness and the docility of his Hounds; and their hunting through sheep and hares, which they did in a very superior manner.

The system by which hounds learn to hunt at the earliest possible age, gradually acquire manners, and hunt in many months of the year, produces great foxhounds.

Hounds raised in a kennel or brought in from walk when ten to twelve months old, and not hunted continuously after that age, are bound to be second rate, as would pampered boys and girls. The survival of the fittest among the young entry, the test in their first season of accounting for foxes in the company of experienced hounds, is the *sine qua non* of admission to the "old" pack. When young hounds first come from the walks, little drafting is done until hunting ability is established; breeding is next considered, then conformation, and, finally, size, no hound being drafted for color.

This system is expensive. It takes much time, not overlooking the keeping of correct records and pedigrees; but it is my conviction that it is the most efficient system when it comes to producing the best possible working pack.

This *exposé* of effort involved brings us to the point of considering the cost and value of hounds in general.

An eminent British authority recently wrote:

Horses can be bought, and the men to ride them can be found; foxes only need to be left alone and there will be plenty of them; but the breeding of a pack of foxhounds takes time, thought, and care.

The hound can hunt without the man, and the man can hunt without a horse, as is actually done both in America and Britain,—thus, in hunting, the hound is the all-important factor, not forgetting the fox. What a fallacy to spend money for horses, kennels, and equipment unless one has the best of hounds.

From the trouble taken by the ancients to import hunting dogs, it must be surmised that their cost and value became at that time a serious consideration. Under the Salic Law for the stealing or killing of a first-class hound, a fine was imposed—actually, 4,500 fr. in gold to-day. Shakespeare's value of a hound in his day, the equivalent of many hundreds of dollars, has been quoted elsewhere.

Lord Althorp, in 1808, *master of the Pytchley, purchased the hounds of Mr. John Warde for* £1,000 (*the probable equivalent of* £5,000 *to-day*).

At the time that 'Squire' Osbaldeston's hounds were sold at Tattersall's, six couple fetched 1,360 *guineas, Mr. Harvey Combe purchasing them for the Old Berkeley country.*

In 1926, the Croome Foxhounds, 38½ couple entered and 18 couple unentered, property of Mr. W. S. Gresson, were sold at auction by Messrs. Tattersall at their Rugby kennels for 4,121 guineas, or $21,758. The average price was $192 with $924 the top price for the stallion hound, *Daystar*. Hence, if in Britain, a country struggling to recoup from a terrible war, such prices can be paid for foxhounds, surely in America the value of a great pack of hounds should be twice the British price. If ordinary terriers, chows, and other dogs that have no working qualifications to be considered sell for $100–$200 each, and show specimens from $400 to $5,000, should not a good working foxhound of good looks be worth at least as much?

In America, hound values have strange and amusing variations. I have known Virginia mountaineers living in log cabins, their children going shoeless in winter, who would laugh at a hundred-dollar offer for a good hound; I have known millionaires to quibble over paying $100 a couple for hounds.

Letters from Mr. Birdsong to Mr. Trigg written in the sixties indicate the great value placed on hounds in America among keen southern foxhunters, at a time when a dollar bill to them was worth $10.00, or even $20.00 in modern money values. In 1866, Mr. Trigg paid Mr. Birdsong $400.00 for four hounds. In 1867, Mr. Birdsong mentioned having sold a fourteen-months-old puppy for $150.00. He sold another dog to Mr. Trigg for $150.00, in July, 1867, when men and animals in the South were all but starving to death on account of hardships caused by the Civil War. Mr. Birdsong wrote: "Thanks to Providence, we will have a bountiful crop this fall, and my poor dogs will soon be fed without stint." Mr. Birdsong finally sold the hound *Longstreet* for $200.00. Mr. R. H. Ward writes of selling a hound, in 1868, for $150.00. In 1870, Mr. Maupin writes, "I have lost my wife and had my house burned, and cannot hunt a great deal. My price for *Towstring* is $100.00."

The man who thinks he can count on buying hounds for a few dollars each who are really good hounds in their work and breeding is, to put it mildly, mistaken. I have quoted the preceding figures, because they indicate something concrete; but it may be definitely stated that a really high-class pack of Virginia hounds is beyond any price valuation, since they cannot be duplicated by purchase. Not only must a pack of hounds be valued for what it can do, but for what it can produce in the future. If the bad ones can be put down fast enough, it is possible in a few years to acquire by purchase a fairly good pack of hounds, but by personal observation nothing will be known of their ancestors' disabilities; hence, the difficulty and extreme uncertainty (even unto remote generations) of good results in breeding such hounds. It must be remembered that "the sins of the fathers shall be visited upon the children," and "consider well his lineage; what his fathers did of old."

In any case, a pack valuation should be at least double the aggregate of its individual hound values. A hound may be worth on its own merits two hundred dollars; nevertheless, if it does not fit into a given pack, it is worth precisely nothing for use in that pack. On the other hand, taking into consideration the laws of supply and demand, plus the probabilities of finding the exact requirements to fit the ideal pack (which is put at a 50% gamble), it is obvious that proven pack values should add 100% to intrinsic individual value.

Once when approached by a young and enthusiastic master to write something that would help him to get the support of his hunt followers toward acquiring a good pack of hounds, the author sent him the following:

I discuss hounds with some trepidation, because it is nearly impossible for uninformed people to understand how essential a good pack is to their pleasure, but I'll let figures talk for me. Say, twenty followers of your hunt own horses representing a capital investment of $30,000; add to this, stables, clothes, etc., and you have a total investment for hunting of perhaps $100,000. The annual maintenance cost per hunting day is very considerable; hence, every hunt day should be the very best possible, and only the best of hounds can make it so. In America, bad scenting conditions are the rule, due to heat, cold, drought, or wind, on five hunting days out of the six. By these premises, hounds should be good enough to give sport every day, be conditions what they may. An indifferent pack will give sport only about one day in six, because they are physically incapable of doing better. More is asked of a foxhound than any other domestic animal. He must have brains, training, manners, nose, symmetry, cry, endurance, and determination ad lib.

It is a pleasure to add that this explanation immediately secured the financial support the master required to provide a suitable pack that would hunt well and reproduce itself properly.

When all is said and done, the points intended for emphasis in this chapter are well expressed by François Villon:

> *For everyone this wise complains*
> *Of dogs and horses, love and war:*
> *Each pleasure's bought with fifty pains.*

CHAPTER VI.

COMMENTS ON HUNTING A PACK

THE skill of the huntsman, in the chase of various sorts of quarry, or the art of venery, is of very ancient origin, and had already reached a high state of perfection before the discovery of America. This we learn from the most famous book of all times on hunting and hounds (previously referred to), written more than five hundred years ago by that great huntsman-author, Gaston, compte de Foix. This may surprise many of the readers of this book who assume that more is known to-day about all phases of hunting than in days of yore.

In America, few people have real knowledge of the technique of hunting a pack of hounds, or the traditions of the chase, apart from riding a horse. Many farmer hunters owning a few hounds have much knowledge of game lore, but the ancient traditions and pageantry, the correct forms and methods of hunting a large pack, are quite unknown to them.

In Britain, hunting to ride is now all the vogue, as opposed to riding to hunt: quick bursts, lifting hounds to halloos, and over-numerous foxes have played havoc with veritable hunting in the old sense.

Calls on the hunting horn and the huntsman's language once had a very definite meaning, but have degenerated to-day in large measure into a meaningless jargon. This should not be so,—huntsmen should try to use language and calls that have significance, as once was the custom generally, and still is the custom in France, a country where the ancient traditions of the art of venery still exist, at least in forms of procedure, horn-blowing, and pageantry. The several packs of staghounds in England still keep up certain ancient forms,—the tufters are used, and numerous expressions and customs remain; but, with the modern general artificiality of hunting conditions, the true art of venery has largely disappeared.

Speed! Drive! These have been the watchwords *ad absurdum*. Less haste, more speed, would account for more foxes, give longer runs and better hunting on many occasions, especially were more stress laid on improving the hunting qualities of hounds, the much overlooked means to the end.

I have seen many huntsmen in my time,—a few of them good, many of them bad, and some of them dishonest to their hounds and to their field. A bad huntsman, if he is not just stupid, is generally a persistent egotist, an egotist of the type that tries to enhance his own importance at the expense of his hounds. He never gives hounds a chance; if they come to a loss, and he can get to them, the run is frequently finished then and there. This sounds odd, but the reason is obvious. He first starts in showing his ability on the horn, gets hounds' heads up, and, as he starts to cast hounds, his whippers-in finish the job properly by unnecessary rating and whip-cracking. By the time this triumvirate of noise-makers has finished impressing their personalities on hounds, the latter have generally lost any interest they may have had in the fox.

In this day and generation, it is quite easy for a huntsman to become egotistical. So few people understand the art of venery as differentiated from "hunting to ride," they become impatient with a huntsman who does not bustle about and fool them into believing that he is the all-important factor to their riding pleasure.

The *deliberately dishonest* huntsman is inexcusable; he ruins hounds and deceives his followers. Cheering hounds to a false line, laying drags, dropping foxes at the end of drag lines, making his field believe hounds are hunting fox when they are in reality hunting the huntsman, express mildly some of his wiles. Unfortunately, there have been several huntsmen in America who regularly practiced such buffoonery. In England, where a huntsman's tips depend largely on his reputation as a "smart" huntsman giving the riding contingent many short, quick gallops, it is also a great temptation for a huntsman to be, euphemistically speaking, a "faker."

With the modern, comparatively mute English hounds, numerous foxes and real or false halloos, this sort of a game is frequent, but it is *not* really hunting. It may be imagined how woefuly detrimental such a practice is to hounds, for with such handling they soon lose all individuality and initiative, and become largely dependent on the huntsman, indifferent to any serious efforts of their own. The try, try, try, stick, stick, stick of the ideal hunting hound is soon lost under such treatment. Where hounds run very mute, it is quite easy for a huntsman to lift the pack and fool his field half the time, if he so desires. In America, there was once a well known huntsman who always produced a grand "foxhunt" on Saturdays and holidays, and little sport on other days. Usually there was a "kill" on these gala days. Odd to relate, the "fox" usually ran through gates, panels, and wood rides. The huntsman, of course, laid drags, and dropped bagged foxes at the end of the drag line. Another huntsman in America would cheer his hounds to cur dogs, and even rabbits, pretending they had a fox line, and, worse still, he had a pet hound that would sling his tongue falsely when cheered, whether there was any line or not. Pathetic as it may seem, the owner of the pack day after day swallowed the lie. Someone may ask what difference does it make so long as the riders have a gallop. The only possible answer is,—it absolutely *ruins* hounds.

In England, a huntsman can handle hounds more accurately than in America. In the latter country, a hunted fox is infrequently viewed; hills and woodlands muffle sound and obstruct vision; hence, a huntsman's difficulties are manifold.

The most clever huntsman within my ken is Charles W. Carver, who hunted my hounds from 1911 to 1925, in which year I began hunting them myself, Carver giving his exclusive attention to the breeding pack. An indefatigable enthusiast in breeding, training, and hunting hounds, he is the keenest man imaginable in his desire to account for a fox once found. Having hunted hounds from the time he was fifteen, his ability from experience to sense what a fox has done or what a hound is up to is second to no man's. Charlie, a bold rider, has been well mounted all his life, and consequently has probably seen more of hound work than any living American huntsman, many of whom are unable to keep close to hounds, because of rough country.

I once saw Charlie by keen thinking perform the greatest piece of huntsmanship that I ever expect to witness. It was in the sandy Overhills country. Hounds had found a grey fox near the Black plantation, between Little River bridge (near Manchester) and Overhills. Grey foxes are sometimes twisters and infinitely more tricky than reds. This particular customer was worse than usual in running a corkscrew line. On that day, a number of followers were out with hounds to whom I was very keen to show sport,—Mrs. Thomas, the Misses Sanford, and Stephen Sanford, Jr. (owner of *Sergeant Murphy*, winner of the Liverpool Grand National, 1922), and Percy Rockefeller. Hounds were running well, when, suddenly, on the edge of the old Plank Road there was a check. For some minutes Charlie let hounds try to work it out themselves, and then he had a try, casting them slowly in every possible direction, with no results until the former Leicestershire thruster began to get very nervous. The fox had apparently escaped on wings.

Charlie turned to me and said, "Mr. Thomas, did you see that automobile drive up the road just before hounds reached it? I think the fox walked the road in the sand rut, and that the car coming along afterwards covered up the line." Whistling softly to his hounds, he slowly cast them up the road, sharply eyeing the sides for fox tracks in the sand. For over two hundred yards he went, when, quickly jumping from his horse, he bent down, and with a satisfied smile gently cheered hounds as he put them on the line where it left the roadway. Reynard had walked the rut just as Charlie thought he had, and the passing car had run over and obliterated the fox track. A good twenty minutes had elapsed, and as scent was none too good at that time, and the country to the north side of the road had been burned over, it re-

ON HUNTING A PACK

quired splendid work for hounds to again get up to that walking fox and get a second run on him. He was killed in proper style, at dusk, in the Ben Thomas swamp, in spite of a fast dropping thermometer.

Charlie is rightly a strong believer in never allowing hounds to give up trying whenever there remains the vestige of a chance to work out a line. To encourage hounds to "quit" is a crime in Charlie's eyes, and justly so.

To have untold patience, to use great self-control, to keep one's head at all times, to act quietly but with decision when one knows definitely what to do, are qualities par excellence in a great huntsman. In addition, he should have health, memory, good hearing, voice, sight, courage, good spirits, perseverance, and activity,—in short, such a man must be *nascitur non fit*. It is not easy to find the super-huntsman.

Referring to huntsmanship, in his *Essays on Sporting*, Blaine wrote, in 1788: . . . . . . *in time of action we ought to be armed with calmness and presence of mind, to observe the various motions and stratagems made use of to defeat us, and furnished with prudent foresight and provision for every new emergency to which the fortune of the day is subject.*

Speaking of calmness, suppose hounds had been hunting a fox hard for one and a half hours, and one suddenly viewed a fox up a tree. Wouldn't almost anyone jump to the conclusion that the treed fox was the hunted one? Not so with Captain Adamthwaite, who was hunting hounds in my absence in the Overhills country, in January, 1926. He showed a remarkably fine piece of huntsmanship by using his eyes, ears, and brains; but, I'll let the reader make his own conclusion by reading Captain Adamthwaite's description of the incident which came to me by letter:

We had a most wonderful hunt on Tuesday last. I only wish you had been here to see it. I send you a copy from my hunting diary. This was undoubtedly the finest hunt I have ever seen in England, Ireland, or elsewhere. Two things stand out as particularly interesting,—(1) a grey fox will run twenty miles without going up a tree, although very tired; (2) a grey fox will go up a tree, although not hunted at all. With regard to (1), we all viewed the hunted fox when found, Marshall two or three times during the run; we all viewed him just before the kill; and we all are confident, owing to his peculiar coloring, his general appearance, and his size, that the fox we found is the fox we killed. Furthermore, from the way the hounds ran, I am perfectly satisfied they never changed. The fox we saw up a tree was quite clean, his sides were not blowing in the least, and his tongue was in. I had a very good view of him, and he was not twenty feet from the ground. I believe he jumped straight out of his lair when he saw us, and ran up the nearest tree. The work on the part of hounds was faultless; once only were they a bit over-anxious at a check. What 'possessed' Antic and Fairy that day, I don't know; they both shone, as also did Liza. She has the makings of a brilliant bitch. They all ran well packed up, and I could not say that any hound was

HOUNDS AND HUNTING

either too fast or too slow; every hound was there when they killed, and, with the exception of perhaps two couple, all came home with their sterns up. I always thought your pack was good, but they excelled themselves beyond all expectations that day. Marshall, Mr. Jordan's old huntsman, says he's never seen anything approaching it. I certainly have not, and I never expect to see anything better—if I see anything equal to it, I shall be lucky. I only wish you had been here, as I feel sure that even you have never seen your hounds accomplish a more brilliant performance.

Extracts from Hunting Diary: January 12, 1926. Found fox 2.40 P.M. Killed, 5.00 P.M. Cold, with signs of frost. Had been hard frost previous night. Distance, as hounds ran, 20 miles.

Hounds had just gone through the fence into Henry Alderman's swamp, when we viewed a big grey fox coming toward us from the swamp; he came through the fence, and as soon as he was well on his legs, I blew my whistle, and at my view halloo, hounds came to me immediately. They settled on the line straight away, and ran the length of the swamp with great cry. They pushed him out of the swamp across the open at a great pace into Crapener Swamp. Here there was a slight check, but righting themselves they went away, led by Antic *and* Fairy *with terrific drive, and carrying a great head they swept across the open up to Monroe Road; crossing the road, they went into Sugar Springs swamp; going through this without a check, they ran into the Flat swamp, and practically up to the Haunted House. Here a check occurred. I think the fox lay down. After giving them time, I held them back, round and behind where the lead hounds had first wavered.* Pride *shortly hit off the line, and they went away with a great burst back to Hurst's place, on through Sugar Springs swamp, and without checking straight across the great burnt country where sand and blackened grass stubble is all that remains to hold scent; forward they drove into Crapener swamp; they never dwelt a moment there, going straight through into the open, where hounds were at fault in a road.*

I tried back, and they very soon settled down again, going to Alderman's swamp, running straight through, then to Macrae's, there swinging slightly righthanded they went through the Scotsman's and straight across the open to Sugar Springs; here the fox turned sharp back and made for Alderman's. The fox was now very tired, and scent was weakening appreciably. Running slowly almost to the end of the swamp, it sounded as if hounds had treed him. A moment afterwards, I saw a grey fox sitting up in a tree. I did not think this was our fox, so sat still and did nothing. A minute afterwards Fly *spoke some distance away, and hounds immediately went to her, and soon settled on the line. Scent on the sinking fox was now none too good, and hounds hunted slowly up the hill towards Alderman's. A check occurred here, but I happened to see* Roman *and* Leppo *running hard some distance ahead, though the other hounds could not hear them. I lifted the body of the pack up to them, and hounds running from scent to view*

ON HUNTING A PACK

coursed him in the open for about seventy yards, rolling him over in Alderman's Lane after two hours and twenty minutes. The distance was not under twenty miles as hounds ran, measured from the map—the point was seven miles.

The cry throughout was wonderful; the pack work excellent; hounds ran well in the open, also on the bare, burnt ground. They went through the briers, cane, and water of the swamps, as if there was nothing to stop them, and ran with terrific dash and drive from view to kill, every hound being up when they ate him.

Had Captain Adamthwaite been in too much of a hurry, and concluded from circumstantial evidence that the fox in the tree was the hunted one, he might have marred the outcome of the hunt by not accounting for the fox that the hounds had strenuously hunted for so long. Jumping to hasty conclusions on the strength of circumstantial evidence, or giving up a hunted fox while there is any chance remaining, is woefully poor huntsmanship, if accounting for foxes is the objective.

On November 10, 1923, while hunting the Millbrook country, hounds found in Peter Flanigan's cover, the fox being viewed away streaking due north. Like a flock of swallows, hounds carrying a great head simply flew away, leaving the field well in their wake. Straight as a string they went, crossing Sloan Avenue away to West Clay Hill, swinging slightly right-handed, a check occurred in the Bangal Road, between the Sackett's Pond schoolhouse and Mr. Cornelius'. The fox evidently ran the road here, for while Charlie Carver was casting hounds easterly, I, who was hunting first whip, heard *Peddler* speaking on the line, which led through Mr. Cornelius' orchard. *Peddler*, '21, a hound of great presence, by *Jolly*, '15, ex *Pinta*, '16, was a wonderful hound in a road, and never lost his head even when crowded by hard riding followers. He was, unfortunately, killed by a motor car, while working a road near Upper Clove, in 1925. His only fault was a somewhat weak voice, but of which he made the best possible use.

On this occasion, I luckily heard him, although he was in the orchard quite out of sight below the crest of the hill where I stood. Charlie soon had hounds where they could hear *Peddler's* cry, and away they dashed north, and still north, quite outdistancing the field. Through the New Country, crossing the Bangal-Hun's Lake highway, the fox turned short back in the ravine just north of the road. Hounds were carefully working out this line when several members of the field viewed him crossing south. Soon the entire pack, well together, went away southeasterly through the woodland and vales of the New Country. Gradually swinging left-hand in a great circle, again swinging northerly and driving rapidly forward, hounds crossed the closely cropped pastures of Mr. Keller, sinking the hill, and skimming along like mad directly toward Hun's lake. I was now alone with hounds, on that grand bay gelding *Acrobee* ('15), by *Oris*. *Acrobee* was then eight years old, and although he had at this juncture been galloping over an hour in a country of steep gradients, was still going strong. As we flew along down the north slopes of the hill, I could see hounds fast outpacing me. Getting into the high road through the Reverend Mr. Bush's farmyard, I galloped madly along the edge of the lake, round its western edge, and, climbing the rising ground toward the northwest, I could just hear hounds driving forward in the direction of Briarcliff. No one else was in sight, and although this country was absolutely unknown to me, I fortunately chanced on several lanes and large open pastures, which hastened my pursuit of the fast receding cry. Fortunately, the wind was carrying the wonderful voices of the pack directly toward me; and often, that day, I blessed the music of those precious hounds, the volume of which prevented my losing track of them in their marvelous progress.

Northwesterly, their course continued as my gallant horse struggled on always at a gallop, his ears pricked listening to the cry, but never could I quite get up to hounds. Finally, I heard them turning sharply left-hand and returning southerly. It was only late that night that I learned from Oakleigh Thorne, Master of the Millbrook, that they had run their fox to within a mile of Stissing station, thus making a point, as the crow flies, from the find in Peter Flanigan's of five and one-half miles, making, however, one complete four-mile circle on the way.

As hounds drew nearer to me, I made a strenuous effort to catch them, but so great was their pace that I just missed them when crossing the Hun's Lake-Bangal High road. The pack all working together, and running to kill, swung westerly into the steep wooded cliffs on the south side of the road, about a mile from Bangal.

At this point, after having galloped continuously for nearly two hours, I was parallel to hounds, and could see on the hilltop above me quite a number of the field with Charlie Carver, who, having been thrown out in the New Country woodlands when hounds circled, had finally gotten up, lured on by the distant cry. Here, hounds in the steep cliffs slowed down to a walking trail, and the fast sinking fox played his best cards to throw them off. He was evidently quite out of his country, and absolutely confused. Slowly the delicate-nosed hounds worked the cliff-side, and then, much to my surprise, several hounds worked a line through a farmyard down to the highway, and even spoke a few times on the north side of the road. Fortunately, no farm dogs, motors, or people were there to confuse the situation, which was most critical at this time. It was impossible for anyone to tell what had happened, and as long as hounds kept trying, the only thing to do was to leave them quite alone and keep very still. The fox had evidently come down to the road and turned back easterly, parallel to the way he had come, for several hounds now worked slowly along the foot of the cliff. Leading my now quite sober horse, I walked quietly along within sight of the pack, and came to a little lane leading diagonally toward where they were working. Going up this lane a few rods (hounds having checked within a hundred yards on my right), I came to a tiny cottage on the left, outside of which stood a scared-looking woman. At first she said nothing, but after I had said, "Good evening," she remarked to me, "I've just been nearly frightened to death—a fox ran into my woodshed." Quickly looking into the darkness of the shed, I could see a pair of shining eyes. That good bitch *Badness*, '22, had come up to me, I cheered her into the shed, and a real tussle ensued, until a mighty whoo-hoop brought the whole pack and the field to a successful conclusion of a great hunt. As hounds ran, the distance was well over seventeen miles.

This long story is related mainly to show that in a rough country, with only the faint line of a beaten fox for tired hounds to work out, how urgently needed is persistency and patience on the part of hounds and huntsman. A spent fox gives out but little scent, and may easily be lost by too much haste or some untoward accident at the crucial moment.

It is sometimes a great temptation for a professional huntsman to take advantage of the ignorance of his field. That was illustrated one day very satisfactorily to several of the Millbrook followers. We had hunted for some time that day without finding. Hounds were drawing westerly through the Butt's Hollow Glen cover, when I heard a few couple speaking on a line at the edge of an open field. The cry did not sound quite "right"; nevertheless, I galloped forward to see what was happening, carrying the main part of the pack with me. The instant the open was reached, it could be seen what the hounds running the line were doing. I decided from the direction of their line that these few couple had jumped a hare, and were having a little unlicensed pastime. My opinion was immediately verified by the hounds with me paying little attention to the cry of the "merry-makers." Up came the field, "hell-bent fer leather," nearly galloping over the top of the hounds with me and not so much as looking at them. They all began telling me that hounds were running hard; and I suppose they were inwardly "cussin'" me for being asleep. I called their attention to the hounds with me, asking what they would be doing if their fellows were really running a *fox*. Then I said, "It's too bad you are not having a gallop, but I will not fool you nor debauch these steady hounds. I could easily gallop on and make you think those rascals are hunting a fox instead of a hare." Fortunately, to prove my assertion, the hare turned straight back toward us, and Singleton, my first whipper-in, stopped the riot. We went on a short distance further, found a fox, had a good hunt, accounted for our quarry, and possibly someone learned something.

Sometimes, when scent is none too good, and a fox is "creeping" ahead of hounds, it is difficult for an uninitiated field to comprehend what is going on. The field gets impatient, some of them return home, but the "stickers" generally get a good "go," if the huntsman has half a chance, doesn't lose his nerve, and has a real pack of hounds.

I had the pleasure of successfully concluding a hunt like this, one day in late December, 1925, in the Overhills country. Hounds had already, in three hours, done great work that day by putting two red foxes to ground, and hunting a grey for one and a half hours, finally treeing him. They then picked up a cold line in one of the "heads," running down into Signal Swamp, and worked it in a circuitous route, now fast, now slow, with beautiful melodious cry, for perhaps an hour when it pretty nearly "pegged out." Several people urged me to return to kennels, but I laughingly told them that I would be older next day and might never hunt again anyway, so I'd not hurry home. It really looked as if hounds were beaten, but, being at a complete loss, I left them absolutely alone. They had spread pretty "wide," when suddenly *Fairy* spoke with enthusiasm. Mr. Fox, not hearing hounds,—they had ceased their cry,—had lain down, and *Fairy* had suddenly gotten up to him. From complete silence and despair the whole scene changed into a wild gallop, hounds leaving thoroughbred horses as if tethered, finally marking their fox to ground in a drain on the Overhills golf course. This concluded with *éclat* a wonderful day's hunting in which four foxes were accounted for in five hours, and comprised the best hound work I ever saw in one day. The last brilliant gallop I wouldn't have missed for anything. It rewarded hounds for their long, long trying, and probably it taught the field that patience on the part of the huntsman has its own reward.

To say just how to hunt a pack of hounds is an impossible task. All one can do is to lay down certain principles, and then allow intelligence, temperament, experience, and observation to do the rest. One must never think that he knows more than a good hound, but one must be *sure* that he has *good* hounds, for without such no huntsman in America can account for foxes with regularity. Learn the traditional language, and use the horn with intelligence. Never excite hounds; never be fooled by inaccurate information nor circumstantial evidence; and teach the field to respect hounds as probably being able to hunt fox better than they can.

The acme of successful form in hunting a pack is to get them away closely packed on a fox, have them run together, and account for their fox collectively. To attain this desired perfect pack work requires an enormous amount of effort in selection and training of hounds as well as mutual understanding on the part of hounds, huntsman, and whippers-in.

Much has been written on how to hunt a pack of hounds in England, and some authors would make it appear that the huntsman is more important than the hounds, and seem to think it extraordinary for a pack to be able to account for a fox unaided. In America, a pack that has once found its fox and cannot account for it unaided seven times out of ten, is not a good pack.

A CAST IN AMERICA.
See page 113.

DRAWING WOODLANDS.

This chart represents a manner of procedure while drawing large woodlands or rough country of bad visibility, as described on page 116.
A, the Huntsman. B and C, the Whippers-in.

ON HUNTING A PACK

What a huntsman can do, is to have his pack under control, with perfect road and field manners, amenable to voice and horn, drafted, and conditioned so they will hunt well as an entity and not as an uncoördinated lot of individuals. He can help them to find their fox by knowing in what locations foxes generally kennel, *help them to keep together when hunting, by intelligent use of voice and horn* (always to be used sparingly, however, if hounds are in difficulties), aided by the proper coöperation of his whippers-in, and sometimes quietly help them at a check, especially if he has information or experience of the run of foxes in any particular country.

It has been remarked that there are comparatively few good packs of hounds in America, and that a high standard of requirements in a good pack is rare; but perhaps the most neglected essential in a good pack and the proper handling thereof is the efficiency of whippers-in.

That very fine art in this country is almost invariably neglected and underrated, although it is perhaps more difficult to play this part of the game properly than that of the huntsman. Let it be understood that a good whipper-in will not necessarily make a good huntsman, and *vice versa;* in fact, the best whipper-in I ever saw disliked to hunt hounds, and became frightfully nervous if required to do so. Bryden relates that Tom Rance, a famous whipper-in to the Cheshire, nearly a century ago, served with that hunt under seven masters and six huntsmen, and would never attempt to hunt a pack of hounds, declaring that he would as soon break stones.

It is much more difficult for a whipper-in to work efficiently in America than in England, where his procedure usually can be fairly well defined. As has been stated before, hunting in the grass countries of England can be conducted in rather a systematic manner, but in America, where foxes may run in any direction, and where hearing and seeing hounds is difficult, the procedure for a whipper-in is hardly ever twice the same. He constantly finds himself in a situation for which there is no precedent, and in which he must use his experience plus intuition. When hounds go away, he may often find himself alone with them, and he must sense whether to carry on with them, or to turn back and urge on tail hounds. A whipper-in, when rating on tail hounds, should never forget that lead hounds may check, and, under such circumstances, unless he is careful, he may get their heads up by cheering from behind.

It should be obvious to either whipper-in that, if he knows his huntsman is held up by bogs, or other circumstances, and lead hounds go away fast over a hill, someone should be with them; in that case, he has no choice but to *go on*. If, on the other hand, he knows his huntsman is close up, and that only part of the pack has gone away, he would be wrong in not *turning back* to cheer on tail hounds, unless they are being brought up by the other whip. If he is certain that tail hounds are being brought up, he should go forward on the down wind flank of the huntsman, for in this position, in a blind country, he can hear better.

In some cases, he must use his judgment in stopping a few couple which may be going away with a fox alone, delaying them long enough to await the coming up of the huntsman and the balance of the pack. In a case where the huntsman and the main portion of the pack have gone away with another fox, every effort should be made by the whipper-in to stop the minor portion, and get them to the major portion, thus reuniting the pack. The difficulties of properly meeting these emergencies of a blind country, where the ear must be depended upon, are evident.

The whipper-in should know the voice of every hound; he must use his sense without direct command to rate hounds on riot at the psychological moment, being firm, yet not over-severe. As mentioned, a huntsman may be thrown out in a woodland, held up by wire, or some unforeseen occurrence may arise, in which case the whipper-in must carry on, taking for the moment the place of the huntsman. These conditions, peculiar to America, make it useful for whippers-in to carry horns, which, however, should be used only with the greatest discretion, and more particularly to help get hounds home, should the pack divide badly in a rough country.

A whipper-in must be an all-round good hound man and a first-class horseman. He should be mounted as well as, if not better than, the huntsman. Such a statement may be astounding to some, because there exists in America the amusing and erroneous idea that a whipper-in is purely a figurehead in the picture, and that anything on four legs is good enough for him to ride; whereas, it is a fact that he should be mounted second to none, for the reason that his horse has to do more work than the horse of the huntsman. If one stops to think, hunt staff horses have to do infinitely more work than any horses out with hounds. While a field is waiting by a covert side, the huntsman and his aids never stop moving. A whipper-in may have to gallop far at speed in pursuit of his duties before any of the field have had their horses out of a walk. He may have to retrace his way for miles in search of missing hounds. Hunt staff horses rarely come home except with the pack; which means, usually, that they are out one or two hours longer in a hunt day than the average hunter. In America, it is usually found impracticable to use second horses, for to stay in touch with hounds they would have to do as much work as the horses they would replace.

All this comment applies not only to the first whip, but to the second whip, if the system of hunting is conducted with the two whippers-in, one on the right and the other on the left flank of the huntsman. In this formation, so important in America, as described on page 116, the second whip is frequently called upon to act in the same manner as the first whip. Therefore, in this case, two extraordinarily clever whippers-in are essential; and they,

ON HUNTING A PACK

in turn, must have complete understanding with their huntsman, which can be acquired only by months, if not years, of working together. They must thoroughly comprehend his ways, signals, and calls, in a word, all must instinctively function as a unit—*exempli gratia*, with the efficiency of a perfectly coördinating polo team.

Masters should not think that they can get satisfactory service from honorary whippers-in, except in the rarest instances. Usually, although the latter may understand the art, their outside obligations make regular attendance improbable. Also, if the huntsman is a professional, he is not in a position to command the honorary whipper-in. In most cases, it might be better to have no whippers-in at all than such a make-shift arrangement.

A master aiming to create first-class hunting, should ponder well and long on the question of selecting his hunt staff and their horses. It is only fair to assume that, without proper *modus operandi*, he can never bring that hunting to the utmost efficiency unless enthusiastic, capable, and complete team work supplements his efforts.

Two excellent dissertations have been written on the art of the whipper-in in England; Beckford handles the matter most intelligently, as well as "Yoiover," in *Hold Hard, Hounds, Please*, both of which should be diligently studied by anyone interested.

The usual routine for a young hound being entered in an English pack is as follows:

On being brought into kennel when about one year old, the hound is broken to couples, and after feeding each day is walked out in a quiet manner in the vicinity of the kennel, by the huntsman and two whippers-in, with the rest of the steady hounds, and is frequently taken across meadows where hare and game of all sorts abound. In many instances hounds are walked in the deer park adjoining kennels, as with the Duke of Beauford's hounds at Badminton. The older hounds are already steady to any kind of riot. The young hounds, each coupled to a steady member of the pack, have no choice but to learn what is taboo, and within a reasonably short time can be handled without couples.

In America, on the contrary, one sees so-called packs of hounds that never leave their kennel for any purpose, at any time, except when taken out to hunt, and then, frequently, it is the huntsman's custom to appear mounted at the kennel door, blowing his horn, and to have the door opened after hounds have been thoroughly excited. The natural result is that hounds rush out, and in their enthusiasm run riot perhaps for half a mile, usually coming back to the huntsman, however, when some of their exuberance has worn off. It is hardly fair to blame hounds that have been handled this way for lacking the manners of hounds disciplined by the English method.

In my experience, American hounds (excepting possibly certain sorts of field trial hounds which are characteristically wild) are amenable to discipline, if reason instead of abuse is practiced in their teaching. The English hound is oftentimes what may be called hard-headed, meaning, very difficult to break of a fault, and frequently has to be chastised with a severity not necessary in the case of his American cousin. It really is not a difficult thing to give almost any pack good manners, even though they never have had any routine training. While it may amuse some of my sophisticated *confrères*, I am sure that a specific formula will be an aid to the man with a wild pack and who has no knowledge of how to correct this condition.

Assume he has twenty couple. For the first few weeks or so, let him begin by spending an hour or more daily, previous to feeding-time, in playing with the entire pack,—first a few hounds at a time, then all together,—having his pockets well filled with bits of meat, calling the hounds by name, until they realize that when they are spoken to and come to him a reward will be theirs. The whippers-in, of course, should be in attendance during this proceeding to rate on to the huntsman (not too strenuously) such hounds as may need admonition. Soon, the entire pack may be easily drafted from one end of the kennel to the other, in and out of the various lodging rooms, passages, and courts, with one whipper-in going ahead of hounds, and one following, to prevent individuals from rushing ahead or lagging.

After this lesson is thoroughly learned, a few couple of the steadiest hounds may be taken quietly outside the kennel, the door having been first opened and one of the whippers-in stationed at it to prevent any hound from rushing out ahead. I have specifically suggested the hour before feeding, because at this time hounds are hungry, and are keen to receive the tid-bits which the huntsman will, of course, continue to give them while calling them by name. When hounds are outside the kennel, the huntsman should have the door closed behind him, and stand still, continuing to dole out the coveted morsels. If any individual hound makes a break, he must be quickly and efficiently stopped by the whippers-in and chastised, but not too vigorously, always being rated by name. No hound should be struck, unless the reason for the rating can be brought home to him. Gradually, the number of hounds taken out may be augmented until the entire pack has learned by experience what is wanted of them. It should not be forgotten that if they never have been handled, they can hardly be expected to know what is desired of them.

The first day they are taken out with horses, they should be walked out of the kennel by the hunt staff in the usual manner. The huntsman's horse should then be brought up to him. He will mount amidst the greatest enthusiasm on the part of hounds, if they have ever previously been hunted. Some of them, in their eagerness to be off, will make a dash, which should be stopped by the as yet unmounted whippers-in. Occasionally tossing a bit of

ON HUNTING A PACK

something to eat to hounds, the huntsman will sit still on his horse until the pack becomes perfectly steady, and realizes that, after all, the huntsman is not going to gallop down the road with them. After some time, the huntsman having moved about on his horse only near the kennels, will dismount, continue playing with hounds, and reënter kennels with the pack for regulation feeding. After a day or two of this routine, the whippers-in may be mounted in the regular manner, and gradually road exercise may be commenced. It is a great pleasure to hunt a pack with perfect manners, under control of voice and horn.

In *The Diary of a Huntsman*, there is a very interesting diagram on how to cast a pack of hounds in England, which doubtless is very useful for England, or any open country where one might act systematically; but, usually in America each case seems to require a different answer. Great stress is laid on foxes running down the wind in England. In America, they rarely seem to pay attention to the wind direction, but only to their "runs." For example, out of the Hog Back covert, in the Millbrook country, rarely has a fox ever gone away anywhere but northerly, regardless of wind, and "points" out of the Hog Back have been from one to seven miles. Out of Young's swamp, in the same country, foxes usually run northerly, regardless of calm or gale.

At a loss, if a huntsman knows positively where hounds last spoke, he may often help hounds after they have failed in their own cast. This is particularly true if he can keep his field form foiling the line. The line of a fox may be likened to a thread. If the thread breaks and a check occurs, the exact location of this check can be determined as the spot where hounds last spoke, always providing that the hounds are strictly truthful. If the huntsman loses the end of the thread, he is seriously handicapped in attempting to aid his pack. If he has the end of the thread, he may be able to help hounds pick up the line again. Even with good hounds that will not overrun, it is sometimes difficult to know just what causes a check, and, lacking evidence, quite impossible to know which way the fox has gone. In an open country, casting hounds is not so difficult and may be made boldly, but in a rough country where a fox may have gone in any direction or lain down in cover, great care has to be exercised.

If scenting is very bad (and a fox is walking as described on page 107), and hounds come to a loss, making their own cast without results, the best bet a huntsman has (if he knows where hounds last spoke) is to cast carefully and quietly without getting hounds' heads up, which causes their interest to lag. The cast may be made after the manner of the accompanying diagram, adapting the cast, however, to circumstances and topography. The whippers-in should remain quiet, so as not to disturb hounds. Their assistance should not be required with a handy, thoroughly amenable pack.

If this cast fails, the only thing left to do is to make a wild gamble in the

.irection most likely to have been taken by the fox; and in such a case the huntsman's "fox sense," or his knowledge of the local run of foxes, will be all-important.

With a really great pack of hounds that have not been excited or disturbed at a check by cattle, cur dogs, or overriding, it is usually best to leave them quite alone and watch them with the utmost attention, as certain hounds with uncanny instinct (or, perhaps, only the barest scent indicating where the fox has gone) may work across the bad scenting ground and suddenly pick up the broken end of the thread. If once a pack of hounds gets the habit of letting the huntsman do it, they soon will be ruined.

There are exceptions to all rules, such as the incident previously described in the sandy road of North Carolina, and no two problems are alike in America; hence, interest is consistently sustained for the huntsman and such members of the field as care for hound work, or who are sufficiently erudite to understand it.

In rough America, another difficult task for the huntsman is to hunt hounds wide enough to find a fox, that may be anywhere, and then get his pack together, and keep it together when a fox is found. Even with perfect hounds, his task is great. To make matters worse, it is extraordinary how little appreciation he will receive from the layman, who often seems quite happy so long as he can gallop after something, right or wrong, with rarely any sympathy for the huntsman who may have unsuccessfully worked himself blind to give sport under impossible conditions.

The orthodox forms and circumstances attending the hunting of a pack of hounds in any open country with small, clean-edged coverts are quite simple and exact. Such conditions, of course, exist in most English hunt countries, and a wonderful description of the procedure is given in Masefield's "Reynard the Fox."

Imagine a beautiful, trim, open country across which one can see for miles; oceans of grass, clean-cut hedges, gates in and out of almost every field, occasional rail fences, and small water courses; every few miles, thick coverts of thorny gorse bushes or trees.

The meet is at some famous country house, or in some delightful village. The well-bred and conditioned, sorty pack (bred and drafted according to show standard for many generations) stands placidly with well-mounted huntsman and watchful whippers-in, awaiting the master's signal to proceed to the draw. Once this signal is given, hounds move off across a few fields, and through several gateways to the edge of a well-known covert, where a fox is almost certain to be found above ground,—all earths and drains of the vicinity having been carefully stopped the previous night when Mr. and Mrs. Fox and all the family were out to dinner. The pack, under perfect control, approaches the edge of the small covert,—of say, ten to twenty acres,—

ON HUNTING A PACK

and at the huntsman's cheer silently dash into where their fox should be waiting for them. In the meantime, the first whip has quietly slipped forward to a vantage point at the end of the covert, whence Reynard is likely to break, and at his view halloo hounds come tumbling out like a shot, the huntsman with them, leaving the second whip to rate on the tail hounds. This is very simple,—hounds are led to their fox; he is generally viewed away; and the waiting crowd of horsemen and women dash forward across beautiful, open grass land like the "Charge of the Light Brigade." All this occurs in a very orderly manner; but this is the ideal hunting ground,—England!

What a different proposition confronts the American huntsman. He is terribly handicapped by a climate most unfriendly to the chase as practiced in Britain. It must be remembered that there is a vast difference, due to heavily wooded, rough terrain, climate, and scenting conditions, between hunting and killing a fox in the well-stopped Shires of England and doing the same thing in the uncouth, wire-cursed topography of America, where in one locality, at least, deer and hare are often more easily found than fox. Practically all procedure must be somewhat different, and, while many expressions and practices have been brought over to America from the mother country, the interpretation must be quite dissimilar.

With recognized hunts, the season begins in America in the month of August, as in England, but the thermometer may often climb to over 80° by 9 A.M. In early October, when the regular season for most hunts opens, heat and drought are frequently annoying, yet the best of the American season, from the viewpoint of the average riding man, is from October first to December fifteenth. In the early autumn it often does not rain for weeks. I remember one such season, when it hardly rained a drop for five weeks. A like condition in England would be considered insupportable. By December, frost and snow are to be expected in all hunt countries north of the Carolinas; and for those countries north of Long Island, the season is usually finished by Christmas.

In the best of countries, it is all very rough, and there are hardly any clean-cut, small coverts. In the Millbrook country, the smallest covert comprises about one hundred and fifty acres, and in no instance is there a mile between coverts. In America, earths and rocky dens are so numerous, it is impracticable to stop them, except on Long Island. After a rainy or snowy night, it is nearly impossible to find a fox above ground (a fact which most laymen do not appreciate); they have all gone in early to avoid the elements, and however pleasant the day may be, they generally remain in until afternoon. This typically American habit of foxes, added to the usual bad visibility and bad scenting, makes conditions far different from England. Under these circumstances, to have good hunts and account for foxes, hounds must have the very best working qualities in the world; and a huntsman must have patience and flexibility of brain to figure out the varying conditions which present themselves every time he takes hounds out. My Virginia hounds can be taken to the edge of a covert as the most bidable English hounds are, but the covert may contain two hundred acres, instead of twenty, as in England, and *rarely can a whipper-in be placed in any spot where he can be certain of viewing a fox away.* The hounds must use their noses to find a fox, and when once found they must have nose, cry, and drive enough to account for him. With bad-nosed, mute, or pottering hounds, a fox would play around a big covert all day, or steal away so far ahead that he would soon be lost.

The method to employ for hunting large coverts to the best advantage requires the huntsman to advance through the center of the woodland with one whipper-in on each side, as per the accompanying diagram. This system permits hounds to be hunted very "wide," thus covering all ground where a fox may be lying still; but it is not always possible to carry out this system exactly according to the diagram, in that often rough terrain, swamps, or wire may seriously interfere with the hunt staff keeping their proper relative positions. (See diagram facing page 109.)

By such a method of procedure, through a woodland even in rough weather, the huntsman A may have little fear of being out of touch with his hounds, because whip B is on his right hand within hearing, and whip C is on his left. If hounds near B or C speak, the huntsman A either hears them, or hears the shrill warning whistle, or the gone-away halloo of his whip. By such a system, the huntsman can always cover a maximum area with his hounds, be within touch of them, and get them together quickly by means of voice and horn (if hounds on either wing find a fox), even if their fellows cannot hear them on account of wind or uneven country. This system, with whippers-in riding on the flanks of the huntsman, also applies when hounds are gone away, the whipper-in on the down-wind side taking care to be well forward.

In so far as possible, a huntsman should always work his pack up wind in hunting for a fox in rough country. Wind in woodlands, especially if the ground is thickly covered with dry leaves, makes hearing very difficult; and, if hounds are hunting down wind in wide formation, it is even more difficult to hear individuals that may suddenly jump a fox and go away at speed. Hounds do not like to be left, and are almost uncanny in their ability to sense the whereabouts of their huntsman, even when he is out of sight and silent for some time. Nevertheless, under bad hearing conditions, frequent use of voice and horn is advisable, especially on changing direction, or when, of necessity, turning down wind.

When hounds find a good line, or are brought to a view halloo, nothing

ON HUNTING A PACK

is so detrimental as excitement. A keen pack of hounds will sense the situation at once, and if their huntsman, or others, get excited, general confusion and catastrophe may result. In taking hounds to a view halloo, the greatest care should be used, because the body scent of the fox may be carried by a stiff breeze in the reverse direction to that taken by the fox. Hounds may catch this scent in the air and run heel with the floating aroma, thus causing a debacle. One should carefully inquire into all possible circumstances before taking advantage of information, and then make haste deliberately.

A good hunting pack of hounds will in no time adjust themselves to circumstances and the will of their huntsman. For some years, as has been stated, my pack hunted the grass and woodlands of the Millbrook country, from June to December, and then entrained for the very dry, sandy Overhills country for the winter season. One country is absolutely different from the other.

At Millbrook, hounds were hunted comparatively close, as foxes were numerous. At Overhills, a huntsman never knows where hounds will find, hence, a pack must be hunted very wide. In moving hounds, we have several times hunted within twenty-four hours of detraining at Overhills, and killed our fox; and invariably within a few hunts, the entire "style" of hunting the pack could be changed. Hounds seem to know whether they are running a grey or red fox, and will work accordingly. They are equally keen on the one as on the other; and, in my opinion, to hunt grey foxes helps a pack—hounds have to be more careful. No one is ever sure what a grey fox is going to do—he may point six or seven miles straight away, or he may point a mile and turn back in cover through a pack of hounds; he may run highlands, climb a tree, or stick to the water in swamps. He's a most diverting sportsman to meet; one individual grey fox sets no precedent for the next one; hence, the huntsman must be more than ever alert when in pursuit of this particular quarry, and very sparing of voice and horn after such a fox is once found, as one may easily encourage hounds to overrun at the numerous twists and turns.

There are sometimes local aids to the huntsman in one country that do not occur in another. In Virginia, crows often will swoop and "fight" a running fox, thus indicating his position in front of hounds. Although there are plenty of crows in Dutchess County, New York, never have I seen them help a huntsman. Apparently, in all countries foxes will run through herds of cattle and sheep to foil their line. A Virginia farmer once assured me that he had seen, a few years ago, in Loudoun County, a fox hard pressed by hounds leap on the back of a sheep and ride the entire length of a field. (This was before the days of prohibition!) Often in Virginia, beef cattle will run after a fox to the side of a field where he has gone out, and stand looking in the direction taken, thus prompting a huntsman to cast forward around them.

HOUNDS AND HUNTING

For some reason, I never have seen dairy cattle do this in New York. In Carolina, no birds or cattle ever help.

In Virginia, clay soil and wet wheat fields that have been limed will yield next to no line, as the soil clings to the fox's pads and spoils the scent. Under such conditions, one must carefully watch wide-casting hounds, or take a chance and hurry the whole pack forward in a wide cast directly around the field. I once owned a hound, *Benjamin*, '14, that under such circumstances would invariably cast forward of his own volition, ignoring the clay field as useless to him in his line of business. He was a great hound, of a splendid strain, and his descendants have inherited his qualities.

In America, practically speaking, there is no such thing as the "cubhunting" season as practised in England, although this term is applied to early autumn hunting. It must be emphasized that, on account of the rough American country, foxes of any age may be found anywhere or nowhere, and it is usually impossible to "stop" hounds on any given fox, young or old. When a cub is found, he will generally run a short time and go to ground, but an old fox may give a hunt of several hours. I mention elsewhere a hunt in August which continued slow and fast for over four hours before the fox was marked to ground.

I have known hounds to find in the early morning in August in my Blue Ridge hunting country in Virginia, and put a fox to ground after several hours, reaching kennels with the thermometer registering over 90°. This is hardly "cubhunting" in the English sense. In America, owing to the preponderance of cover, if hounds once find, as stated above, it is nearly impossible to stop them, which is the regular practice in England when anything but a cub is being run. It can be seen that under American conditions there can be, so far as hounds and foxes are concerned, no appreciable change in the manner of hunting throughout the season.

The only similarity between cubhunting in England and the so-called cubhunting in America, is that in both countries this season is devoted to preparation for more serious events. In both cases, those who come out with hounds are supposed to do so only by special invitation. Informality in announcements, dress, and procedure is the rule. As already mentioned, in England, foxes are usually found in very small woods or coverts. The country surrounding such coverts is carefully cultivated, or consists of closely-cropped pasture land. Every fox earth in a given covert is known to the local gamekeeper, or earth-stopper, whose business it is to "stop" the same when hounds are to hunt this given vicinity. In Britain, the theory of cubhunting is to train both foxes and hounds. It may be well to explain that the English fox is rigorously protected, lives in a country where game, especially rabbits, are much more plentiful than in America, and is rarely disturbed by dogs of any sort, aside from the infrequent visits of the foxhounds. The American

ON HUNTING A PACK

fox has no such protection, has to travel many weary miles each night for food, and is, in consequence, always fit, and undoubtedly much more difficult to kill than the well-fed fox of England.

When hounds go cubbing in England, a large number of spectators, afoot and mounted, usually surround the covert selected for the excitement. Hounds are brought quietly to the covert side and cheered in. The earths being stopped, they of course find at once. Naturally, the quarry attempts to escape from the covert, but the spectators permit only old foxes (recognized by their size) to break. Cubs are frightened back by all sorts of marvelous noises,—voices, tin pans, rattles; of course, some get away across country, but, until crops are harvested and the country is ridable, hounds are stopped by the whippers-in from leaving the vicinity.

This procedure is, of course, unknown in America. In no American country is it physically possible to find foxes as in England, or for whippers-in to stop hounds in the same systematic way, which fact is unquestionably advantageous to American hounds, as it gives them much more opportunity of sticking to the business in hand without interruption.

In a word, what is "sauce for the goose" is not, in this case, "sauce for the gander"; and only intelligent adoption of the best technique to be learned from all practical sources will bring about the best results in any given American country. This applies to hounds as well as to huntsmanship.

Coöperation between the huntsman, his whippers-in, and followers of hounds—a point upon which stress has already been laid—is, of course, very dependent on signals. Suggestions for signals adapted from French and English tradition but yet suitable for American requirements may be classified as:

Silent signals, which are useful when the spoken word will not carry. A huntsman may point in a given direction to indicate to the whipper-in that he desires him to get forward toward a certain locality; or, he may point back, to indicate the position of an absent hound. A whipper-in may use the arm to indicate the position of invisible hounds that he hears running a line when the huntsman, being up wind, perhaps cannot hear them. Holding the cap (or hat) above the head is the time-honored manner of indicating where a fox has been viewed; but to avoid delay and confusion, anyone so holding the cap should place himself as nearly as possible in the line of the fox, facing the way the fox has gone.

Vocal signals are used by huntsmen, whippers-in, occasionally by members of the field when a fox is viewed, and, in England, almost too frequently by people on foot. These latter cry "Tallyho," to indicate that they have viewed a fox. English hounds are so accustomed to this call, and go to it so readily, that when it is used by someone far from the line the fox has taken, much confusion is sometimes caused, especially when several foxes have gone away from the same cover and tallyhos emanate from opposite points of the compass.

Following the precedent of Lord Lonsdale, with the Cottesmore, my hunt staff is provided with whistles, which are used when a fox is viewed. This unique signal is unmistakable, as emanating from the hunt staff only, and the sound carries farther, perhaps, than any other. It has the added advantage of attracting the attention of hounds as nothing else will.

Calls on the horn should be orthodox, so far as possible, as well as hunting cries (some of the latter still bear evidence of their Norman origin); but when all is said and done, it is the inflection and quality of voice that makes or mars the cry and has consequential effect on hounds and field. Nothing can be more soul-stirring than a fine voice convincingly used; nothing is quite so dull as a voice conveying only a monotonous, unconvincing sound.

A pack brought up to the edge of a cover, under complete control, hears the huntsman softly cheer them, "Leu-in, Leu-in", and quietly breaks into the wood; but, should the huntsman scream the same command, hounds would probably become so excited that they would sling their tongues falsely.

Working through a cover, the main use for the huntsman's voice is to let his hounds know where he is; although his language should always be of a cheery character. If the expression, "Try on, try on," is used to encourage hounds which are "questeying" for a fox in cover, let it be given as if it meant something, interspersed, perhaps, with, "Wind him, my beauties, find him," and an occasional note on the horn not too long: thus,

When the huntsman turns sharply right-handed, two such blasts repeated at intervals several times will indicate to his whippers-in that the direction has been changed to the right, and that hounds on the left wing should be turned to him. If a huntsman turns sharply left-handed, three such blasts may be used to indicate the reverse procedure.

A huntsman in crossing a ride, or sharply changing his direction from one part of the cover to another, as a signal to both hounds and whippers-in should, with the utmost volume of sound possible, cry, "Yoi-over," following this by the regular in-cover cries, and use of horn. Should a reliable hound speak on the taint of a fox, a scream, "Hoick" ("Ed-Hoick," or "Yoicks"), followed by, "Hark" (to Ranter) should be used, with a few quickly rendered short notes on the horn: thus,

This will bring the pack flying; but, let the huntsman be certain that Ranter

ON HUNTING A PACK

is right before he encourages. When hunting in woodland as outlined in the diagram on page 109, a whipper-in who sees hounds feathering on a fox line, or hears them speaking to it, may properly call his huntsman's attention by the cry, "Forrard," repeated as necessary, intoning the cry vigorously or otherwise, according to the urgency of the situation. To indicate that the signal has been heard, the huntsman may reply by a couple of short blasts of his horn; thus,

▬ ▬

As other hounds speak on the line, cheer after cheer of "Hoick—Hoick—Hoick," should be used to get the pack together, with a succession of sharp blasts on the horn: thus,

▬ ▬ ▬   ▬ ▬

It is an excellent practice to blow this call when hounds pick up the line after a check, for if the field have confidence that they will be thus notified when hounds go away again, they will be less inclined to follow hounds about.

When hounds have settled on the line, "Hoick—Hoick—Gone away—Away—Away—Away—Away," is the cry, with a sharp "Gone-away" signal on the horn (3 shorts and a long, repeated several times, ending with a succession of short notes, as long as one can conveniently blow): thus,

▬ ▬ ▬ ▬   ▬ ▬ ▬ ▬   ▬ ▬ ▬ ▬

In this cheer the whippers-in may join, that the waiting field may be advised that their "coffee-housing" had better cease, and if they came out to hunt, now is the time to be at it. A huntsman with an exhilarating "Gone-away" cheer has an effect as of strong wine, bringing boldness into the heart of the most apathetic.

A huntsman hearing a "Tallyho," or the whistle of a whipper-in, may encourage hounds forward to the signal with the cheer, "Hark—Hollar—Hoick—forrad-away," using the "Gone-away" call on his horn.

For calling hounds from a cover drawn blank, a series of long intonated cries are useful: "C-o-m-e—come aw-a-a-a-y—come," "C-o-m-e—come aw-a-a-a-y—come," followed by a series of long drawn out, rolling calls on the horn; thus,

〰〰〰   〰〰〰   〰〰〰

Thus, it will be indicated to whippers-in and field that the huntsman is moving on. On such an occasion, a whipper-in behind hounds in cover should rate them in no uncertain manner, "Get away—Hark," while on the road, the expression "Get away—On," may be used.

If the huntsman should have occasion to draw his whippers-in to him,

[121]

or to indicate that all his hounds are "on," he may use some call, such as five slowly rendered, medium blasts: thus,

▬ ▬ ▬ ▬ ▬

As a signal to stop hounds running riot, the cry, " 'Ware—Riot," with a series of long-sustained notes on the horn is distinctive: thus,

▬▬▬ ▬▬▬ ▬▬▬

Whippers-in should rate rioting hounds with but one expression, such as " 'Ware Riot," and not attempt to vary the sound, as,—" 'Ware—Deer," " 'Ware—Rabbit," " 'Ware—Hare"; but a sharp, rebuking tone should be used as hounds, of course, do not comprehend what a man is saying, while the inflection of voice means everything to them. It would behoove the hunt staff, therefore, to systematically use distinctive calls for voice and horn, especially in America, where it is incalculably important that interpretive cries and calls of definite meaning be used, not only as signals for hounds and whippers-in but for the edification of the field. In a country where followers of hounds are confronted with limited visibility, they are likely to crowd huntsman and hounds unmercifully, in their desire to avoid being left behind, unless they can depend on signals for any emergency.

In unstoppable American countries, kills are rare, and it is hardly necessary to have two different signals to indicate a kill and gone to ground, either manner of accounting for foxes under the circumstances being equally important. So, it would seem advisable to adopt for both cases the extremely distinctive, "Whoo-hoop," accompanied by sharp blasts on the horn that end with a tremulo (produced by slightly shaking the horn on the lips):

▬ ▬ ▬ ～ ▬ ▬ ▬ ～ ▬ ▬ ▬ ～

An individual "going home" call is also most useful, such as, two long blasts, followed by two short blasts, repeated *ad lib:*

▬▬ ▬▬ ▬ ▬   ▬▬ ▬▬ ▬ ▬

In England, there are two schools of hunting. They may be termed the "cheery" and the "silent"; but there is no doubt that in a country of bad visibility the "cheery" system, with generous use of both voice and horn, is essential, if hounds are to be kept together and gotten away together, with the field not left behind.

The secret of getting a pack all together out of a big woodland with lightning-like rapidity, depends largely on hounds understanding the methods of their huntsman. All in all, on this understanding hangs the art of hunting a large pack "as a pack," and giving full value to the same; for, if they are not

ON HUNTING A PACK

gotten away together, the effort of maintaining a goodly number is hardly worth while.

There are certain occasions when care should be used in the blowing of the horn, notably, at a check. When hounds are on a line under difficult scenting conditions, discretion should be used with voice and horn in bringing tail hounds up to the body of the pack. Use of voice and horn should likewise be avoided when hounds are on the line at some distance from the huntsman, lest hounds be confused into believing they are wrong, and that the huntsman is encouraging them to come to the position in which he stands. Again, it must be emphasized that the horn and voice should be used very sparingly while the pack is running a twisting fox, especially the grey fox of America, unless a huntsman positively knows the position of his fox; otherwise, he is unwittingly, liable to cheer hounds the wrong way.

> *Then, as he listened, he heard a 'Hoy,'*
> *Tom Dansey's horn and 'Awa-wa-woy.'*
> *Then all hounds crying with all their forces,*
> *Then a thundering down of seventy horses.*
> *Robin Dawe's horn and halloos of 'Hey*
> *Hark Hollar, Hoik' and 'Gone away,'*
> *'Hark Hollar, Hark Hollar'; then Robin made*
> *Pip go crash through the cut-and-laid,*
> *Hounds were over and on his line*
> *With a head like bees upon Tipple Tine.*
> . . . .
> *Bold Robin Dawe was over first,*
> *Cheering his hounds on at the burst;*
> *The field were spurring to be in it,*
> *'Hold hard, sirs, give them half a minute,'*
> *Came from Sir Peter on his white.*
> *The hounds went romping with delight*
> *Over the grass and got together;*
> *The tail hounds galloped hell-for-leather*
> *After the pack at Myngs' yell;*
> *A cry like every kind of bell*
> *Rang from these rompers as they raced.*
> Masefield.

CHAPTER VII.

THE ECCENTRICITIES OF SCENT

TO any one of the million hunters who annually go out with any kind of dog that uses his sense of smell while hunting, the peculiarities of scent are an ever-changing mystery. Since Nimrod, man has no doubt been trying to solve these strange phenomena. For over two thousand years observations have been recorded; but as yet there is no conclusive solution.

In the fifth century B.C., Xenophon in his *Cynegeticos* observed of hunting hare in Greece:

In the winter there is no scent early in the morning, when there is either a hoar frost or ice . . . the south winds also hurt it, but the north winds, if not too severe, strengthen and preserve it. Rains and drizzling mists drown it . . . . In the spring, on account of the mild temperature of the air, the trail would be very strong, if the earth, being full of flowers, did not puzzle the dogs by mixing with it the odour of the blossoms. In the summer it is slight and imperfect; for the earth being hot, it destroys the warm particles it contains; and the scent itself is not only slight, but the dogs also smell less, on account of the relaxation of their bodies. In the autumn it is pure; for of the productions of the earth, the cultivated part is carried off, and the weeds are withered, so it is not at all injured by the scent of the fruits of the earth . . . The scent is also stronger in woody places than in open ones, for there, sometimes running and sometimes sitting, she (the hare) is touched by many things. . . . . . .

Under certain conditions, in certain countries, scenting is always bad. Rarely can anyone say positively that it will be good under any given conditions until the hunting dog puts these conditions to the test. Any and all kinds of dogs from cocker spaniels, pointers, and setters, to beagles, foxhounds, and staghounds, hunting all sorts of game from quail to deer, are limited by circumstances imposed by the strange and changeable phenomena of scent. A dog having an extra good nose, with experience to use it, can do much on a bad scenting day that an ordinary dog cannot do; therefore, stress should be laid by all users of hounds and sporting dogs on *nose*. This is particularly true in America, where scenting conditions are usually worse in the hunting season than in Europe.

ECCENTRICITIES OF SCENT

If modern science ever can give a formula by which a good scenting day may be accurately recognized, it will do something which the experience of hunters through the ages has been unable to solve. When it comes to telling anything very precise about scent, I am afraid I cannot do it; no more can any man, for the oddities of scent are apparently inexplicable.

Scent seems to depend upon the degree of moisture in the ground and on foliage, as well as on atmospheric conditions. Scent is not always good when dampness prevails. Scent must be "lying," not "rising," to use a common hunting expression. Possibly the theory of "vertical winds" has some bearing on the verbiage. In New York State, Virginia, and North Carolina, I have observed that scent is almost invariably very bad and very "spotty" whenever the breeze is due south. Almost always, a south wind brings execrable scent,—the day may be sunny or cloudy, still or windy, the ground moist or dry, or in melting snow. These observations include experience with bird dogs, foxhounds, harriers, and beagles. In ancient Greece, as previously noted, Xenophon mentions bad scenting with a south wind; but, in England, conditions are said to be the opposite. Nevertheless, to quote from one British writer,

"What kind of sportsman was that poet who gets into his stride with the descriptive line:

'A southerly wind and a cloudy sky proclaim a hunting morn.'

As a matter of fact, there are few hunting districts where hounds ever run properly under these conditions!

Give me the verses which start:

'With the wind at north-east, forbiddingly keen . . .' "

Melting conditions usually give good scent: freezing, the reverse. I have known Virginia hounds to run like mad in frightful gales of wind, even in very dry weather when there has been no rain for weeks, and account for their foxes with the utmost precision. Scent must have been carried in the atmosphere at a point easily reached by hounds' noses. This condition may be likened to that of low-lying smoke in the wake of a railway train which disappears slowly. Under such circumstances, hounds can run a fox well, even when they are far behind their quarry. Again, hounds can often run a fox hard when they are close to him, but have difficulties if he gets well ahead of them. This condition may be explained by again using the "smoke" simile, as when smoke lies low but quickly disappears.

On the contrary, often have I noted hounds having the greatest trouble in apparently perfect conditions of moisture and calm. In the latter case, scent was doubtless "rising," and while a man on horseback could smell ground odors easily, hounds at the ground level were having difficulty. One often observes smoke rising rapidly and quickly disappearing, as scent doubtless does when it is said to be "rising."

It is conceded that there are two methods by which a hound follows its quarry,—that of the body scent floating in the air, and that of the pad scent on the ground, which latter is sometimes augmented by scent on the grass and bushes which have come in contact with the hunted animal. Often one may notice clever hounds smelling leaves and grass blades for "ends of scent":

> *But as he trotted up to cover*
> *Robin was watching to discover*
> *What chance there was, and many a token*
> *Told him, that though no hound had spoken,*
> *Most of them stirred to something there.*
> *The old hounds' muzzles searched the air,*
> *Thin ghosts of scents were in their teeth,*
> *From foxes which had crossed the heath*
> *Not very many hours before.*
> *'We'll find,' he said, 'I'll bet a score!'*

Wild animals seem to know when scent is bad. A fox, for example, will sometimes apparently amuse himself hugely by keeping just a short distance ahead of hounds, knowing perfectly well that in bad scenting hounds cannot run hard, and that he will not have to hurry. Often he will walk on his toes, putting as little of his feet to the ground as possible. In doing so, he will sneak forward at a walk the pace of which is with difficulty exceeded by hounds. On such occasions, the cry of hounds will be "queer," as if they were uncertain as to whether they are right.

Determined hounds hunting under peculiar scenting conditions are most interesting to watch in their efforts. To quote from a letter that Captain Adamthwaite once wrote to me about hunting in North Carolina on a cold, dry day:

Even where they could trail slowly in the swamps, the whole show collapsed when they got out on a sandy ridge; and it was pathetic to see hounds literally pushing their noses into the sand to try to get a smell of something in their keenness to get forward on the line.

It has been my observation that a hare sitting quite still in its form, or a fox curled in its lair, will often be passed over by a whole pack of hounds. If the quarry remains perfectly quiet, it often gives off no scent. This, it is said, applies to ground birds also, especially in the nesting season. If the fox loses his *sang froid* to the point where he starts to run and gets "warmed up," so to speak, the body scent plus the full imprint of the pad on the ground makes

ECCENTRICITIES OF SCENT

conditions immediately better for hounds. The body scent is doubtless augmented in a fast running fox by exhalations from the mouth, especially due to the fact that perspiration in foxes is through the mouth, as in dogs.

Speaking of body scent (in the air), a pack swimming a river, all giving tongue, must be smelling the aroma of the fox that has emerged on the opposite bank, otherwise the pack certainly would not give cry while in the water.

I once saw my *Blaze*, '22, coming up from behind the pack, running a narrow ride very fast and parallel to the line. The fox suddenly crossed, but not within her vision. Reaching the precise spot, she caught the fox taint, and in her frantic effort to turn in the right direction, she rolled completely over; she did not overrun an inch, having sensed and taken the direction within the fraction of a second. How did she know the direction the fox had taken? Was it from the body scent in the air?

On a windy day, hounds often run far to the lee side of the line where they are near enough to their fox to catch the body scent in the air. One day, in October, 1926, a fox went away from Pugsley Hill, in the Millbrook country, in full view of the field, although he was not in sight of hounds. He ran northwesterly, on the windward side of the road, while hounds, two hundred yards behind him, were coming at full cry one hundred and fifty yards on the lee side of the same road, where the body scent was blown by the gale.

I have heard it said that in England a falling barometer indicates bad scenting; a hygrometer showing plenty of moisture in the atmosphere is said to indicate good scenting; but I have never definitely proved either of these contentions, although I believe that both theories may be correct. Conditions that apply in one country do not necessarily apply in another. For example, if it is true that in England, as the old saying goes, "a southerly wind and a cloudy sky denote a hunting morning," certainly it is not true in eastern America, as has been stated.

To mention some paradoxical examples of good and bad scenting conditions:

Miss E. Œ. Somerville, author, painter, musician, and M. F. H. of the West Carbery, in *Wheel Tracks* relates an incident that occurred while she was hunting her hounds among the eternally green hills of Southwestern Ireland that overlook the expanse of sea wherein ships of the Armada as well as the Lusitania found a grave:

We had not found, but the hounds were very busy, feathering, and obviously sure that a fox had been about. But we could not find him. Then one of the Field rode up to me and said, with the icy calm that so often masks the fullness of pride: 'There's your fox, Master!'

He pointed with his whip to something that looked like a rusty can, lying under a furze bush.

HOUNDS AND HUNTING

A fox! Not, as I first feared, dead, but very much the reverse, as I found when I cracked my whip at him. He slid away over the hill, crossing, after half a dozen yards or so, a wide blackened patch where furze had been burnt. In an instant we brought the hounds to the place where he had lain. They said nothing. They were interested, and thought it was worth looking into, but no more than that. We took them on, and crossed the burnt patch, and suddenly, on its farther verge, they all put down their heads and went away with a shout, and we had a brilliant forty minutes, till he beat us on the edge of the sea, getting into a slit in the cliffs (whence an obliging fisherman offered to extract him with a boathook; but the offer was declined).

Why should the fox's bed have been less fragrant than his light feet, and why could not hounds acknowledge him until he had crossed the burnt bit of hill? These things are a mystery.

One day, with my bitch pack in the Overhills country, in 1922, it was terribly dry; there had been no rain for a long time, and it was blowing a violent gale. Hounds went out under protest, but in three hours they ran three foxes, one after another, and killed them all. The last fox made a point of six miles, and swam the Little River ahead of hounds, who plunged in carrying a head of a hundred yards, all giving cry in the water. Toward the end, this fox ran in full view for over a mile with twenty couple right on his brush, until *Quickstep* went to the front and rolled him over. Although the wind was blowing probably forty miles an hour, scenting conditions never seemed better.

On one occasion in the Piedmont country, Charlie Carver was hunting hounds, which were just over the crest of a hill from me, rather closely packed. It was about three o'clock in the afternoon, calm and cloudy. We had not found that day. Suddenly, my horse nearly stepped on a fox lying asleep in wheat stubble. I hallooed; Reynard ran for about two hundred yards in my full view, through a gateway, and then dodged behind a wall. Hounds were quickly brought up and put on the line; two or three of them spoke, but the hunt "stopped before it began," as the Irishman would say. There was no scent. Charlie Carver still believes that I never could have viewed a fox at all. Strange to relate, we found again, twenty minutes later, and had a splendid hunt with a five-mile point, accounting for our fox. Apparently, the scenting conditions had entirely changed. I have known four such instances in which hounds could not own the line of a viewed fox. Scent is, indeed, a subject for serious contemplation!

An instance of variations of scent within a few hours recently appeared in an account of a day with the Isle of Wight hounds (January 6, 1928):

After meeting at the Lodge, Brightstone, a fox found on Grammar's Common was hunted very fast to ground on Row Down, and was bolted and killed. The next fox was found on Castle Hill, and hounds ran him hard by Grammar's Common up on to Westover Down, when scent which had been good, *suddenly*

ECCENTRICITIES OF SCENT

changed and became non-existent. *Another fox was found in Ferny Bottom, but hounds could not walk after him. At 2.30 the weather and scent suddenly changed, and finding a big dog-fox in Monkham hounds raced after him, on a breast-high scent, for forty minutes without a check and killed him.*

Animals, including man, leave a distinct scent, and there is no reasonable doubt but that the odor of individual foxes varies just as that of human beings does. The scent of vixens may vary, too, according to the time of year or their condition; but, I do not believe the yarns that dog hounds will sometimes not run them as hard as scenting will permit.

What is more perplexing and wonderful than the ability of hounds to follow a line in the right direction and unravel its tangled thread!

> *Soon the sagacious brute, his curling tail*
> *Flourish'd in air, low-bending plies around*
> *His busy nose, the steaming vapour snuffs*
> *Inquisitive, nor leaves one turf untried,*
> *Till conscious of recent stains, his heart*
> *Beats quick; his snuffing nose, his active tail*
> *Attest his joy; then with deep-opening mouth,*
> *That makes the welkin tremble, he proclaims*
> *Th' audacious felon; foot by foot he marks*
> *His winding way, while all the list'ning crowd*
> *Applaud his reas'nings. O'er the wat'ry ford,*
> *Dry sandy heaths, and stony barren hills,*
> *O'er beaten paths with men and beasts distain'd,*
> *Unerring he pursues, till at the cot*
> *Arriv'd, and seizing by his guilty throat*
> *The caitiff vile, redeems the captive prey:*
> *So exquisitely delicate his sense!*
>
> *Should some more curious sportsman here enquire*
> *Whence this sagacity, this wondrous pow'r*
> *Of tracing step by step or man or brute?*
> *What guide invisible points out their way*
> *O'er the dank marsh, bleak hill, and sandy plain?*
> *The courteous Muse shall the dark cause reveal.*

How can a hound sense instantly and positively which way its quarry has gone? Never have I seen in print any discussion or explanation of this most interesting and, to me, marvelous ability on the part of the hound. The theory that the older end of a line is more faint is not always true, because the ground conditions may alter this, and rarely does a good hound hesitate more than an instant in coming on a line before deciding *which* way to go. Some advance the theory that one end of the foot gives off more scent than

HOUNDS AND HUNTING

the other. Would that I could solve the riddle. There seems to be no known scientific or practical explanation of how a hound can "sense" the direction taken by its quarry. The following interesting comments, however, are made in "Hold Hard! Hounds Please!" by that astute observer the anonymous writer "Yoi Over," who was for 40 years Huntsman and Whipper-in to well known English packs:

"I fail to find words fully to express the character of those truly wonderful nose-nerves of the foxhound; but you cannot have it every day from the hound. Let's see if I can support, by a case, my contention that it is not only that the scent must fit the nose but the nose fit the scent.

"The incident I quote is one of several. A bitch, a cross from an American hound by an English foxhound, jumped a gate close by where a stonebreaker was breaking stones. He swore the fox had not passed him on the road. But it had. This bitch was in her first season. She was solitary. I was watching her. She put her nose down. The weather was bleak but dry. For a full six or seven minutes she stood, and, so to say, nose-searched in a straight line no longer than six feet, with her stern going all the time, and her long, pendulous ears touching the ground. At last, out rang a note, then another and another, and on she went for about fifty yards. Up came her head, she charged another gate, topping it like a red deer; on the other side she galloped off in full cry, and I halloa'd on the pack. In twenty minutes this fox was pulled down.

"Now I maintain that during the six or seven minutes this bitch was nosing that line of six feet she was tuning her nose as the fiddler does his strings, until, at last, she got the right tension, and was able to feel the pad-scent of that fox. Slow work I admit, but true hunting nevertheless. She must have fitted her nose to a soil which had absorbed the taint of the fox-pad. Then she felt it to such a degree that she was warranted, joyously, to tell the watching whipper-in, and her nearby fellows of the hunting pack, that the fox had gone that way. Indeed, when the pack caught her up they were on soil far more favorable to the holding of the fox-taint than was the case when she so persistently, and patiently, struck the scent-wave that moved her to give from bosom and throat the clarion call.

"One can say that a hound who had not the determination such as this bitch-hound had would not have felt the fine silken thread of scent that the fox had left behind. Now critics or cynics may remark, 'well, what does one keep hounds for but to hunt? There is nothing wondrous or clever about that. She was bred to hunt, not to be looked at.' But I am trying to show, or prove, by a case how that, if they get the chance, those nose-nerves make the very utmost of the fox-taint, be it strong or weak. On a real good day folks say, 'a rattling good scent.' I say, 'wonderful nose-nerves of the pack.' On a bad scenting day, 'rotten scent,' say they. I say, 'wonderful nose-nerves to have been able to hunt the fox at all.'

"Some critic may say, 'you wish folks to draw the inference that the breeding of the hound, or its study, leaves much to be desired?' I do nothing of the kind.

ECCENTRICITIES OF SCENT

My story of that American–English foxhound shows that hounds are bred with most wonderful noses."

Certain ground rarely holds scent, and this fact seems to be known to wild animals. A striking example has been given me by Captain Miller, whose bobbery pack in India frequently hunted jackals. When hard pressed, these animals would often run to a dried-up salt lake bottom filled with underbrush where scent was always *nil*. Here hounds invariably lost, unless someone were placed on the far side to view away the quarry, which, on coming out on to normal soil, would again leave a screaming scent.

It is remarkable for how many hours scent will sometimes remain distinguishable to hounds; and stories told of the extraordinary ability on the part of bloodhounds to track men on old scent are almost unbelievable. Mr. W. Shovelton, of Alberta, Canada, has kindly sent me the following sworn statement concerning a couple of hounds which he himself handled in 1910:

Worthing, S. D., County of Lincoln, ss: We, J. W. Dickens and Agnes A. Dickens, husband and wife, of said county and state, first being duly sworn jointly upon our oaths, depose and say that we are the parents of Millard Dickens, who lost his life by drowning in Beaver Creek. On March 7th, 1910, at about 4.30 o'clock P.M., our little boy wandered away from home and was lost. We organized searching parties, who scoured the neighborhood, but without avail. Finally a ray of hope came to us through having heard of the wonderful work of the Fulton bloodhounds at Beatrice, Nebraska, and telegraphed to Dr. J. B. Fulton, the owner and proprietor of the bloodhound kennels at Beatrice to send us a pair of these dogs immediately. In answer to our message, Dr. Fulton at once sent us a pair of these famous bloodhounds. These dogs reached our home at 5 o'clock P.M., on March 10th. They were given the scent of the child from clothing previously worn by it, and when taken out of the house immediately took up and followed the trail of the child in a wandering way, about one and one-half miles to a stream known as Beaver Creek. The stream was running almost bank full, on account of recent heavy rains. We were horrified and loath to believe that our child was drowned, and asked the trainer to run the trail again. This he did three times, the dogs taking the same course each time. The trainer showed us the footprints of our child leading into the stream. Each time when coming to the stream, the dogs could hardly be kept out of it. The evidence now before us pointing strongly to the lamentable fact of our beloved child, we then dragged the stream, and found the body of our little boy a short distance below where it had fallen in. We count it as near seventy-two hours from the time the child wandered away until the dogs were placed upon the trailing where the scent had lain so long. We recommend these wonderful and sagacious animals of Dr. J. B. Fulton to anyone in need of like service. Further the affiants sayeth not.

In the eighteenth century, Somerville enlarges on the theory of scent as follows:

HOUNDS AND HUNTING

The blood that from the heart incessant rolls
In many a crimson tide, then here and there
In smaller rills disparted, as it flows
Propell'd, the serious particles evade
Thro' th' open pores, and with the ambient air
Entangling mix. As fuming vapours rise
And hang upon the gently-purling brook,
There by th' incumbent atmosphere compress'd,
The panting chace grows warmer as he flies,
And thro' the net-work of the skin, perspires,
Leaves a long-steaming trail behind, which by
The cooler air condens'd, remains, unless
By some rude storm dispers'd, or rarefied
By the meridian sun's intenser heat.
To ev'ry shrub the warm effluvia cling,
Hang on the grass, impregnate earth and skies.
With nostrils opening wide, o'er hill, o'er dale,
The vig'rous hounds pursue, with ev'ry breath
Inhale the grateful steam, quick pleasures sting
Their tingling nerves, while they their thanks repay,
And in triumphant melody confess
The titillating joy. Thus on the air
Depend the hunter's hopes.

Beckford offers no explanation of the phenomena of scent, but simply records numerous very intelligent observations, of which the following comments are of particular interest:

Scent is, I believe, what we sportsmen know least about. I cannot agree with Mr. Somerville in thinking that scent depends on the air only. It depends also on the soil. Without doubt, the best scent is that which is occasioned by the effluvia, as he calls it, or particles of scent, which are constantly perspiring from the game, as it runs, and are strongest and most favorable to the hound when kept, by the gravity of the air, to the height of his breast; for then, it is neither above his reach, nor is it necessary that he should stoop for it. At such times scent is said to lie breast high. *Experience tells us, that difference of soil, occasions difference of scent; and on the richness and moderate moisture of the soil, does it also depend, I think, as well as on the air. At the time leaves begin to fall, and before they are rotted, we know that the scent lies ill in cover. This alone would be a sufficient proof, that scent does not depend on the air only. A difference of scent is also occasioned by difference of motion.*

I believe it is very difficult to ascertain what scent actually is: I have known it to alter very often in the same day. I believe, however, that it depends chiefly on two things,—*the condition the ground is in; and, the temperature of the air; both of which, I apprehend, should be moist, without being wet: when both are in this condition, the scent is then perfect; and* vice versa, *when the ground is hard, and the air dry, there seldom will be any scent. . . . It scarce ever lies with a north, or an east wind; a southerly wind without rain, and a westerly wind that is not rough, are the most favorable. Storms in the air are great enemies to scent and seldom fail to take it entirely away. In some fogs, I have known the scent to lie high; in others not at all. When the dogs roll, the scent I have frequently observed seldom lies; for what reason I know not. . . . I have also observed that, in some particular places, let the temperature of the air be as it may, scent never lies.*

In all I have quoted from Beckford, I concur as correct according to my own observation in the Eastern United States, except that the wind usually concurrent with the worst scenting comes from a different direction, namely, due south. I have also proved to my satisfaction that the fact of bad scenting before a storm (mentioned by Beckford and others) is true in New York, Virginia and North Carolina. Not only is scent lacking, but often foxes will be trailed to their earths, since they apparently have the natural instinct to anticipate the coming tempest. Once it actually begins to rain, if scent has been poor previously, conditions sometimes seem to change for the better; although if it rains hard, scent will be washed away:

William Blaine wrote in his *Cynegetica* (1788):

I have frequently heard the good Housewives complain, that, against rain or thunder, their milk will turn, and their larders taint; and I have as often perceived, that a storm approaching, the scent will, in a moment, change and vanish.

J. Otho Paget, in his *Memories of the Shires* (1920), refers to the effect of an impending storm on scent. He writes that during an excellent hunt with the Quorn from Baggrave in which hounds had run very well, "the sky then clouded over and scent entirely disappeared."

A wonderful example of this phenomenon occurred in January, 1922, in the Overhills country. That keenest of huntsmen, Samuel L. Wooldridge, of Kentucky, had brought a number of his best Walker field trial hounds to Overhills (including the famous *Big Stride*). A little snow had fallen, but by noon it was melting fast in the brilliant sunshine. On that day, to test hound characteristics, a mixed pack of hounds from Kentucky and my Old Virginia hounds were being hunted. A grey fox, found about 1.30 o'clock, gave hounds the fastest kind of a hunt for some twenty-five minutes. Suddenly, with a quick change of wind, the sky clouded over, and hounds were brought to their noses. The Virginia hounds held to the line for three hours, unable to drive the fox faster than a walk until, finally, a freezing condition coming on made further efforts useless. The Kentucky hounds were quite unable to own the line, after the change in atmospheric conditions.

HOUNDS AND HUNTING

Once in Loudoun County, Virginia, in the Peidmont country (in 1914), hunting with me were two hunt-to-ride men, H. P. and A. C. They cared nothing about *hunting*, except as an excuse for jumping fences. Being young and ambitious, it was my hope that if I showed them good hound work they might become interested in hounds *per se*. The pack was by no means a poor one, the day was damp and cloudy, and conditions seemed to presage a storm. To make a long story short, hounds drew every likely place over the best country,—the beautiful grasslands of Messrs. Gatewood, Glascock, and Slater included, for hours without uttering a note. Suddenly, I viewed a fox slowly trotting across a grass field. The fox did not hurry at all. He knew a thing or two about scent, even if I did not. Within two minutes, hounds were put down on his line, but never a whimper did they give; either that fox had rubbers on, or there was not a particle of scent. Not even those experienced noses could own the line. Obviously, the hunt ended then and there, and I never saw those two "riding" gentlemen out again.

The entire season of 1925, at Millbrook, was unusual as to scenting, and many opportunities presented themselves to verify the phenomenon of bad scenting just previous to rain. During October and November, on each of twelve hunting days, when hounds met it was cloudy, without much wind; in local parlance, "a storm was brewing"; and it invariably rained before night. Throughout each of these days, scent was obviously bad until after it began to rain, when a slight improvement was noticed. This condition was repeated in the autumn of 1926, which had the worst hunting days, atmospherically, in all my experience. On innumerable other occasions, in various American countries, I have observed similar conditions, and have had the correctness of my observations verified by masters of beagles and other packs.

With a leaden sky and an impending storm on a still day, sound carries badly, as if there were a pressure or lid, so to speak, on the atmosphere—and I have heard it said that this apparent atmospheric pressure (which condition is an acknowledged detriment to scenting) likewise appears to affect even the flight of golf balls. How different on a still, clear morning, when sound carries with freedom through the atmosphere, and hounds simply fly on the line of a fox!

"Nimrod" (C. J. Apperly) remarks, referring to England:

There is a very peculiar circumstance attending hills which has often been a matter of observation: and that is, wherever a fox has reached them after a run over lower country, the scent has generally failed on running over them. This must be attributed partly to atmospheric causes, and partly to the difference in the mean temperature of the earth.

Often, I have noticed a strange phenomenon which seems to occur identically in all countries: to wit, should a fox or hare, hard hunted by hounds,

ECCENTRICITIES OF SCENT

suddenly be coursed by a stray dog or unduly frightened by meeting men unexpectedly, scent will almost entirely disappear for some distance on the line the quarry takes. Of this, Beckford says:

... *if the game should have been run by a dog not belonging to the pack, seldom will any scent remain.*

In Masefield's marvelous poem, "Reynard the Fox," there is given a wonderful description of this strange fact:

> *And young Jack Cole peered over the wall*
> *And loosed a pup with a 'Z'bite en, Saul,'*
> *The terrier pup attacked with a will,*
> *So the fox swerved right and away down hill.*
> *Through the withered oak's wind-crouching tops*
> *He saw men's scarlet above the copse,*
> *He heard men's oaths, yet he felt hounds slacken*
> *In the frondless stalks of the brittle bracken.*
> *He felt that the unseen link which bound*
> *His spine to the nose of the leading hound,*
> *Was snapped, that the hounds no longer knew*
> *Which way to follow nor what to do;*
> *That the threat of the hound's teeth left his neck,*
> *They had ceased to run, they had come to check,*
> *They were quartering wide on the Wan Hill's bent.*
> *The terrier's chase had killed his scent.*
>
> . . . .
>
> *The threat of the hounds behind was gone;*
> *He breathed deep pleasure and trotted on.*
> *While young Kid Kissop thrashed the pup*
> *Robin on Pip came heaving up*
> *And found his pack spread out at check.*
> *'I'd like to wring your terrier's neck,'*
> *He said, 'You see? He's spoiled our sport.*
> *He's killed the scent.' He broke off short,*
> *And stared at hounds and at the valley.*
>
> . . . .
>
> *He watched each hound for each small sign.*
> *They tried, but could not hit the line,*
> *The scent was gone.*

On August 17, 1926, an interesting occurrence with my hounds in the Millbrook country coincided almost identically with the incident related in the poem just quoted. Hounds had found a cold line at seven o'clock in the morning, and worked it cleverly until the fox was up and running for his life.

HOUNDS AND HUNTING

In his efforts to throw off hounds, the fox deliberately ran through William Hall's farmyard, and happened to be viewed by Mrs. Hall. Incidentally, the fox was coursed by her house dog, and when the pack reached the spot shortly after, scent was *nil*. A check occurred here which would have been final, had not the fox been viewed a half mile further on and hounds put on his line, after nearly thirty minutes had been lost—but more of this hunt elsewhere.

The possible explanation of this often observed fact is that the hunted animal is suddenly so frightened that its normal status, including that of emitting a scent, is completely changed: witness the effect of fright on the human body—cold chills, faintness, teeth chattering, "goose flesh," and so on. Fright may possibly cause a sudden drop from normal body temperature to sub-normal, momentarily checking the emission of scent.

Failure to give scent has often been noticed in a sinking fox or hare. Sometimes, just as hounds are about to kill, scent will greatly diminish. When a huntsman thinks that hounds are about to run into their quarry, let him take care to make haste slowly, for that moment is most critical. Possibly loss of scent under such circumstances is due to sub-normal temperature in the exhausted animal.

Scent is no respecter of persons, and often will be bad day after day, as George Washington testifies in the notes of his personal diary: to wit,

1775—January 25—Cold scent
" 30 " "
February 2 " "
" 3—Hunted 1 hour
" 6 " ¾ "
" 9 " "
" 10 " 7 hours—lost
" 11 " 6 " killed

1785—December 5—It being a scenting morning, I went out with hounds. Run at 2 different foxes. Caught neither.

1786—January 23—Went out with two Mr. Hansons and Mr. Alexander when they set out on their return after breakfast with the dogs, just to try if we could touch on a fox as we went along the road. This we did, but the scent being cold and seeing no great prospect of making it out the dogs were taken off and the gentlemen went home.

Thus, it is to be assumed that the Father of his Country, were he present, would agree with the sentiments of the Glorious Grocer (as does this most humble author), when he said:

Scent is a weary, uncomprehensible, uncontrollable phenomenon, constant only in its inconstancy.

CHAPTER VIII.

KENNELS AND STABLES

THE subject of hound kennels and kennel management is one which the layman may pass in disdain. If one were discussing hunt stables, a more attentive hearing might be obtained—but, "Kennels! why, anything will do for a kennel," is the feeling of many. This, however, should not be the case. If hounds are to be kept at all, certainly they should be kept in the best possible way. If a remarkable, or even a respectable, pack is the objective, a well designed, handy kennel kept in a neat, workmanlike manner is essential. This truth cannot be stressed too vehemently, and what a pleasure it is to visit such an establishment, for those who are able to discriminate.

Xenophon treats in his *Cynegeticos* on the training and hygiene of the Greek pack. Arrian gives wise precepts on the training in health and care in sickness of hounds. He mentions among other things the habit of having an attendant sleep in the kennel, and the advisability of taking hounds out for exercise each day.

Gratianus and Nemesianus, the Latin writers, describe in detail the manner of feeding, training, and healing hunting hounds. Among the hunt equipment of their day are mentioned "couples," and spiked collars, sometimes hung with amulets to keep the dogs from madness. The Romans in caring for their dogs went so far as to take them for sea-bathing to cure the mange. In the case of certain sicknesses, pilgrimage was made to the Temple of Vulcan in a grotto of Mt. Ætna, and baths were given the dogs in a fountain of naphtha, which completed the list of religious practices. As did the Romans, the Franks made pilgrimages with their horses and hounds to the Chapel of St. Martin, in Tours, and made vows for them. It was their custom to couple their hounds when taking them to the hunt, in the manner of the present time. A decree of Charlemagne read, *Any one finding a hound branded on the right shoulder, bring it to the King*, evidently indicating the mark of the Royal pack.

One hundred and five years before Columbus sailed on his memorable voyage across the western ocean, the versatile Gaston de Foix wrote in his famous book the first description in the Christian Era that I have been able

HOUNDS AND HUNTING

to discover of how to plan a kennel and take proper care of it, and to his words little in principle can be added to-day. In the quaint French of the period he writes: "*Du chenil où les chiens doivent demourer, et comment il doit être tenu*"; but, to continue from a translation of the fifteenth century, *The hounds' kennel should be ten fathoms in length and five in breadth, if there be many hounds. And there should be one front door and one behind, and a fair green, where the sun shineth all day from morning till eve, and that green should be closed about with a paling or with a wall of earth, or of stone, of the same length and breadth as the hounds' kennel is. And the hinder door of the kennel should always be open so that the hounds may go out to play when they like, for it is a great liking to the hounds when they go in and out at their pleasure, for they are not likely to get the mange so soon. Also, a kennel should have a gutter or two, whereby all water may run out that none remains in the kennel. The kennel should also be in a low house, and not in an upper chamber, but there should be a loft above, so that it might be warmer in winter and cooler in summer, and always by night and by day I would that some child lie or be in the kennel with the hounds to keep them from fighting. Also, in the kennel should be a chimney to warm the hounds when they are cold, or when they are wet with rain, or from passing and swimming over rivers.*

As to hound management, Gaston Phœbus has to say: *Thou, Sir, whatever you be, great or little, that would teach a man to be a good hunter, first he must be a child past seven or eight years of age or a little older, and if any man would say that I take a child in too tender age for to put him to work, I answer that all nature shortens and descends. For every man knoweth well that a child of seven years of age is more capable in these times of such things that he liketh to learn than was a child twelve years of age (in times that I have seen). And therefore I put him so young thereto, for a craft requires all a man's life ere he be perfect thereof. And also men say that which a man learns in youth, he will hold best in his age. And furthermore from this child many things are required, first that he love his master, and that his heart and his business be with the hounds, and he must teach him, and beat him when he will not do what his master commands him, until the time that the child dreads to fail. And first I shall take him and teach him for to take in writing all the names of the hounds and of the hues of the hounds, until the time that the child knoweth them both by the hue and by the name. After I will teach him to make clean every day in the morning the hounds' kennel of all foul things. After I will learn him to put before them twice a day fresh water and clean, from a well, in a vessel there where the hounds drink, or fair running water, in the morning and in the evening. After I will teach him that once a day he empty the kennel and make all clean, and renew their straw, and put again fresh straw a great deal and right thick.* [Note: Evidently Gaston did not realize as we do that straw breeds fleas more quickly than hay or shavings.] *And there where he layeth it the hounds should lie, and*

HUNTLAND, LOUDOUN COUNTY, VIRGINIA,

Built by the author. The kennels are in centre foreground, stables to the left, and Huntland House to the right.

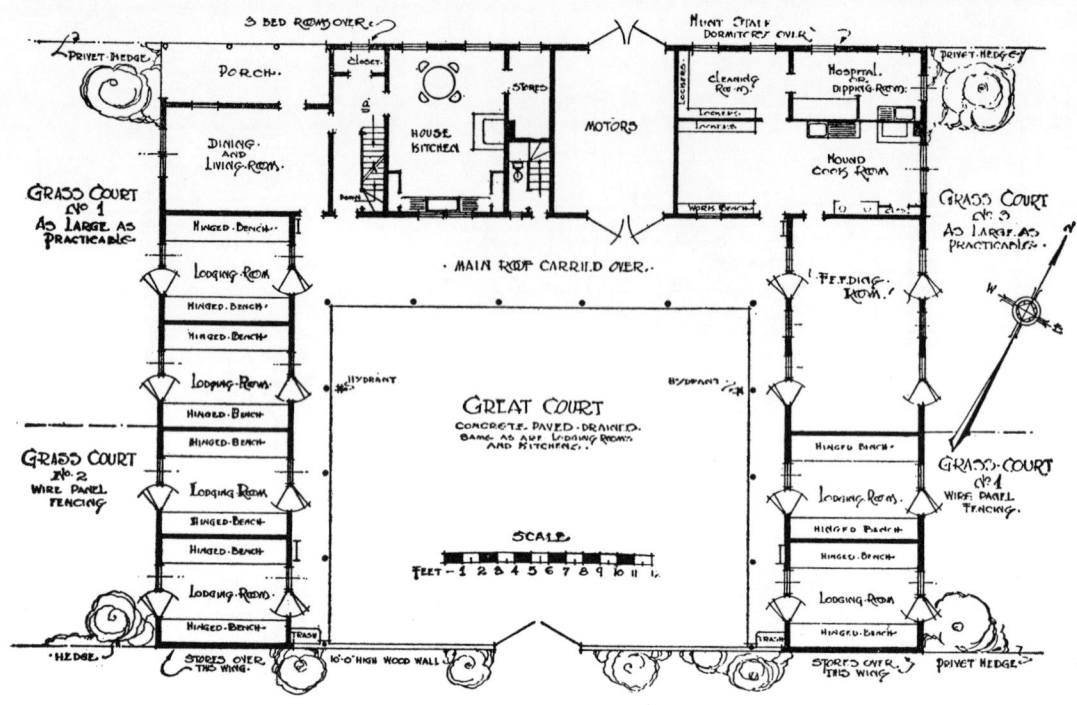

KENNELS BUILT BY MR. P. A. ROCKFELLER FOR THE OVERHILLS HUNT, NORTH CAROLINA.
These kennels were designed by the author and are similar in plan to those at Huntland, Virginia.

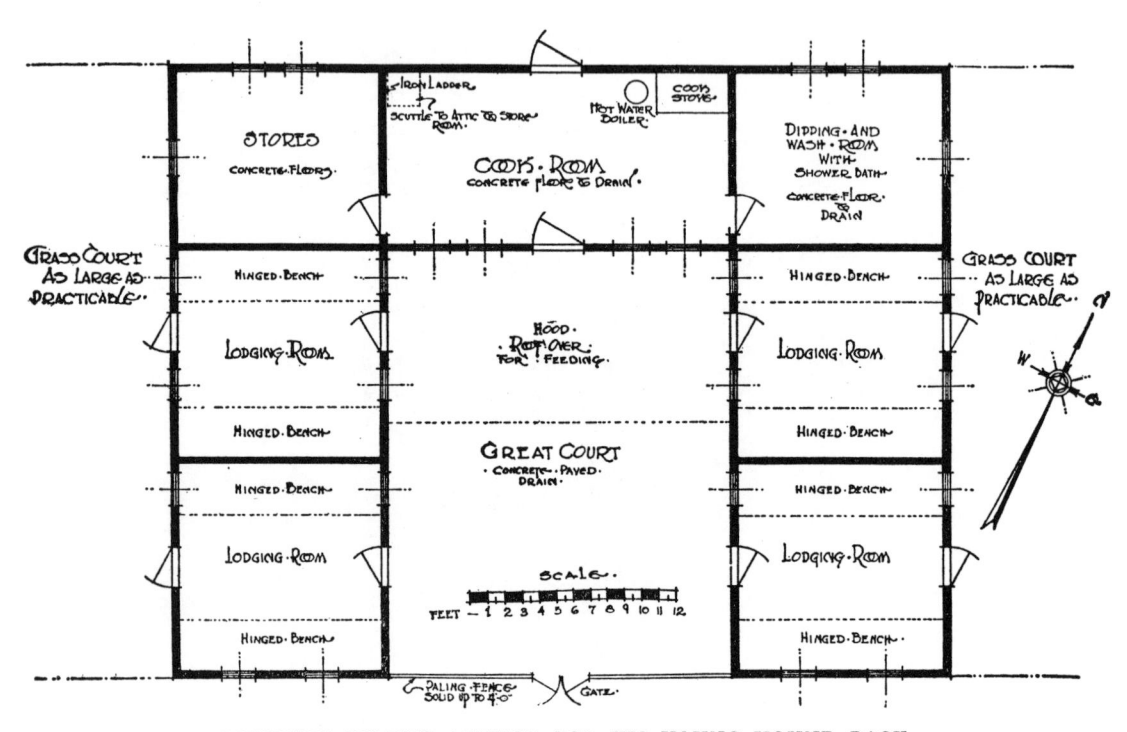

DESIGNED BY THE AUTHOR FOR HIS YOUNG HOUND PACK.
The plan indicates every facility for lodging and handling hounds, but in this case it was unnecessary to provide living quarters for the hunt staff.

KENNELS AND STABLES

the place where they should lie should be made of trees a foot high from the earth, and then straw should be laid thereupon, because the moisture of the earth should not make them morfunder nor engender other sicknesses by the which they might be worse for hunting. Also that he be both at field and at wood delivered (active) and well eyed and well advised of his speech and of his terms, and ever glad to learn and that he be no boaster nor jangler. . . . Also, I will teach the child to lead out the hounds to scombre twice in the day in the morning and in the evening, so that the sun be up especially in the winter. Then should he let them run and play long in fair meadow in the sun, and then comb every hound after the other, and wipe them with a great wisp of straw, and thus he shall do every morning. And then shall he lead them into some fair place where tender grass grows as corn and other things, that therewith they may feed them(selves) as it is medicine for them, for sometimes hounds are sick and with the grass that they eat they void and heal themselves.

Do we, of the twentieth century, so often satisfied with our "up-to-date" ideas, really know any more or always care for our hounds as well as this very great nobleman, huntsman, warrior, and writer, whose bones had crumbled to dust long before America was ever heard of?

Louis XIV, of France, as keen on building as he was on hunting, constructed at Versailles, and at Fontainebleau, magnificent buildings, designated *kennels*, designed to lodge the masters of his hunt, the hunt staff and entire *équipage*. The kennels at Versailles, located behind the large stables (*grande écurie*) cost at least 200,000 *écus* ($1,000,000.). The large and small stables, superb buildings which had nothing to resemble them in Europe, had already been built by the King on the Avenue de Paris. In the small stables, according to Manesson, 1683, were ordinarily to be seen five hundred horses kept for hunting and the pleasure of the King. His master of hounds, the duc de la Rochefoucauld, had under his direction sixteen lieutenants, forty-eight gentlemen of the hunt, many pages, one hundred *valets de chiens*, and farriers; and the packs numbered more than five hundred couple.

Nothing so quickly exposes the type of mind of the *deus ex machina* of a hunt as the kennel and its management. No self-respecting master who really knows or cares about hounds *per se*, and who believes that his hunt should represent certain dignified standards of excellence, will have other than a well-planned, well-ordered kennel. Unfortunately, in America we have few examples to guide us, and few traditions or hereditary standards of excellence in such matters. This lack of standards makes many of our kennels anything but what they should be. A few American kennels are excellent and their management first class, but these are exceptions. Makeshift buildings and slipshod methods are more often to be found. To "get by" with the least possible exertion and cost seems to satisfy, rather than to demonstrate pride and pleasure in doing "the best ever."

HOUNDS AND HUNTING

In England all is different. The hundreds of kennels,—foxhound, staghound, harrier, beagle,—are almost invariably well planned and conducted in a smart manner. In every instance within my ken, from the wonderful kennels of the Belvoir foxhounds, built by the Duke of Rutland, scores of years ago, down to smaller and less famous establishments, they are well managed; and this was so to my personal knowledge even in February, 1919, when England had been struggling for years under war taxes and innumerable discouragements to hunting.

An efficient kennel, well laid out, has many a practical advantage. In the first place, it has a tendency to sustain the morale of the hunt staff, it is easier to handle hounds in, it is easier to keep clean. A huntsman cannot feed hounds properly nor give them proper kennel manners—not to mention separate them to his liking and to the best advantage,—unless he has proper lodging rooms, courts, and grass courts, with adequate appurtenances.

In 1911, when my first foxhound kennel was built, I had been a large breeder of Russian wolfhounds since 1898, and had visited dozens of famous kennels in England, France, Belgium, and Russia, had seen the really good hound kennels in America, and had read everything obtainable on the subject. My objective at this time was to create a great pack of foxhounds, and, following Somerville's admonition, "First let the kennel be the huntsman's care," I proposed to build for the pack and the hunt country the best and most workmanlike quarters that thought and experience could produce. My point of view was that only the best possible hounds, hunt staff and kennels were good enough for any country worth hunting, and that all of these must of necessity be good to produce a perfect working organization.

To this end, many months were spent working on plans for a kennel to be used by the Piedmont and the Middleburg foxhound packs, and the Piedmont beagles. The accommodations were of suitable dimensions for 60–80 couple of hounds.

This building, completed in 1911 at Huntland, four miles from Middleburg, Loudoun County, Virginia, was built of poured concrete, stuccoed on the exterior, with the interior walls plastered where essential. On several walls are inserted panels with raised letters, giving admonitions on kennel management in the delightful verse of, "The Chace." The roofs of cypress shingles, stained black, the cream-colored stucco walls with handmade brick pilasters supporting arches, with white shutters and black detail, produced a very satisfactory ensemble, especially when in a few years ivy, trees and shrubbery judiciously planted completed the picture. The general effect is that of a building in the eighteenth-century manner.

The general form is that of a hollow square, facing southeasterly. The northerly side contains the huntsman's quarters (two floors and six rooms), also the hound cook room and the feeding room; over these, two hunt staff

KENNELS AND STABLES

bedrooms, livery lockers, feed bins with chute to cook room, and storage space; a cellar under both ends for coal bins and the house-heating furnace.

The east side contains a trophy room and office, two hospital rooms, motor shed, and five lodging rooms. The west side contains dipping room, two store rooms, shed for motors, and five lodging rooms. The square is completed on the southerly side by a ten-foot wall and gate, the interior of this hollow square being divided into concrete paved courts. The concrete paving is of a brick-color to obviate glare. All divisions of space are of stout wire panels and doors stretched on steel frames set in concrete. A passage wide enough for vehicles leads from the south gate through an archway and sliding doorway in the center of the north side. A court into which hounds may be drafted before feeding gives access to the feeding room through one door, while another door gives exit to the court after feeding. By this arrangement hounds can be drafted in and out of the feeding room by name, one at a time, shy feeders and thin hounds first. The lodging rooms in the east and west sides, ten in number, are approached from the inside by corridors running the entire length of each side, with doors into each lodging room, and doors to the outside grass courts. Each paved court, feeding room, and cook room, has a water hydrant and drain for quick sluicing-down with hose. This general arrangement makes it possible to draft hounds at will, individually or collectively, from any lodging room in the kennel to any other part without delay or confusion; it also makes possible the division and subdivision of the pack *ad lib.*

In such a kennel, hounds can be controlled with precision and become very obedient. Young hounds coming in off the walks learn their names quickly, and soon come to hand, realizing that there is no escape from doing what is asked of them. Incidentally, the hunt staff has no excuse whatsoever for not doing their work to the very best advantage and not having a pride in it.

> *. . . Well-bred, polite,*
> *Credit thy calling. See! How mean, how low,*
> *The bookless saunt'ring youth, proud of the skut*
> *That dignifies his cap, his flourish'd belt,*
> *And rusty couples jingling by his side!*
> *Be thou of other mould; and know that such*
> *Transporting pleasures were by Heaven ordain'd*
> *Wisdom's relief, and Virtue's great reward.*

The hunt stable which adjoins the kennel at Huntland is of similar proportion and design, and, together with the mansion laid out in relation to the stable and kennel, makes a very efficient working establishment, the general plan of which can best be visualized by reference to the bird's eye view.

HOUNDS AND HUNTING

Another very handy hunting establishment, and perhaps the prettiest one to look at that I ever saw, is the property of P. A. Rockefeller, at the Overhills Club, sixteen miles west of Fayetteville, Harnett County, North Carolina.

The rectangular-shaped kennels unit faces a similar-shaped hunt stables unit. The intervening space, about two hundred yards in diameter, termed, "The Circus," and circled by a drive, is equipped with divers jumps, and is used for a schooling ground. This "Circus" is surrounded by a white paling fence with gateways in the center of each side, whence a broad drive straight as an arrow stretches away easterly and westerly, and is eventually lost in the distance. The entrance gate posts are surmounted by figures of a fox and a hound originally brought from Huntland.

The *toute ensemble* of this very practical hunting establishment is very charming, the white, black, and scarlet coloring of the buildings being well set off by the planting of numerous flowering trees and shrubs which grow ever so well in this mild climate.

These stables and kennels, built of wood, are similar in plan to those of Huntland, except on a somewhat smaller scale. The kennel's central court is used in good weather, instead of the proper feeding room, one lodging room being used as a court before feeding. The doors to the lodging rooms enter directly from the central court, and another door at the far end of each lodging room gives exit directly from the lodging room to an outside grass court. There is one grass court for each two lodging rooms.

This is a very efficient working kennel, simple in plan, and free from dampness. On the whole, I find wooden kennels less prone to dampness than when built of more solid material. The dampest kennel in which I ever kept hounds was one built at great expense of hollow tiles with stuccoed exterior and interior. The ceilings were unusually high, and theoretically it should have been perfect, but such was not the case.

A kennel smaller in every way than those already described was designed for my young hound pack, in 1926. The accompanying plan indicates every facility for lodging and handling hounds, but in this case no living quarters had to be provided for the hunt staff. If men's quarters must be built, it is well to incorporate them in the kennel rather than to have out-buildings scattered here and there, with the hunt staff consequently removed from their charges.

Serious consideration should be given to this general matter of quarters for hunt staff, hounds, horses, and equipment, for if new edifices are to be constructed, certainly it is advisable to think of all necessities in advance, and to make provision for all such requisites in the first place, all under the roofs of not more than two buildings. Thus, one can perfect an establishment not only suitable for the best results, but also pleasing to the eye. The oppo-

KENNELS AND STABLES

site of this, of course, would be a heterogeneous group of buildings of all sorts and sizes, disadvantageously placed and wasteful of space, material, and time.

Kennel management is largely a matter of proper standards. If inefficient, careless, second-class, irresponsible service is good enough to satisfy the master of a pack, that is the service he probably will get. Naturally, no first-class results can be obtained without intelligent, ceaseless effort on the part of all concerned, and such results depend, obviously, on personnel—and in America that's the rub!

In America a good hunt staff is hard to find. Usually it has to be trained here from raw recruits or imported from England. The trouble with this latter course is that the average English hunt servant—the typical professional,—if he has been schooled for conditions in England, is frequently incapable of changing his methods in order to adapt himself to American conditions, topographical and climatic. He is inclined to believe that the fashionable English foxhound is the only hound suitable for hunting anywhere, and he is prone to follow set rules of procedure oftentimes useless here. On the other hand, most Americans who engage themselves to work with a pack of hounds have had no training whatsoever, and may have taken up this work thinking that it would be more pleasant than some other kind of work; in other words, not as a vocation. Such men are inclined to be impatient of discipline or of doing anything systematically, and while their native wit and adaptability may serve them in some measure, only if the master really knows his business can an organization composed of such be successful.

Never have I seen a kennel in England, large or small, that was not conducted with a definite standard,—which delights me in the thought that there is long experience and years of tradition behind this pride in well-doing; for example, hound lists are always available, hounds are taught proper manners, they come when they are called by name, are accustomed to being drafted, and show themselves magnificently, individually, and collectively. When anyone is inspecting hounds, he sees the hunt staff in smart coats, and caps or round hats; the feed-hour and the walkout afterwards, at which the master generally is present, is invariably considered a daily function of importance rather than a necessary nuisance.

There is plenty of precedent for careful kennel management. For a thousand years it has been recognized as important: kings, queens, emperors dukes, knights, and squires have been keenly insistent on careful methods, so, why not *cives Americani?* In fact, our First of First Citizens exercised just such thought and care when he built his kennels at Mount Vernon. They were situated adjoining the mansion, and about one hundred yards south of the family vault where his remains now repose. A bubbling spring was in the midst of the paled-in-grass court which fronted the hound quarters.

HOUNDS AND HUNTING

Gaston de Foix in the fourteenth century wrote very explicitly of kennels, as well as the medical care of hounds, as quotations from his MS. prove. In the fifteenth century, the hunt records of King Charles VI of France give evidence of careful management. The King's hounds that fell ill were fed on bean soup, seasoned with salt and lard; they were fed mutton, also quite large amounts of oil of flaxseed; sulphur and mercury were used in the composition of ointments for skin irritations. The feet of lame hounds were bathed with salt and vinegar. Wooden combs for cleaning hounds, needles for sewing up those wounded by wild boar, cows' milk for puppies, also appear in the expense accounts.

Following the Roman practice of supplication for celestial aid, the French took both scenting hounds and greyhounds to the Chapel of Saint Mesmer, near Maintenon, where for their benefit a mass was sung and offerings of wax and silver made before the altar of the Saint, as a protection from hydrophobia. Again, the archives show that over four hundred years ago Louis XI was equally solicitous for the welfare of his hounds. In the expense accounts of his hunt appear items for ointments, powders, and medicines. Wounded hounds were sent to the home kennels from the hunting front, carried in two-horse wagons, in litters, or boats. A special bathing instrument was used to wash the greyhounds which lived in his rooms and which slept on decorated feather beds.

Du Fouilloux, Salnove, and many other ancient writers dwell at length on the subject of hound management, giving in great detail the treatment of their packs by all classes of hunters, pointing out the system of feeding, physical and mental training. They mention well ventilated and spacious kennels, watered by living springs, with grass courts, rooms for the accommodation of attendants who slept near the hounds, also bake ovens for making the hound bread. The principal feed in early days consisted of bread from barley and bran flour, except in the case of the famous white hounds of the French king who alone enjoyed the privilege of being fed on wheat bread.

Through the ages, simple hound remedies have remained very much the same, for, alike with Charles VI, George Washington records in his diary, January, 1770: "Annointed all hounds and puppies with mange with hog's lard and brimstone."

It does not seem essential to enlarge in detail on the subject of hound feeding and treatment of diseases, for at least in the latter case there are innumerable books which one can study in detail; but it must be remembered that, after all, experience is the best teacher. For example, there seems to be in England a very rigid system of feeding in which horseflesh is an important factor. The most important cereal in an English kennel is oatmeal, and without it some kennelmen would believe hounds incapable of hunting at all. It

HUNTLAND KENNELS, LOUDOUN COUNTY (VA.).
Built by the author in 1911. *See p. 140.*

COURTYARD OF HUNTLAND STABLES,
Built by the author in 1913. *See page 141.*

KENNELS AND STABLES

would astonish them to know that many hounds in America never touch flesh, except that which they pick up in a casual manner in the field, and that most American hounds, at least those owned by farmers, never have tasted oatmeal but are fed very largely and satisfactorily on baked cornmeal (maize). Some people think that dog biscuit, of which there are numerous brands, are essential to proper hound feeding; others never use it, preferring to obtain the same ingredients for less money in other forms.

As to cooking methods: the regular English system is to boil the meal in a large cauldron directly over the fire, which necessitates constant stirring by the kennelman to obviate the danger of burning the meal. Traditions and customs are often great things to cling to, but new methods should be employed where common sense dictates. For example, this stirring of the boiling meal is done in England by a most cumbersome method whereby the kennelman has to get up on a stool, and push up and down in the cooking meal a very heavy iron tool with a grilled end. The use of this tool, termed a mixer, is a hot, back-breaking procedure, and in consequence, no doubt the meal is sometimes burned. In my kennels the stirring is done with a paddle three feet long, cut with a strong knife: the paddle costs nothing, weighs little, and can be easily handled even by a boy, and with it the cooking meal is easily stirred from the boiling room floor, and hence is not neglected.

In a small kennel where the kennelman may have duties in addition to that of cooking, it is, in my experience, advisable to use a double boiler in which the meal may be cooked for hours without stirring. This system makes the work of cooking less onerous, consequently it can be easily and thoroughly performed each day, so that the hound pudding in warm weather never has time to sour: to give a hound half-cooked or sour food is almost as bad as to give him poison.

Biscuits, when used, should be fed either hard (so that the hounds have to chew them thoroughly) or soaked for several hours, and thus made very soft—any half-measures will surely cause serious digestive troubles. In cases where digestive troubles do arise, it is well to cook all feed in lime water; and I might also suggest that if the kennelman can be induced to separate hounds so they will not fight, it is most advisable for the benefit of their teeth to occasionally give them bones to gnaw and hard biscuit or even hard corn bread to eat.

On the subject of using horseflesh, I never have been able to get the best results by its use—it has laxative effects. I much prefer meat trimmings from the local markets, or cracklings, which are the boiled-down dried meat scraps obtained from certain abattoirs making lard. Cracklings will stay fresh and wholesome in any climate for months. They come in the form of enormous round cakes resembling a car wheel, and as much as may be needed from day to day can be cut off with an axe. By their use the vicinity of the kennel is kept free from "noisesome smells," as Somerville would say, and one is relieved from the sight of ancient equines in nearby paddocks awaiting swift-approaching fate.

> *O'er all let cleanliness preside, no scraps*
> *Bestrew the pavement, and no half-pick'd bones*
> *To kindle fierce debate, or to disgust*
> *That nicer sense on which the sportsman's hope*
> *And all his future triumphs must depend.*
> *Soon as the growling pack with eager joy*
> *Have lapp'd their smoking viands, morn or eve,*
> *From the cistern lead the ductile streams,*
> *To wash thy court well-pav'd, nor spare thy pains;*
> *For much to health will cleanliness avail.*

Since feeding of hounds is of the utmost importance as well as the prime factor for keeping them in condition, I append some specific data that may be useful. The late Lord Willoughby de Broke said, "If the question were asked as to what shows the most sport and kills the most foxes, the magic word, 'condition' would be a safe answer."

The feed should be varied according to season,—cornmeal in winter may be replaced in the summer by well-cooked rice. An occasional quarter of fresh meat from some animal that has met with an accident and has had to be destroyed is, of course, good. Vegetables in quantity, as will be seen in the following formulae, are essential.

First of all, quality and not quantity is the most important thing in hound feed, and on no account should the quality be reduced in summer, as is done in so many kennels. I have known of the same quantity of feed being given in the summer as in the hunting season, while the quality has been sadly reduced, the thick oatmeal and flesh being watered down to the consistency of "hog swill." I believe this to be bad policy, as sloppy food does not "stay by" hounds and does little good: it dulls their spirits as well as the shine of their coats; whereas, good stiff feed will keep them in health and muscle—in other words, "Condition!" Since the natural feed of dogs is solids, it is incomprehensible to me how hounds can hunt for any length of time on the sloppy feed so frequently fed to them. Obviously, then, the drier the feed is, the better. The quantity (not quality) should be reduced in the summer as well as when hunting has to be curtailed in season.

An excellent aid to the health of hounds is the regular use of Glaubers salts,—two pounds to thirty couple given regularly in the feed will help keep the blood cool, and will in a remarkable manner prevent skin trouble and itching. Furthermore, it will tend to do away with that "doggy" smell which

KENNELS AND STABLES

is noticed in so many kennels, and reduce the necessity for dipping in disinfecting solution for skin irritations.

Cod liver oil in the quantity of a tablespoonful to each hound, mixed in the feed every other day, is excellent. The oil should be as crude as possible.

Epsom salts is an excellent physic when necessary.

Bran, thoroughly boiled, one-half bucket in the feed regularly given, is particularly helpful when hounds are shedding their coats. It is unquestionably an excellent conditioner.

One cannot over-estimate the daily use of green vegetables of almost any sort except potatoes—twelve pounds daily in winter to thirty couple. Carrots, cabbages, and onions are excellent. Very little green feed is given to hounds in England, but they are allowed to eat all the grass they want while being walked out. The American method seems preferable, assuring each hound of his share.

Winter Diet for Thirty Couple of Hounds

Approximate dry measure

Meat (cracklings)	1½	buckets boiled until quite soft.
Vegetables	12	pounds, chopped fine and boiled with meat.
Oatmeal	2	buckets thoroughly boiled until quite thick.
Cornmeal	1½	buckets baked into bread, then crumbled, and mixed with boiled feed.
Common salt	2	handfuls.
Glaubers salts	2	pounds every other day dissolved in cold water, mixed in feed (not cooked).
Cod liver oil	1	tablespoonful per hound every other day.
Bran	½	bucket thoroughly boiled.

N.B.—In summer, rice in lieu of cornmeal or oatmeal is used. Rice and oatmeal must positively be boiled until thoroughly soft, the water to be cold when cooking is begun.

Summer Diet for Thirty Couple of Hounds

Approximate dry measure

Meat (cracklings)	1 bucket	Oatmeal	2 buckets
Vegetables	16–18 pounds	Rice	1 bucket

Remainder of diet same as in winter

Common salt should be used in the cooking of food—a large handful when the meat starts boiling, and a second handful mixed in the cooked meal.

It may be suggested that, to prepare the cooked feed for use, shortly before feeding time, say, 3.30 P.M., all the ingredients should be thoroughly mixed in large tubs, and sufficient cornmeal bread, baker's bread, or soaked dog biscuit added to thoroughly thicken same. When it is available, stale baker's bread (if not moldy) may be used instead of, say, oatmeal; but the bread must not be added until just before feeding, since, if it stands there is danger of fermentation in hot weather, and consequent souring of the feed. Rice is excellent for summer use, but must be properly cooked by having been first placed in cold water, which is gradually brought to the boiling point. One cannot be over-particular in such matters.

As to the medical end of kennel management, there are certain troubles which exist in America that are perhaps unknown in England, and *vice versa*,—e.g., kennel lameness, so prevalent in England, seems unknown among American type hounds; hence, it is my impression that kennel lameness is due largely to the over-straight forelegs of English hounds; but it may be accentuated by the dampness of the English climate,—possibly a form of rheumatism unknown in America.

Hookworm, the same minute pest that is so prevalent among the human race all over the world, especially in warm climates, is the greatest menace except distemper that one has to guard against in American kennels. Of course, there are various other kind of worms, but hookworm, on account of its subtle power of debilitating the entire system in hounds of all ages, is fundamentally the cause of many deaths through pneumonia, distemper, black tongue, etc. Hookworm infection occurs through open cuts and through the mouth. It is difficult to detect, although sometimes the eyeballs of the victim turn white, and the gums lose the natural red color. It must be fought constantly in all sections of the United States to-day, for it occurs in all ages and all sorts of canines, including foxes,—at least, those that are kept in confinement on fur farms. Its cure, as in humans, following the formula of the Rockefeller Institute, is quite simple, but must be constantly repeated to be definitely effective.

In an approved hunt organization, stable and stable management are of great moment; yet, in the best sense of the word, these essentials are little understood in America. For this reason, the excellent available precedents and standards with regard to these allied subjects should be carefully studied. It is, perhaps, not surprising that in a country where many people have only known horses kept in the free and easy manner of the range and corral that the complications of keeping horses in stables are often overlooked.

KENNELS AND STABLES

How quickly, in entering a stable, the trained eye can tell whether or not the master is a real savant in horse matters, or merely a *dilettante*. It may not be suggested here how any individual stable should be conducted, but it may be permissible to call attention to this phase of hunting that is often badly managed.

Stables should be designed for best working results. This does not necessarily mean that they should be expensively built, but it does mean that they should be planned so that there will be a place for everything; consequently there can be no excuse for things out of place—a cleaning room, a separate tack room, that saddlery may stay clean; a proper place for grain, to protect it from rodents; suitable lofts, preferably over the boxes, for hay; and a convenient and neat method for disposal of litter.

As in kennels, a real difficulty is that of personnel. In these days, every boy is familiar with motors, but, few are the men available as grooms who have a practical knowledge of horses and stable management. The mysteries of proper feeding, conditioning, grooming, the care of steel, leather, and equipment, is all a closed book to them as it is, in many cases to their masters. Knowledge in traditional standards of how to properly keep a stable is rare. One constantly sees horses bought at high prices ruined by ignorant management, or, perhaps, so over-fed and under-exercised as to be unsafe for children or women to ride.

The highest product of the ancient art of saddlery is to-day found in certain English saddles. The leather is perfection; the workmanship meticulously correct; yet how infrequently is saddlery given commensurate care in America. Good leather well cared for will last a lifetime, and this fact is appreciated in England. Leather uncared for will soon dry up, crack, break, or disintegrate, which usually is its fate in America. How rarely does one find an American stable in which the art of properly caring for leather is understood or practiced?

Cleanliness is an important requisite in stable as well as kennel management, which harks back to the necessity of properly-built and equipped buildings, managed by intelligent, well-thought-out methods, the execution of which naturally depends on the human equation.

> *For forms of government*
> *Let fools contest,*
> *What ere is best administered*
> *Is best.*

CHAPTER IX.

RIDING TO HOUNDS AND HUNT UNIFORMS

IN this chapter, other commentators will be freely quoted, because, in making caustic criticisms for frequent lack of circumspection in riding to hounds, I do not wish to weaken the arguments by allowing myself to be considered a lone fanatic on the subject. To express the opinions of others may tend to drive home my own appeals for fairness to hounds and huntsman by those keen enough to play the game to the best advantage, and who should always remember that, fundamentally, the objective of foxhunting is to account for foxes. Beckford, even in the eighteenth century seems to have discovered four species of foxhunters: "dress," "around the mahogany," "health hunting," and "genuine."

This chapter decidedly does not tell how to jump fences—in fact, it is annoying to a *bona fide* hunting man to have jumping considered as the main reason for riding to hounds. Even horses are not essential to hunting. These statements will shock the hunt-to-ride contingent, but it will be readily understood by the advocates of riding-to-hunt. In 1823, it was sung of John Warde (who hunted hounds for fifty-seven years, and was called one of the fathers of modern English hunting), then with his noted pack in the Craven country:

> *Here is health to John Warde and success to his hounds:*
> *Your Quornites may swish at the rasper so clever,*
> *And skim ridge and furrow, and charge an ox fence;*
> *But will riding alone make a sportsman? No never!*

To enlarge: beagles are usually hunted on foot, both in America and abroad; harrier packs often are hunted on foot in Britain; several foxhound packs in the Fells of Cumberland, John Peel's country, are hunted on foot, while in Great Britain and Ireland, many people follow all sorts of packs, on foot, bicycles, and as best they can.

RIDING TO HOUNDS

Myngs riding hard to snatch an innings,
. . . .
Then last of all, at top of rise,
The crowd on foot all gasps and eyes
The run up hill had winded them.
Masefield.

If an act of Parliament could be passed that no one should ride foxhunting unless and until they had served an apprenticeship with a pack of foot beagles, it would be the finest thing in the world for modern hunting. In no other way are the science and the manners of hunting so completely attained.   Bryden

Often in America, the farmer-hunter, owner of a small pack, sits upon a hilltop enjoying the cry of his hounds as they follow the twists and turns of the fox in the vale below. There is, in North Carolina, one informal hunt where hounds are brought to the meet in the motor cars of their respective owners, and these owners stay within hearing or sight of hounds, in their cars, or on foot, as circumstances permit.

The conclusion is, horses are but a pleasant means to an end. As this is written, I can almost hear the epithets that are to be hurled at me; but in baldly pointing out certain facts, it is desired only to arouse interest in the fundamental object in hunting, that is, the work of hounds. If the novice can gain this understanding, and if eyes and ears are trained to hound work, even the hunt-to-ride man or woman will have immensely more fun when hunting than will be the case if his or her interest is limited to horses, or jumping, or gossiping. To further arrest attention to hounds, I am moved to cite the fact that the great and much-occupied George Washington was never too busy to think of his hounds and their hunting ability—his horses he rarely mentions: his interest in hound work was that of a true foxhunter—a rare *genus* among those who ride to hounds in our day. Many people spend an infinite amount of time and patience to become proficient in sports, such as tennis and golf—taking lessons and practicing to perfect themselves. The same people, strangely, often take up hunting with little or no serious consideration for the art.

It takes attentive intelligence to ride well to hounds. A thoughtless, unobserving person who lacks concentration cannot be really successful nor enjoy the sport to its utmost. What a worry and annoyance the unthinking hunt-to-ride contingent is to the huntsman and master! If such people actually do no wrong, often it happens that the finest hound work under difficult conditions may be entirely unappreciated by them. Huntsmen and masters

HOUNDS AND HUNTING

are only human, and intelligent appreciation from those who hunt with them of the merits and demerits of the pack is but their just due.

It is hardly correct to call unthinking riding to hounds, "hunting"; yet, it is really extraordinary how many people of average intelligence can ride with a given pack for years and rarely know one hound from another, nor have proper comprehension of hound work and huntsmanship. I once read the "hunting" diary of a well-known hunt-to-ride man, and from one end of the record to the other the work of hounds was not mentioned; the weather, the number of people out, the duration of runs, yes, but no comment on hound work, and no mention of accounting for foxes. The result of such a lack of comprehension in the case of the average organized hunt is indifferent sport, because followers do not understandingly applaud nor constructively criticise the work of hounds.

The height of the art of hunting and accounting for foxes with a pack of hounds should be looked upon in the light of any "team" game, and should be played accordingly by hunt staff, hounds, and followers of the hunt. Followers may enter into this spirit of team play, amusing themselves not a little, and at the same time helping hounds and huntsman to account for foxes (which in America, at least, have all the odds in their favor), if they will remember the following:

In a hilly, woodland country, where the earths and dens cannot be stopped, and where foxes may be found "anywhere or nowhere," to play the game to the acme of perfection, to produce perfect pack performance, and to give the maximum pleasure to the field, are goals not easily reached. In a gently rolling, open, grass country, with foxes to be found in small coverts with earths well stopped, it is quite another matter. The main difference is that in one case hunting must be largely a matter of "hearing" hounds, and in the other case of "seeing" hounds. In the early autumn, with sound deadened by heavy foliage or confused by echoes, the difficulties of playing the game accurately are greatly enhanced.

It takes an extraordinary pack of hounds to kill foxes above ground in a rough, unstopped country—one, two, or three couple can hardly do it; so, if the objective of the game is to kill foxes with a pack of hounds, do not start to gallop after a *few* hounds, should they speak on a line—wait for the pack to get together, and then stay with them, if you can. When a hound is heard to speak, be sure it is "right" (puppies, for example, often will speak on hare or rabbits). Remember that this desire to run hare is particularly true on bad scenting days, or after a rainy night, when most foxes are hard to find, for following a storm, in an unstopped country, they are usually tucked away in their earths. If a hound is heard to speak or a fox is viewed, try to notify the huntsman, if he is uninformed.

Man is a gregarious animal; sheep are also gregarious; if one animal starts

RIDING TO HOUNDS

to run, the whole flock may do likewise without reason. This sort of stampeding by followers of hounds often causes the loss of a fox at a check. To get across country with hounds to the best advantage requires individual, intelligent thought.

In attempting to acquire knowledge of hound work, the first thing to remember is that one is out *hunting* and not *Sonntag* riding in Central Park. If a person hunts thrice weekly for a total of twelve hours, that person has many times twelve hours in the week left for horse-talk, gossip, and laughter; so, why not, when hunting, keep the tongue from wagging and eyes and ears concentrated on hounds. Of course, if one is an indifferent rider, and all energies are required to stick on a horse, there may be some excuse for lack of attention to the pack.

If it is desired to become proficient in the understanding of hound work, and thereby add to the pleasure of riding by having two strings to one's bow, the first thing to do is to learn something about the *virtues and vices* of hounds (see Chapter V), and try to understand some of the problems that confront the huntsman (see Chapter VI). Having acquired a bit of the theory, make yourself known to the huntsman of your pack. He will be delighted to tell you all he can. Because of the lack of interest in hounds shown by most people, a huntsman is generally hungry for signs of intelligent interest in his charges. Be able to recognize the best hunting hounds; take them for your guide; watch them closely, and you will learn much. If the pack is hunting, or, as the ancients would say, "seeking for a fox," and you observe *Ruin, Docile, Charmer, Rueful,* and *Pride* with sterns feathering, their noses glued to the ground, it is the sign that a fox has walked there. Stop, instantly! Do not let your horse move at all, even if hounds come in your direction. Remain quietly where you are, for the direction of a horse's movement will influence the cast of a hound. *Captain* speaks in his deep, melodious voice; *Docile* speaks; they have the best noses in the entire pack, and will cry a line when other hounds can hardly honor it. At *Captain's* voice, the entire pack has rushed instantly to the scent, all heads down, sterns waving madly, all intently working out the direction in which Charlie Fox has walked. At this juncture, be ready for anything, all alert, but not in a hurry; hounds may work a cold line for quite a distance, and then suddenly check; so, keep your eyes on the pack, and your ears wide open to their cry. The instant cry stops, check your horse in his tracks; stand still; and always remember that any hunter you cannot rate had better be left at home, or kept out of harm's way, several fields off. You have no right to spoil the sport of others by riding an uncontrollable horse.

If you hear a hound speak, but see the huntsman standing still, or perhaps blowing his horn, and most of the pack quietly standing about, do not gallop after the single hound; he is running a hare, or doing something he

[153]

should not be doing. No doubt the huntsman and the hounds know what the matter is, even if you do not. So, watch hounds, listen to them, and watch the huntsman. A huntsman always can tell from the way his steady hounds act if others are speaking to riot.

To illustrate, may I quote from Izaak Walton?

What pleasure doth man take in hunting the stately Stag, the generous Buck, the wild Boar, the cunning Otter, the crafty Fox, and the fearful Hare! . . . What music doth a pack of dogs then make to any man, whose heart and ears are so happy as to be set to the tune of such instruments! For my Hounds, I know the language of them, and they know the language and meaning of one another as perfectly as we know the voices of those with whom we discourse daily.

Once, I owned a very good bitch who never spoke falsely, but she had a dashing style of her own. At a check she was very busy, often casting herself in a quick manner, and somewhat wider than most hounds. During one season, I had to keep her in kennels most of the time, because an over-ardent sportsman knew this bitch by sight, and the instant she began her cast he would exclaim, "*Fairplay* has it," and away he would go after her, regardlessly. Nothing would induce my friend to listen for *Fairplay's* voice indicating that she really had the line; and as for the rest of the pack, they did not interest him.

In the case when hounds do go away with a great burst, as when they are brought to a view halloo, and go away at speed—give them a chance to really settle to the line.

Hold hard, sirs, give them half a minute.

As a matter of fact, good hounds are frequently stepped on by horses, generally through sheer thoughtlessness or stupidity on the part of the riders. It is a rider's business to keep out of the way of hounds and not to expect hounds to look out for them. A hound may be running a line in a ride—to keep out of his way is only fair. Hounds are running to the huntsman's cheer: to keep out of hounds' way, to ride wide of them—not behind, with the risk of running over them—is the duty of all.

The fox takes precedence of all from the cover:
The horse is an animal purposely bred
After the pack to be ridden—not over;
Good hounds are not rear'd to be knocked on the head.

Furthermore, if one really wishes to ride close to hounds, it is best to take a quartering position at one side. There, one can see the pack better, and ride closer without being an infernal nuisance to the huntsman and a menace

RIDING TO HOUNDS

to hounds. In riding thus, one can observe and hear hounds the second they begin to waver and check, and can easily turn away from them, to avoid the stupid act of riding into them.

If you live with hounds, turning as they turn, but never turning among them, keeping your distance, but losing no yard, and can do this for seven miles over a grass country in forty-five minutes, then you can ride to hounds better than nineteen men out of every twenty that you have seen at the meet, and will have enjoyed the keenest pleasure that hunting, or, perhaps I may say, that any other amusement can give you.
Trollope.

If you can't stop your horse when hounds check, turn the brute's head away from the pack, for in that direction you can do little harm; possibly you will be able to run down a fox by yourself; but if you wish hounds to do it, give them a chance.

Nothing is so grossly stupid, unintelligent, and sport-spoiling as over-riding hounds at a check; yet, it frequently happens. The results may be personally dangerous, as the following epitaph indicates:

> *Green grows the grass*
> *O'er the sporting old stager*
> *Who overrode hounds*
> *Of an ex-Indian major.*

One of the most exciting hunts in which I ever participated was utterly ruined in its conclusion, when hounds were overridden at a check, the story of which follows:

One day, in November, 1925, hounds met at a famous covert in a country I hunted for five seasons. A little snow lay here and there; a slight breeze was blowing from the wood; hounds were very restless at the meet;

> *Most of them stirred to something there;*
> *The old hounds' muzzles searched the air.*

As later events proved, there was good reason for their restlessness, for, no sooner had the pack been cheered into cover than they spoke in chorus, and Charlie Fox was viewed crossing a ride—such a fox! nearly white in color, so white, in fact, that when viewed later on a woman screamed, "Look at the fox with snow on him." A true ghost fox it was, even to the final vanishing of the ghost; straight away north, up hill and down dale, crossing Mr. Haight's meadows, leaving the big Brook earth on the right; 'cross Kinney's lane; 'cross the Shunpike, went fox, hounds, and riders. Never shall I forget how a newly-imported Irish grey attempted to kick off from the top of each rail fence as he would have from a bank. One, two, three miles still due north, through the Stick Heap covert; still north, four miles, five miles, without a check. At this juncture, hounds swooped into a covert, but as they emerged from the wood, I viewed the fox, his white coat gleaming in the sunlight, not two hundred yards ahead of hounds, and just disappearing over the crest of a grassy hillock. He had swerved due east, and crossed a narrow road which was in a depression flanked by wire fences. Hounds checked momentarily in the sunken road. At this moment, several well known hunt-to-ride people dashed up through a lane which emerged just where hounds had checked. Without observing, or trying to observe, what was going on, these scatter-brains began galloping in the road which led north—the previous direction of the fox's line. No one had seen the fox go east but myself; no one paid any attention to hounds, the idea of each thrusting rider seeming to be only to beat the other fellow. The galloping horses all dashing north, got hounds' heads up, and as they were wildly excited (being close to their fox), the whole pack followed the horses, as highly strung foxhounds of any kind will do, if horses move at a check.

Between the line of the fox and myself was a five-strand wire fence, and there was no open access to the field for a considerable distance either way. There was nothing for me to do but to have my horse held, climb the wire fence as best I could, and run on foot to the crest of the hill where I last viewed the fox. In the meantime, by means of horn and whistle, and what voice I had left, I got hounds back on the line, which they ran at great pace for another twenty minutes directly away from the road-galloping thrusters. Unfortunately, being about done, "Charles" apparently became confused, and again changed his direction, crossing in view of the road-galloping field, who soon finished the hunt completely and irrevocably by overriding the pack a second time, in the middle of a muddy, plowed field, where hounds had checked momentarily.

The next hunting day I had my innings. *La revanche est un plat qui se mange froid.* No hounds were visible at the meet. When people began to inquire where hounds were, I advanced on foot, with several volumes under my arm, and, referring to the woeful incident of the preceding day, I begged leave to cite the opinion of the Ancients on this particular subject.

From the *Cynegeticos* of Xenophon, I read as follows:

The huntsman . . . should follow the dogs, taking care to keep behind the hare, and not to head her, which is unsportsmanlike. . . . The huntsman should restrain himself and not follow the dogs too near, lest, through emulation, they should overrun the scent.

Taking up my First Edition of Beckford, I continued:

Gentlemen, when hounds are at fault, are too apt themselves to prolong it.

RIDING TO HOUNDS

They should always stop their horses some distance behind the hounds, and, if it be possible to remain silent, this is the time to be so; they should be careful not to ride before the hounds, or over the scent; nor should they ever meet a hound in the face, unless with a design to stop him. Should you at any time be before the hounds, turn your horse's head the way they are going, get out of their track, and let them pass by you.

In dry weather, foxes, particularly in heathy countries, will run the roads. If gentlemen, at such times, will ride close upon the hounds, they may drive them miles without any scent. (No one should ever ride in a direction, which if persisted in would carry him among the hounds, unless he be at a great distance behind them.) Highmettled foxhounds are seldom inclined to stop, while horses are close at their heels.

An acquaintance of mine, a good sportsman, but a very warm one, when he sees the company pressing too close upon his hounds, begins with crying out as loud as he can, 'Hold hard.' If anyone should persist after that, he begins moderately at first, and says, 'I beg, Sir, you will stop your horse; Pray, Sir, stop; God bless you, Sir, stop; God d—n your blood, Sir, stop your horse.'

I am now, as you may perceive, in a very violent passion; so I will e'en stop the continuation of this subject, 'til I be cool again.

Finally, I read from Commander Forbes' *Hounds, Gentlemen, Please:*

I have just heard a delightful little anecdote from a southern English country. Hounds after a sharp gallop checked. A lady, who had certainly ridden well to the fore, came up to a well known sportsman who was intently watching for the recovery of the line, and in excited tones exclaimed, 'Wasn't it grand? Talk to me! talk to me!' and because he failed to comply with what she, no doubt thought a reasonable request, that well known sportsman got himself very much disliked. . . . I have heard it said of late years that the tempers of amateur huntsmen are often unbearable; but though I most strongly deprecate the use of violent or unseemly language in the hunting field, it appears to me that the modern M. F. H. is the most highly tried of human beings.

After reading these rather definite illustrations of why one should be careful at a check, I thanked the company for their attention, and ordered the pack brought up. A good day's sport occurred; and subsequently, in that particular country, more attention was given to the work of hounds.

Nothing is so exasperating to a huntsman, or expresses so well the egotism of many hunting people, as their thoughtlessness regarding hounds, the *sine qua non* of their sport. It must be remembered that a hound working a line in underbrush and fallen leaves cannot hear or see as well as a man on horseback. Also, a tired hound cannot get out of the way as easily as the rider can keep out of the hound's way. To deliberately ride between hounds and the huntsman indicates the height of ignorance.

Once, I saw a huntsman standing by the side of a covert at the end of a day, calling hounds out. Several couple emerged from the wood through a barway, and were coming along a ride flanked with thick, prickly bracken difficult for hounds to go through. After these hounds came several members of the field, who jumped the barway, and charged at a gallop down the ride and through the hounds, quite regardless of the fact that the "going home" call was being sounded on the horn, and the huntsman and pack were standing in full view. These thoughtless people, when asked in no unmistakable language what the hurry was, seemed quite hurt.

Oftentimes, in wood rides, one has seen the entire field madly galloping away from hounds like cattle in a stampede, no one person having sufficient individual initiative to stop and listen long enough to ascertain which way hounds were headed. MORAL: if you do not see hounds, and cannot hear them, do not gallop wildly about, just because someone else is doing so—use your brains!

Some persons, especially if they do not know the country thoroughly, have a most annoying way of riding almost on top of a huntsman. Nothing is more aggravating to the huntsman; he needs to have all his senses concentrated on hounds, and any nearby rider is bound to distract him more or less. In some woodland or hilly countries, if the pack gets out of sight, sense of hearing alone can indicate the direction they are taking. There is an art in listening to cry. If the huntsman is riding alone, he may be able to hear hounds distinctly, whereas, if a group of people are galloping at his very heels, instead of a hundred yards away, the thunder of hoofs often makes hound voices inaudible. If a huntsman stops to listen under such circumstances, followers should instantly stop in their tracks, and not ride up to him, thus adding the noise of their panting horses and creaking saddles to that of his own horse. One's horse even when standing, by his breathing and pawing will make so much noise that it is often necessary to dismount, and have him held while one walks away several yards to listen for hounds. Whippers-in should never be spoken to when in pursuit of their duties, for, as intimated, they need all their wits for the business in hand.

Riding to hounds long ago became an integral part of country life in Great Britain, and remains such in spite of many handicaps only because the most fundamental responsibilities are understood and lived up to. In America, only wide usage and broad understanding of these responsibilities will make the growth of hunting successful. This great sport has reached its zenith in the British Islands, because it is everywhere conducted with due consideration for all.

As much as it hurts to acknowledge it, we Americans sometimes are woefully superficial in our sporting knowledge. Unfortunately, we have little custom or precedent to guide us. Hunting cannot be maintained or improved in the future unless hunting people realize their responsibilities and their re-

LORD LONSDALE AT BARLEY THORPE IN THE COTTESMORE COUNTRY,
of which he has been three times Master. An ancestor of this famous sportsman first
brought hounds to Leicestershire, in 1666.

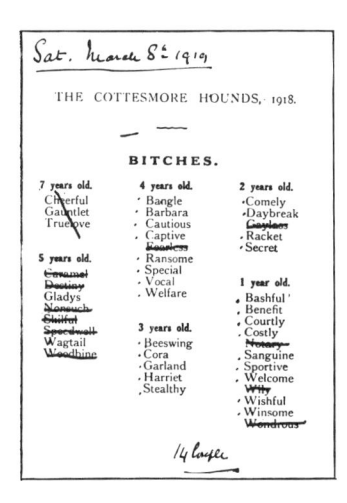

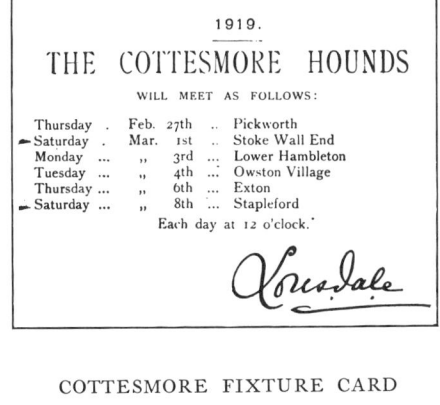

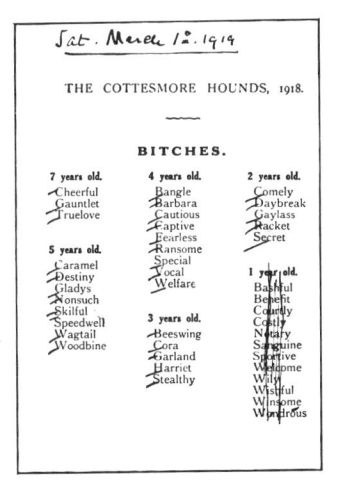

COTTESMORE FIXTURE CARD
AND HOUND LISTS, 1919.

The lists indicate the care with which packs as a semi-public institution were maintained
in England even after four years of war.

GOBELIN TAPESTRY SHOWING FRENCH HUNT UNIFORMS, HORNS, HOUNDS, AND HORSES OF THE EIGHTEENTH CENTURY.

RIDING TO HOUNDS

lation to the landowner, the relation of guest to host. It is pathetic to think of the asinine actions that have been from time to time perpetrated by ignorant and selfish people. Townspeople are prone to imagine that the broad fields of the country belong to no one, because no one is in sight; they too frequently forget that their hunting is made possible only through the courteous hospitality and sporting spirit of landholders, and that every fence that is knocked down must be replaced by someone. Landowners while standing in their own fields have been cursed and threatened for no vital reason, fences have been broken, and stock turned loose without a word of apology, while at times, when protests have been made, patronizing answers have been forthcoming.

Few Americans know, and few stop to realize, that it costs tens of thousands of dollars annually to properly maintain a three or four-days-a-week country and support a fencing and paneling system, without which expenditure there will be no foxhunting in the near future. In England, costs are realized and the responsibilities squarely met; but with us, standards are low, and the payment of subscriptions is consequently often minimized or avoided. He who cares a straw about the real advancement of the sport should support his master in every way, not forgetting to subscribe to hounds with which he regularly hunts at least the equivalent of one-half the amount it costs him per annum to feed his hunters—for what good are the hunters without good hunting?

A newcomer in a country who desires to hunt should inquire of the master or hunt secretary if he would be *persona grata* in the field; he should inquire what regular subscriptions would be satisfactory for him to give, and if there are special funds; he should send his check at once, and write a note asking if the master has any objection to his coming out cub-hunting. The master will, of course, answer the letter in a gracious manner, doubtless calling attention to the fact that in his country, at least, hunting is made possible only through the sporting spirit of landowners whose crops must never be trampled nor their cattle disturbed, also, that gates must be closed, and damage reported.

Where one rides, the way one rides, and the quality of one's horses are of infinite importance; members of the field should come to the meet and not anticipate the draw; larking across the property of others is a practice that causes much trouble, and in some American countries is strictly vetoed; keenness is, of course, excusable, but the less conspicuous a member of the field makes himself, the better it is for sport.

I've just a word, a warning word to whisper in your ear!
When starting from the covert, should you see bold Reynard bust,
We cannot have no huntin', if the gemmen go fust.

HOUNDS AND HUNTING

Great care should be exercised not to rush at jumps coincidently with others. Nothing is more dangerous or more likely to make a man or woman unpopular. Women are, unfortunately, prone to be heedless in this particular.

The injuring of a hound by one's horse through carelessness, is an unpardonable sin which can hardly be atoned for. It takes years to perfect a good pack of hounds, of which individuals may have cost hundreds of dollars and be invaluable.

Sufficiently forward, yet still keeping bounds,
His wish to ride after, not over the hounds,

has often been quoted as a warning to impatient people.

Any horse, especially a young one, is liable to kick hounds or riders. Great care, therefore, should be exercised in this regard, and animals especially given to this trait should have a bit of red ribbon tied in the tail, and be kept at a safe distance.

A member of the field should never halloo nor attempt to make hunting noises when any of the staff is present. Hunting people when crossing fields, or on the road in remote country districts, should always salute anyone they may meet with a pleasant word or a bow. Should one come to a gate carelessly left open and there is no one else in sight behind him, he must always shut it. Should someone be following, the cry "Gate please," should be passed back. It is the very particular business of everyone who wishes to hunt in the future to see that fence damage done by himself or others is repaired or carefully reported to the master as soon as practicable. Young horses as yet improperly schooled should hardly be taken out hunting to break rails at the expense of friendly landholders.

There is no class of persons which brings more disrepute to a hunt than grooms. They, as a rule, are extremely thoughtless, noted for leaving gates open, and causing other damage. The strictest orders possible should be given to them, not once, but several times during the season. In some American countries they are forbidden the field at all except by express permission of the master.

Every man or woman who has the slightest interest in the local hounds should consider it their personal, sacred duty toward the sport to help build up hunting by generously supporting the hunt organization, and attempting by word and deed to smooth its none too easy path; do not criticize harshly or unjustly—gossip not at all.

Hunting people should remember: that the task of the master of foxhounds is not an easy one, and that it is as impossible to find a perfect master of hounds as it is to find a perfect man or woman; that the responsibilities of the master and field to the community and to the welfare of the sport are many; that upon their own individual words, actions and subscriptions depend present and future conditions; that when they have complaints to make they should ask themselves, "what have I personally done to help matters, and how much do I subscribe to hounds?" *Noblesse oblige!*

When a master of hounds is inducted into office, it must be remembered that if he is at all keen on giving the very best sport, he may of necessity be called upon to enforce certain measures that will tend to make him unpopular. Nevertheless, he must always keep in view the fact that the primary object of foxhunting is accounting for foxes; the field must be kept in control, accordingly, so that the fox may not be headed nor hounds interfered with at checks, nor hunt staff hindered; over-aggressive members of the field should be quietly but firmly told of their errors, for their actions are generally due to ignorance of hunting technique. A field master who really understands hunting can do much to instruct his field in what they should or should not do to enhance their own sport, and if he can work in complete understanding and coördination with the huntsman—not tagging him around too closely, especially at a check,—results should be of the best.

Cubhunting should be considered a private matter conducted by the master for the purpose of conditioning and educating hounds; at this season it is the master's sole prerogative as to whether fixture cards shall be sent out, and at what place and hour hounds shall meet. A master undoubtedly has the right to take hounds home at his own volition,—in other words, a master is absolute. He has been selected for the purpose of hunting the country to the best of his ability. If for any reason, such as over-soft condition of ground, or because of the field overriding hounds, or riding over crops, he elects to take hounds home, it is his privilege to do so. In countries where valuable stock (for example, blood horses) are pastured, or where particular attention is paid to the shooting, a master should have a clear understanding with landowners as to what might be considered detrimental.

Meets should be held punctually, and should be regarded most seriously. Nothing but the most extraordinary circumstances or weather should warrant the abandonment of an advertised meet or the change of its venue. Should such an emergency arise, every possible effort should be made to notify any and all who may be interested; in addition, someone should be at the appointed place of meeting to inform any who may come there. Nothing creates greater lack of confidence in a hunt organization than missing hounds owing to negligence of the hunt.

A master wishing to resign should notify the hunt committee sufficiently early to give the country opportunity of securing the services of the best candidate available; it is also only fair to the hunt servants that they should be given a proper chance to make future arrangements.

HOUNDS AND HUNTING

Where the hounds belong to a club or trustees, having either been purchased by, or presented to, the hunt, an incoming master takes over a certain number, and he is morally bound to leave the same number on his retirement.

A master eager to improve conditions in his country should keep his hunt committee as personally interested and informed as possible, so that when necessity arises the members may be in touch with the *status quo*.

A map of any hunt country, having the location of meets carefully designated thereon, is most valuable. Such a map may be divided into sections, and so far as possible definite days designated for hunting them; for example, let the westerly section be hunted on a Monday, the easterly section on a Wednesday, so that the one-day-a-week man, if he lives in the Monday country, may make his arrangements accordingly and keep that day open for sport.

Interested individuals in each section, may be appointed to act in the interest of the hunt, keeping the master informed of conditions in their section, and holding themselves ready to coöperate with him when necessary.

A master should, *ad infinitum*, attempt in the following order of precedence to make the hunting popular with all in his community: evolve a fencing and paneling system; have a plentiful supply of foxes; improve the pack in ability and appearance; finally, indulge in the luxury of perfect horses and perfect equipment for his hunt staff.

Through the ages, human relations have evolved certain customs and manners, or unwritten laws; so, in organized riding to hounds, an unwritten code has developed for the relationships between hunts, the salient points of which may well be reviewed.

It is obvious that where damage to fences and agriculture may occur from riding horses over a country, one organization only should hunt, and thus be responsible for damage in a given district. This custom exists and is regulated, both in Britain and America, by having certain boundaries recognized and registered with the Masters of Foxhounds Associations. Taking precedent from Britain, the hunting of other packs (say, beagles or harriers) in any such countries may properly be done only by courtesy of the recognized local master of foxhounds.

A fox found in a hunt's own country may be followed anywhere beyond its boundaries.

Should a pack run a fox to ground in a neighboring country, he should under no circumstances be dug out; but it is permissible to get him out by the following means: the pack's own terrier may be used, the fox may be drowned out, twisted out, poked out with a pole, or smoked out. If there is more than one fox in the earth, only one of them is fair game.

If a pack should run a fox into a neighboring country and, apparently losing him, turn to go back within their own boundaries, and a fox is viewed near where hounds lost, it is quite correct to hunt that fox, as it is not possible to say that the viewed fox was not the hunted fox which had lain down; but, where a pack has moved off a mile or two from where the fox was lost, and information came to hand of a fox having been viewed, such a fox should not be hunted, for it could hardly be considered the hunted quarry. Lacking definite evidence, such a situation, however, must be left to the sportsmanlike instincts of masters and huntsmen. In cubhunting, hounds should be kept as much as possible within their own country.

As regards neutral areas, an exact understanding should be had between the hunt committees interested. As to the moving of cubs from near the boundary of another hunt, this should not be done, unless a master is in complete accord with the neighboring master, as the latter may have a covert close by where he expects these cubs to kennel.

When going out with a pack of hounds which are maintained by its master in a first-class manner, the question of dress should be given due consideration. That the subject may be thoroughly understood, I shall enlarge to some extent on the development of hunting dress, daring to express my sentiments, even though such famous writers as Xenophon have made suggestions on this subject for over two thousand years.

The wearing of special hunt uniforms is an ancient custom from which certain precedents have developed conventions of dress that lend dignity to the chase, and have now become generally *de rigueur*.

As long as Americans elect to turn out with an organized pack of hounds after the conventional English manner, it is perhaps well that they should know something about the evolution of hunting clothes as now worn.

There are very patent reasons why color should be worn by the hunt staff and principal members of any hunt; for example, they can be seen better, which is ofttimes useful for various reasons. The hard velvet caps worn by the hunt staff indicate to any observer their positions of responsibility.

Tradition has much to do with the wearing of color, but, aside from tradition, the pageantry of hunting should not be overlooked, for, if the picture can be made delightful to the eye, it may give keen pleasure to many people.

In France, as far back as the twelfth century, there appears to have been special clothing used for hunting, and grey seems to have been the customary color at that time. In the thirteenth century, we have in the romance of Partonopeus de Blois a detailed description of a hunting uniform, the colors being green and grey, a belt of Irish leather, an ivory horn, and spurs of gold and silver.

In his fourteenth century manuscript, Gaston Phœbus refers to uniforms of green for stag hunting, and grey for boar hunting. These uniforms appear

HOUNDS AND HUNTING

in the illuminations of the manuscript, and are highly ornamented, as are the trappings of the horses. In 1316, Philippe le Bon is described as being dressed for hunting in forest green. In *Canterbury Tales*, Chaucer describes a yeoman's hunting dress:

> *And he was clad in cote and hood of grene;*
> . . . .
> *An horn he bar, the bawdrik was of grene.*

Uniforms of this color seem to have been general from this date up to the sixteenth century. In the late fourteenth century, during the reign of Charles V, the royal hunt uniform of France was green. Certain Flemish tapestries, after the pictures of Van Orley, represent the de Guise huntsmen wearing livery of all colors, striped in a bizarre manner. In *Sir Gawayne and the Green Knight*, the following description appears:

> *His blue robes trail to ground right as they should,*
> *Brave is his furred surcoat and noble hangs his hood.*

An ordinance of 1427 indicates that the hunt servants of Phillipe le Bon wore livery all in the same color, by the wishes of the king. The hunt servants of the duc d'Orléans, afterwards Louis XII, wore yellow.

In the sixteenth century, Henry IV of France went hunting in a red cloak. This is, perhaps the earliest mention of red for a hunt uniform. In the memoirs of Fleuranges, 1525, it is shown that the hunt staff livery of Francois I was of traditional green.

In the seventeenth century, the livery of the duc de Maine was of red and gold.

In the early eighteenth century, the hunt of the prince de Conti wore yellow broadcloth, trimmed with silver and blue velvet. Scarlet was the royal style, when Louis XV made his famous entry into Parliament in hunt uniform, with red doublet, grey hat, and great boots. About the same time, the livery of the duc d'Orléans was of scarlet, blue and silver. *Circa* 1740, the French royal hunt uniform, according to the beautiful pictures of Van der Meulen and d'Oudry, consisted of doublet of turquoise blue, lined with red, trimmed with gold and silver; and this was the uniform worn down to the time of the Revolution. Under Louis XVI, the illustrious Chateaubriand relates that when he hunted with the king, in February, 1787, he wore a grey coat, which was the required uniform of novices (debutants) in the sport.

Of hunt uniforms under the First Empire, when the forms and uniforms of court life were being revived, Ludwig relates:

After hours of deliberation, it is possible to decide what colors the Empress and the highnesses (Napoleon's relatives) must wear when they go out hunting.

RIDING TO HOUNDS

Up to the nineteenth century, a great variety of colors was used in the general dress of men, and many hunts in Britain which adopted divers gay-colored uniforms more than a hundred years ago, have never changed them. Although the wearing of scarlet is generally foxhunting color, tradition is so strong in Britain that in some cases the wearing of forest green (the color of the ancient huntsman) still persists. The hunt servants of the Duke of Beaufort's foxhounds still wear green as they did when the pack hunted stag far back in the eighteenth century; the members of the field with the ducal pack wear blue, the reason for which was recently kindly explained to me by the present Duke. More than a hundred years ago, the Beaufort household livery was blue with yellow facings. This livery was worn on all state and public occasions, including racing and hunting. Little by little the privilege of wearing the blue and buff coat was given to relatives and friends, and is to-day extended solely by the Duke of Beaufort to regular followers of his hounds.

Blue appears to have been the uniform of the Royal Buckhounds, as George III (who is said to have ridden 19-stone) often hunted in a light blue coat with black velvet cuffs, tricorne hat, and top boots. After 1786, he is portrayed wearing a cap similar in shape to the modern huntsman's cap. Of the Marchioness of Salisbury, who was master of the Hertfordshire Hunt from 1775 to 1819, it is written:

Clad in a habit of blue, with black collar and cuffs, and with a hunting-cap upon her head, she was the hardest rider in the hunt.

The oldest hunting uniform in common use seems to have been green, possibly because stag hunting was so prevalent in ancient days, when hounds and greyhounds were held in slips in the runways of the deer, and the green color helped to conceal the presence of the huntsmen from the quarry. In 1351, King Jean of France, who had an imposing organization for those days, turned out twenty-eight, all told, in his hunt staff. They were dressed in green in summer and grey in winter, suggestive of camouflage. It was customary for him to uncouple fifty hounds. The green conventional uniform which had so universally been used for stag hunting in earlier days, continued in use for hare hunting when that form of sport began to supersede in large measure the chase of the stag.

Scarlet uniforms came into use with British foxhound packs in the eighteenth century, to distinguish them, no doubt, from harrier packs, which were then more common. At that period, when foxhunting was in the ascendency, and new packs were being formed, scarlet was extensively used in English army uniforms, and, thus, its adoption as a foxhunting uniform color was perhaps only natural. There is one foxhunting pack in America which hunts a country that was overrun by British Redcoats a century and a half ago (and in this region prejudice against redcoats still exists), so this hunt

HOUNDS AND HUNTING

adopted green for its uniform. There are, of course, exceptions to all rules, and in choosing a hunt uniform color, common sense should be applied. However erudite one may be as to the reasons for scarlet being a popular hunting color, one must always defer to the point of view of John Jorrocks, Esq., M. F. H.,—"but for which many would never hunt."

As far as America is concerned, scarlet is the usual color for foxhunting uniforms; but there are uniforms of other colors,—notably blue, grey, green. Probably the first prescribed uniform for use in America was that adopted in 1774 by the Gloucester Foxhunting Club. It was a dark brown cloth coatee, with lapelled dragoon pockets, white buttons, and frock sleeves, buff waistcoat and breeches, with a black velvet cap. In writing the Memoirs of George Washington, Custis stated that Washington hunted in a blue coat, scarlet waistcoat, buckskin breeches, top boots, velvet cap, and whip with a long thong.

Tradition seems to have some influence on each item of the hunting uniform. Boots, the progenitors of the modern, smart, soft-legged hunting boot, have been worn for many centuries. In the twelfth century, high boots were worn with golden spurs—

Heuses chausciees et esperons d'or fin.

Also, as far back as the fourteenth century, de Fouilloux mentions "great, high boots." He further mentions that the boots "should come up over the knee and be attached with straps to keep water, leaves, insects, and other things from falling down inside the legs." This is the first mention of the boot garter. Two hundred years ago, boots were of soft leather, and worn very loose with the tops turned down. The relic of this turned-down top still exists in the pink, or brown, tops used with scarlet uniforms. In the eighteenth century, they became more like modern boots, but were still so loose-fitting and soft that they had to be held up by a strap over the knee, which strap is represented to-day by the garter used below the knee, and without the use of which no boot looks properly finished.

Breeches were, of course, worn in the eighteenth century, and their use has never lapsed in Britain; hence, the art of making them was never lost in that country. In America, from the early part of the nineteenth century until quite recent years, breeches were entirely unknown. Even in the American cavalry, trousers were worn thrust into boot-tops, or with a strap under the boot. The difference between breeches and trousers is still a little indefinite in the minds of some Americans: even the tailors, in many instances, are so uninformed that they sometimes crease breeches down the middle of the leg as they would do with "pants." Tradition is useful, even in the tailor's art! How many tailors know that the buttons on the back of a frock coat were once used to button back the long embroidered coat tails while riding?

RIDING TO HOUNDS

According to de Maricourt, writing in the time of Louis XIV, hats were equipped with a cord braided by the huntsman from the hair of his ladylove, with silk of a color selected by her, the use of which was to hold the hat if it fell off. Apparently, this is the first mention of a hat guard. The modern hard huntsman's cap is an adaptation of the jockey caps which came into use in the eighteenth century. These caps were kept on the head by a ribbon tied with a bow, which is suggested today by the bow on the back of hunting caps, now worn purely as an ornament, pendant ends indicating professional hunt servants.

Possibly enough has been said to thoroughly illustrate the evolution and antecedents of twentieth century hunting dress, and to give a broad idea of the reasons why certain clothing for the chase is sanctioned by custom.

Some emigré returning from the Island of Juan Fernandez may hope to find in these pages a series of detailed directions as to how to turn himself out, or what the ladies should wear when hunting; but, in such necessity, a study of the English illustrated sporting press is recommended. This study should be a careful one, with later recourse to the best English bootmakers and other outfitters. One should not wander from the narrow path. The best equipment possible will be useless, however, unless properly taken care of and correctly worn.

In America, due to the heat of early autumn, it is wise to make certain deviations from hard and fast rules. In this connection, something must be said anent the so-called cubbing season, which is a misnomer under American conditions, as explained in Chapter VI.

Since the American master is confronted with a trying climate, in the late summer months it is always advisable to turn out even at 5 A.M. in clothing of tropical weight. For some years, my hunt staff used white linen coats, white breeches, regular hunting caps, and black topped boots. At one time, the use of white helmets was tried; but they are quite useless, on account of the noise made by the wind striking the brim, preventing one from hearing hounds well. White coats can be easily seen in leafy woodlands, and are comfortable. After the regular hunting season begins, even in October, it is often too uncomfortably hot to wear the regulation scarlet hunt coats which are so practicable in England. Special light-weight scarlet coats made of dress coat material are useful for such warm weather.

Nothing can be so incongruous as inattention to details. Few would think of wearing brown boots to a ball, but I have actually seen brown polo boots worn without garters and spurs in combination with a scarlet coat.

One sees other odd sights now and then in the field; hunt servants in filthy livery, unpolished buttons and boots (signs of honorable wear are permissible, but not indications of sloth); sportsmen in un-cared-for toppers, hard hats too small, soft hats remindful of the rodeo, and hatless riders (unworkmanlike, and unsafe in case of striking branches or in falling); spurs worn upside down, or dangling loosely from the heel, spurs with chains, *à la grande armée;* stoutish ladies with limbs of uncertain dimensions encased in "sewer pipe" (stiff) boots, and baggy breeches, with buttons on the side reminding one of old-time pantaloons; whip handles without thongs, often held upside down; boots without garters; unpinned stock ties; coatless riders (again, unworkmanlike and impracticable. It is positively dangerous to be coatless, if one is to be out several hours with hounds in hot weather, as one may become heated, and then cool off). One of the outré "fads" is the sleeveless riding coat, sometimes worn by women at summer resorts and recommended by "expert" salesladies in department stores who have never seen a smartly turned-out woman on a horse. *De gustibus non est disputandum.*

Comments of this kind would, perhaps, be unnecessary in any country other than America, but for some strange reason there appear to be people in these United States who, on most occasions, dress appropriately, but when riding array themselves (may it be said, *dis*array themselves?) in unique manner. Frequently, not only will their clothes be inappropriate, but, what is worse, they will be unworkmanlike, and to appear unworkmanlike in one's sporting clothes is inexcusable; or, to quote Whyte Melville in *Riding Recollections*, "To be correctly dressed is a compliment to society."

If a pack of hounds is to be turned out by a master with English equipment, and in the most approved manner possible, with consideration for every detail—hounds fit, horses fit and well done, saddlery spotlessly clean, and livery *ditto*—if this is the standard expected, then anyone not suitably turned out who hunts with such an organization is certainly failing to do his part to keep up the standard of the whole. If he is at all a prominent person, he is doing much to spoil the morale of the hunt staff, and will bring ridicule on himself; in fact, any member of the field, if not suitably dressed under such circumstances should be considered a *persona non grata*, as he would be were he to attend a formal evening function in street attire.

In Wyoming, I have had great pleasure in hunting in a stock saddle, dressed in chaps and flannel shirt, and riding an ungroomed, unshod pony in true western fashion; but such is the custom of that region!

Precedent and reason have, in many instances, created standards of what is done and what is not done. For example, when I say "suitably dressed," I do not mean fancifully dressed or necessarily turned out in scarlet. Nevertheless, the wearing of a hunt uniform when one has been invited to do so by the master of a creditably equipped pack should be taken as a matter of course, and not regarded as an affectation. The question sometimes arises as to whether one who has the privilege of wearing scarlet with his own pack should wear scarlet or black when visiting another pack. This question of etiquette is difficult to answer, depending, as it does, on the circumstances.

RIDING TO HOUNDS

But, in hunting, as in other sartorial attire, a gentleman is better underdressed than overdressed. If in doubt, therefore, always wear black. By keeping to quiet, conventional standards, one can never be wrong, provided that each item of clothing from hat to spurs is right. Do not try to improve on adopted English custom, with years of precedent behind it.

Est modus in rebus.

CHAPTER X.

HUNT COUNTRIES AND QUARRY

TO an American who has never been to England or Ireland, it is nearly impossible to describe a good hunt country, because there exists nothing comparable in North America. The best way to explain the natural hunting facilities in Britain is to call attention to the ancient and modern English hunting pictures, especially the series depicting famous localities which have been so ably portrayed by Lionel Edwards and Cecil Aldin.

In visualizing the possibilities of a hunt country anywhere, one must always estimate the available area, its fox-holding properties, the inevitable wire question, and the ridable assets of its topography,—whether it is too hilly, too rough, or too boggy for horses to follow hounds, the percentage of woodland to open fields, the percentage of grass to plow, and the percentage of wheat and rye (riding on which is taboo both in England and America). There is no country in America which can compare favorably with the average British hunt country, typical descriptions of which, picked at random from *Baily's Hunting Directory*, read as follows:

North Cotswold. The country, which covers some 250 sq. miles, lies in Gloucestershire and Worcestershire. On the N. it adjoins the Warwickshire; on the W. the Croome; on the S. the Cotswold, and on the E. the Heythrop. In the hill district walls are the only fences; in the vale country, Leicestershire fences. About 40 per cent. of the whole is pasture, the remainder equal parts of plough and woodland. Wire is almost unknown in the season, as the occupiers are extremely fond of hunting, and remove it before November 1st. A small well-bred horse is best for the hills, and a bold powerful horse for the very strongly fenced vale.

Of the Cottesmore it is written: *The country, which lies in Leicestershire and Rutland, is about 18 miles N. to S. and 22 miles E. to W. On the N. and E. it adjoins the Belvoir; on the W. the Quorn and Mr. Fernie's, and on the S. the Fitzwilliam. The fences vary; posts and rails and blackthorn hedge in the smooth pastures of the Oakham district; very big and formidable fences on the Leicestershire side, where are steep ascents and descents; blackthorn hedges and walls on the plough in the E., where also are large woodlands. Wire practically* nil. *There is a scent in all weathers. The best horse bred is indispensable for the Leicester-*

HUNT COUNTRIES AND QUARRY

shire side and the Oakham country; a stout one on short legs for the eastern side. . . . The first records appear to be of hounds being taken down by road from Lowther (Westmoreland) by Viscount Lowther for the purpose of hunting the Cottesmore country, 1666–70.

Agricultural England reflects in its well-kept appearance the age-long loving care of landed proprietors for the beauty of their estates, and superior standards of farm maintenance; hence, a condition naturally exists which can hardly be expected in those parts of America which were forest wildernesses only a few generations ago. Moreover, pride in the traditions of the sport is so universally ingrained in the British soul that it is the most natural thing in the world for hunting to receive the loyal support of all classes. A reflection of this condition is the interest shown at meets of English packs, a typical sample of which is recorded in the diary of the author under date of November 14, 1921:

Kirby Gate is the famous 'opening' meeting place of the Quorn, and people come in crowds from Leicester, Melton, and other towns to see this sight—perhaps a thousand people gathered on foot or 'bikes,' in motors, and charabancs to see the show. The bitch pack graced the occasion—twenty couple, symmetrical, but not as even in color as some packs. To-day the first draw was a thick covert about six or eight acres in extent, on the eastern side of a hill with a bare top (like Round Hill, at Greenwich, Connecticut). Hundreds of spectators stood on the hill. The hounds, master and field, trotted out from Kirby Gate about two and one-half miles. It looked like a cavalry regiment hundreds strong—most of the men and women in toppers and black coats. Hounds were thrown in one end of the wood. The field largely remained at one end. Among the hundreds on the hill were Clara, the Sanfords, Hopping and myself. No sound except the huntsmen in cover. Suddenly, the first whip at the far end halloaed, and away we went, Clara and myself among the first few. We reached the crest of the hill; below us spread a most beautiful country with fox, hounds and riders streaming across it.

Another splendid proof of much that is fundamentally behind English hunting to-day is a second entry in the author's diary:

November 3, 1921. The Blankney. Last night we arrived at Scopwick House to visit Lieutenant-Colonel Vernon Willey, M.P.—a real 'live wire' who used to play polo at Narragansett. He went to Gallipoli as Lieutenant-Colonel of Yeomanry; was later wool controller of England; is now M.P. for Bradford, M.F.H., plays polo, steeplechases, shoots, etc. Colonel Willey took over the Blankney just after the war, during the latter part of which a sporting farmer named Spencer had acted as huntsman, and kept the show going. The Blankney hounds are a picture, and the pack in beautiful condition of coat.

The meet to-day was at Blankney Hall, seat of Lord Londesborough, a typical Victorian house—surrounded by beautiful green lawns and wonderful trees. Blankney is only a tiny village, but a crowd of several hundred gathered for the

HOUNDS AND HUNTING

meet, and although it began to rain no one paid any attention to that—all stood about and looked critically at hounds and horses and did much talking. The 'meet' was set for eleven, at which time appeared the hounds and hunt staff very well mounted on blood horses, all looking very smart and fit. Sandwiches, with port and other drinks were passed around to all the assembly, and about 11.15 the master gave the word to draw. We trotted slowly off across the park over the most delightful grass imaginable.

In Chapter I, a word-picture of a typical English hunt has been given, but to more clearly inform the layman about the wonders of British countries from a hunting point of view, it may be well to further state that the average hunt country suggests the well-kept appearance of a golf course; all winter the grass stays green; there are practically no rough spots, few holes, and in most countries rarely does one see a rock; a large percentage of the hedges and stone walls are well kept, and, after November, ditches are comparatively free from blindness; there are few post-and-rail fences, no worm or snake fences, and, from observation of scores of countries in Britain, the author has never seen a plank fence. Miracle of miracles! almost every gate can be opened from a horse's back, and closes and latches of its own weight, while there is hardly a gate in any American country I have ever seen that can be opened or shut without super-efforts, and to even move them one must frequently dismount.

There are British countries that have a fair percentage of plowed land; but, in Leicestershire, at least, there is perhaps less than ten percent of plow. Nowhere are woodlands extensive, and the coverts where foxes are found usually contain but a few acres, which are jealously guarded for their fox-holding properties. These may be of small woods, or consist of gorse or privet bushes. A famous example of such a covert is Ranksborough Gorse in the Cottesmore country. A fox leaving this covert must travel straight away several miles before he can find natural cover of any size other than hedges and ditches. One may stand on the grassy pasture land of Ranksborough ridge and view the fox that is driven out of the thick, prickly covert by hounds, then watch the hunt streaming away for miles across beautiful open country, spreading out like a panorama below—an unforgettable memory picture.

> *Oh, glory of youth! consolation of age!*
> *Sublimest of ecstasies under the sun;*
> *Though the veteran may linger too long on the stage,*
> *Yet he'll drink a last toast to a foxhunting run;*
> *And oh! young descendants of ancient top-sawyers!*
> *By your lives to the world their example enforce;*
> *Whether landlords, or parsons, or statesmen, or lawyers,*
> *Ride straight as they rode it from Ranksboro' Gorse.*

HUNT COUNTRIES AND QUARRY

Though a rough-riding world may bespatter your breeches,
Though sorrow may cross you, or slander revile,
Though you plunge overhead in misfortune's blind ditches,
Shun the gap of deception, the hand-gate of guile:
Oh, avoid them! for there, see the crowd is contending,
Ignoble the object—ill-mannered the throng;
Shun the miry lane, falsehood, with turns never ending,
Ride straight for truth's timber, no matter how strong.

I'll pound you safe over! Sit steady and quiet;
Along the sound headland of honesty steer;
Beware of false halloas and juvenile riot,
Though the oxer of duty be wide, never fear!
And when the run's over of earthly existence,
And you get safe to ground, you will fear no remorse,
If you ride it—no matter what line or what distance—
As straight as your fathers from Ranksboro' Gorse.

Even in Sir Edward Curre's Welsh country—which from the English point of view is very rough and hilly,—the coverts are clean edged, and a fox viewed away can be seen for a long distance as he crosses the green pastures. Hilly and rough as this country may seem to a Britisher, it would be considered a huntsman's paradise if it were on the western shores of the Atlantic Ocean.

In England, the typical jumping is over hedges with a ditch on one side, or both sides, sometimes having in addition single, or double, oxers—which pleasant (?) device is a low rail to keep cattle out of the ditches flanking the hedge; hence, English jumping is broad rather than high, so a horse must be schooled quite differently than for America, and ridden in a different manner.

The most common type of hedge in England is made from a quick-growing thorn bush, which formerly was protected with rails for a few years after planting, but now that rails are scarce and labor high, wire is commonly used where hedges need strengthening. After the hedge grows to a certain height and strength, stakes are driven in the ground, the tallest and strongest shoots are bent down and woven through the stakes. As the hedge grows older and the shoots grow taller and stronger, they are frequently partially cut through with a pruning knife, and woven horizontally through the hedge, making what is known as a "cut-and-laid," *vide* Masefield:

> *. . . then Robin made*
> *Pip go crash thru the cut-and-laid.*

It must not be assumed, however, that such hedges can be brushed

HOUNDS AND HUNTING

through, because if a horse pecks hard enough on the entwined binders, he may land in the far ditch, or be turned over by the far oxer, if any exists. To quote again from Davenport's beautiful and descriptive poem:

> *Oh! gently, my young one; the fence we are nearing*
> *Is leaning towards us—'tis hairy and black,*
> *The binders are strong, and necessitates clearing,*
> *Or the wide ditch beyond will find room for your back.*

Especially before the war, on a well-kept English estate, the hedges were constantly trimmed; but, in such instances where trimming has not been done for years, they have grown up into tall, thorny barriers known as "bullfinches," which are, indeed, unpleasant obstacles to encounter.

> *He grasped these things in one swift look*
> *Then dived into the bullfinch heart*
> *Through thorns that ripped his sleeves apart*
> *And skutched new blood upon his brow.*

In certain areas of England, such as the country hunted by the High Peak harriers in Derbyshire, near Haddon Hall, the Cotswold in Worcestershire, and that part of the Duke of Beaufort's country which is in Gloucestershire, there is a large percentage of stone walls. The stones are mostly flat, and laid up without mortar, similar to many walls in Virginia and Kentucky. Several Irish countries, also,—notably, the Galway country,—have a large proportion of such walls. In the country of the Galway "Blazers," the walls are high, running up to five feet, and many of the fields are so small that the most ardent hunt-to-jump enthusiast can easily have more than his fill of "lepping."

Water jumps are frequently met with in England and Ireland and are from a few feet to a few yards wide; the banks are generally clean, but one must be able to sense where they are strong, for if a horse takes off from a rotten edge, he is almost bound to land in the stream bottom which is usually deep and muddy. Perhaps the most famous water jump in England is often encountered when a fox goes away from Ranksborough Gorse, the description of which is best left to Davenport's inimitable picture:

> *. . . Now far down the pastures*
> *Of Ashwell the willows betoken the line*
> *Of the dull-flowing stream of historic disasters;*
> *We must face, my bold young one, the dread Whissendine!*
> *No shallow-dug pan with a hurdle to screen it,*
> *That cock-tail imposture the steeplechase brook;*
> *But the steep broken banks tell us plain, if we mean it,*
> *The less we shall like it the longer we look.*

HUNT COUNTRIES AND QUARRY

Then steady, my young one, my place I've selected,
Above the dwarf willow, 'tis sound I'll be bail,
With your muscular quarters beneath you collected,
Prepare for a rush like the 'limited mail.'

Oh! now let me know the full worth of your breeding
Brave son of Belzoni, be true to your sires,
Sustain old traditions—remember you're leading
The cream of the cream in the shire of the shires!
With a quick shortened stride as the distance you measure,
With a crack of the nostril and cock of the ear,
And a rocketing bound, and we're over, my treasure,
Twice nine feet of water, and landed all clear!

What! four of us only? Are these the survivors
Of all that rode gaily from Ranksboro's ridge?
I hear the faint splash of a few hardy divers,
The rest are in hopeless research of a bridge;
Vae Victis! the way of the world and the winner!
Do we ne'er ride away from a friend in distress?
Alas! we are anti-Samaritan sinners,
And streaming past Stapleford, onward, we press.

Another realistic picture of the tragedies attending water jumping is vividly described by Masefield:

> *And there before them ran the grey*
> *Yell Water, swirling as it ran,*
> *The Yell Brook of the hunting man.*
> *The hunters eyed it and were grim,*
> *. . . they could see*
> *(Each man) his pollard willow tree*
> *Firming the bank, they felt their horses*
> *Catch the gleam's hint and gather forces;*
> *They heard the men behind draw near.*
> *Each horse was trembling as a spear*
> *Trembles in hand when tense to hurl,*
> *They saw the brimmed brook's eddies curl.*
> *The willow-roots like water-snakes;*
> *The beaten holes the ratten makes,*
> *They heard the water's rush; they heard*
> *Hugh Colway's mare come like a bird;*

HOUNDS AND HUNTING

A faint cry from the hounds ahead,
Then saddle-strain, the bright hooves' tread,
Quick words, the splash of mud, the launch,
The sick hope that the bank be staunch,
Then Souse, with Souse to left and right.
Maroon across, Sir Peter's white
Down but pulled up, Tom over, Hugh
Mud to the hat but over, too,
Well splashed by Squire who was in.
With draggled pink struck close to skin,
The Squire leaned from bank and hauled
His mired horse's rein; he bawled
For help from each man racing by.
'What, help you pull him out? Not I.
What made you pull him in?' they said.

In Ireland, there is a certain proportion of hedges, especially in countries such as the Duhallow, near Cork; but the typical enclosure is, of course, the Irish bank. This is a formidable-looking obstacle to one who is unused to it, especially the bank found in Tipperary and Meath. Ireland apparently never had much timber for fencing, and doubtless at one time there was much surplus labor, or, probably, the Irish banks never would have been brought into existence. They are not only enclosures, but the ditches which usually flank them help to drain land that might otherwise be too wet for agricultural purposes. The surest way for a novice to cross an Irish country is to ride an Irish horse, and leave it to the horse, which has been used to this particular game—scrambling over the gaps in the banks—from colthood, and perhaps later ridden bareback by some gossoon with more enthusiasm than discretion.

A typical Irish bank is anywhere from four to seven feet high, frequently several feet wide at the top. It has a deep ditch filled with muddy water on one or both sides, and often a hairy hedge on the top which may or may not contain a gap. The sides of the bank are quite steep, but are usually covered with luxurious strong sod, except those which, as a diversion from the commonplace, are stone faced. Woe betide the ambitious Nimrod who attempts an Irish bank on which the sides and top are not firm. Such a bank is known as "rotten," and frequently precipitates the unwary horseman into the yawning Slough of Despond before or behind him.

A big, strong bank is better to jump than a little one, as a horse properly "in the know" will jump onto the bank, scramble to the top, change legs, slide part way down the opposite side, and pop over the ensuing ditch; while in the case of a small, clean bank, he might come to grief in a hurry. This was

The *Allées* of the Forest of Chantilly—A Typical French Hunting Forest.

Typical English Hunting Country—large fields, well-kept hedges, and clean, rolling grass land.

Mrs. Thomas on the Thoroughbred Mare *Pipe Dream*,
negotiating a Virginia stone wall.

The Snake or Worm Fence with Stakes and Riders. *Commodore Gaunt*,
a perfect ladies' thoroughbred hunter carrying
Mrs. Thomas in proper form.

once aptly pointed out to me by that famous character, P— D— of Dublin, who, in describing a local hunt point-to-point, in 1926, said to me: "Sure, th' banks was too shmall; they wint too fast an' thried to jump thim in their sthride; three horses an' one man was kilt. Begor', me darter was ridin' in the race, an' if her horse hadn't run away, she'd have bin kilt, too."

There was once a man who went to Ireland for a rest cure. According to that clever authoress Dorothea Conyers, he fell in love, and was inveigled onto a horse; he began to think hunting was a tranquil pursuit, when

'Tally ho!' yelled voices from the gorse. 'Go—on—away . . . !' screeched someone else, and the whole world appeared to go mad. . . . He was content to gallop on until he saw an unbroken line of green bank in front, and then he decided to go back to the road through the fields he had come to, and jog along to see what happened. He was much impressed by all the excitement, had even shouted a little himself, crying joyously that the dogs had found the trail; but he had no intention of going on. He pulled at the reins to get around, and—found he was mistaken; Blackbird, who had gone easily when her bridle was slack, took this as a sign to take hold and quicken her pace, and did both immediately. The thing upon her strong back rocked and bumped strangely, but she meant to carry it as near hounds as possible. The mare had a mouth like iron when she chose. Acland found that he could in a manner guide her, but she did not mean to stop; she dashed on, straight for that high bank, while his heart pumped like a steam piston, and he used exceedingly bad language. It rose, high and unbending; his endeavours to turn were now frustrated by horses to right and left, heels in front went up in a sickening fashion, another horse rolled back.

'Great God!' said Alexander Acland, with whimpering wrath, 'and I must jump it. I must. He wreathed his hands in the mane. 'Great—— Oh-h!'

Blackbird dropped to a trot, crouched on her powerful quarters, and rose. Acland rose with her, gripping the mane as the good mare lighted on the bank; next moment, with a sensation of being kicked into the next world they went off. He lost both stirrups in the downward swoop, and grovelled on the beast's neck, praying for help. She shook him back, and strode away, until, with a certain sense of elation, Acland realized that the fence lay behind and he was still upon the back of the animal which had jumped it; moreover, that he was very close to the flying pack.

It is not difficult to understand that with such necessity for so much jumping up, balancing, changing legs, and jumping down, a particular type of horse has been developed in Ireland especially suitable, by virtue of good shoulders and strength of loin and hocks, to meet the requirements of the country. Hence, in Ireland, a horse which on the average is not quite so quick as the thoroughbred horse, yet one that has plenty of blood seems to suit most people best; although the greatest horses are said to be thoroughbred in this game as in most others.

[177]

HOUNDS AND HUNTING

One must not entertain the belief that England and Ireland are without some drawbacks, for although in each country hunting is infrequently stopped by frost, there is much wet weather, and the going at times becomes frightfully deep. During the past few years many countries have had their hunting stopped for brief periods to avoid contagion from the dread foot-and-mouth cattle disease; also, since the war, wire has in many sections become a menace. With the agricultural depression and the high-priced farm labor, a strand of barbed wire is the quickest and cheapest means of repairing broken fencing. Herculean efforts are made by the hunting organizations in Britain to combat the use of wire, and untold sums are spent each year, with the sporting coöperation of farmers, to remove it during the hunting season, even though it has to be replaced in the spring.

As to the use of wire, it does not seem to be generally understood by many people either in England or America that it is the quickest and most efficient means the farmer has of keeping live stock within bounds. Almost universally to-day farms are undermanned, and nothing is so wasteful of time to the generally harassed farmer as searching for lost animals which have escaped through inefficient fencing. Even on fairly well-fenced farms, certain animals have a predisposition to jump almost anything, and no one would ask why farmers use wire (as if it were being done purposely to spoil sport) if they themselves had to spend dreary hours trudging about a country looking for stray stock.

British hunts are marvelously well run, and British hunt countries are splendidly managed. Previous to the days of financial stringency caused by the war, there were more packs than at present, which were owned and largely supported by individuals. Even to-day there are but few "hunt clubs," as known in America, but each hunt country, as a rule, has a self-perpetuating "committee," composed of prominent landholders, who run the country as a supreme oligarchy. As a result of this system of benevolent despotism, the great packs of early days were developed. Precedent and custom are so strong, experience has taught so much, and so many people are vitally interested, that there is little opportunity for matters in this well-worn path to go radically wrong,—in fact, much that is best in the tradition of the sport, with its unwritten laws, regulates as if with strictest discipline what "is" and what "is not done." When a master is appointed by a hunt committee, he has tremendous prestige behind him, and, consequently, can work in an untrammeled manner to maintain the sport. As a rule, a hunt committee guarantees a definite subscription obtained from local supporters of hounds, according to their means and interest in the sport, and from hunting visitors who are expected to pay a "cap" of so much per horse per day when they hunt. An understanding is arrived at with an incoming master as to how much he personally is to supply, whether in funds, horses, or hounds.

HUNT COUNTRIES AND QUARRY

This marvelous system of hunt organization is the direct result of British continuity of policy intelligently handed down, in many instances from father to son through numerous generations. It is, indeed, a lesson that should be seriously taken to heart in America, if riding to hounds is to progress and hunting countries are to be developed and improved.

In France, the fairly numerous packs are almost invariably owned privately. They are located in widely separated parts of the country, and although revolutions, wars, and financial upheavals of the past hundred years have made continuity of breeding difficult, nevertheless, keen enthusiasm for the true art and practice of venery in the ancient sense has not been suppressed. French hunting is largely in forests where the hunting rights are leased from the government. These forests are often extensive, but cannot be likened to American woodlands, as the rides are broad, cut straight from "round points," like the avenues radiating from the Arc de Triomphe, in Paris, and in these rides one may gallop at speed. Game and hounds can be seen crossing, and in large measure it is possible to see through the forest as much of the underbrush is kept trimmed from the local necessity of using fagots for fuel. The origin of this marvelous system of rides is very ancient, and doubtless was inaugurated in the royal forests, in order to facilitate the hunting pleasure of the kings. These wide, straight rides, carpeted with green grass, form excellent fire protection, and are marvelously beautiful to behold, especially when shadows formed by the filtering sunlight add variation to the intriguing vistas. As one canters along, pheasants, rabbits, hare, and perhaps a distant stag, or roe-deer, can be seen.

Although such forestry in America would be of much economic and aesthetic value and very useful, especially in hunting countries, it is nowhere done, except in the Overhills country, where it has proved its value.

At this juncture, it might be well to outline the general features of those American countries where riding to hounds with packs is at all possible. There is unquestionably a vastly increasing interest in the sport in America, but, largely on account of the advent of wire and the disappearance of rail fencing, due to economic causes, less natural hunting country remains available each year. Under the circumstances, the only possibility in many localities is drag hunting. Where sufficient enthusiasm exists, however, artificial development of a foxhunting country by means of panels may be possible, but only through a deliberate policy intelligently pursued, and at great expense. It may be well to explain to our uninitiated *confrères* beyond the seas —where I believe the practice is entirely unknown—that a panel is an artificial jump built in a wire fence, and has numerous forms, as will be explained anon.

The earliest reference to wire being detrimental to hunting was in connection with an accident to one of the whippers-in of the Pytchley country,

HOUNDS AND HUNTING

I believe, sixty or seventy years ago; but the general use of wire in England has increased very slowly. In America, however, during the past fifty years, its use for fencing has entirely superseded in many localities the original split-rail fencing, which cost nothing except time and energy on the part of the farmer or his (then) generally numerous sons.

In a country which had to be cleared of trees before it could be plowed or used for pasture, the use of split-rail fencing was originally, of course, quite natural. It was the one way of disposing of the trees, except by fire. In many localities there was no market for timber, and even trees now valuable for expensive veneers, such as black walnut, were hewn into rails. Such fencing would have, in many cases, long ago disappeared, were it not for the lasting properties of certain timber. I know of an instance in Rappahannock County, Virginia, where chestnut rails on a farm owned from father to son for several generations are known to have been in certain fences for over a hundred years. They are still quite strong, although the work of the elements has gradually worn away the outside, until they have been reduced in size. Unfortunately, the chestnut blight which started on Long Island some fifteen years ago, has killed every chestnut tree on the entire Eastern Seaboard, and no other variety of tree—not even oak—which is available and splits properly, lasts as long; hence, the use of the rail fence as an economic possibility is now fast disappearing.

On Long Island, the original fencing consisted of two locust posts set side by side; an augur hole was bored through the two posts, and a stout locust peg driven through the holes. In more recent years, this wooden peg was supplanted by an iron rod turned down at the ends. On these pegs, or rods, were placed the stout chestnut rails.

In New Jersey, Pennsylvania, and Maryland, mortised locust or cedar posts were carefully set, with chestnut rails sharpened at the ends, cleverly wedged into the mortised holes. This forms the best and strongest type of post-and-rail fence.

In Virginia, Carolina, and Kentucky, and generally throughout the country as far west as the natural forest line, snake or worm fences were most common. These were made by laying rails alternately on top of each other in zigzag fashion. Two sharpened stakes were driven in the ground opposite the ends of the rails and about two feet from the line of the fence, so that they inclined across the top of the rails forming an "X"; on this "X" was placed a rail known as a "rider," to increase the height and help hold the stakes together. Near Sperryville, Rappahannock County, Virginia, where my young hounds are walked, the average fence of this type is over six feet high, and is, of course, not jumpable except where partial gaps occur. The reason for this enormously high fence is to safely keep in the young cattle, horses, and mules. The farms are very large, and stock getting into a corn (maize) field would be hidden in tall stalks, enabling them to do much damage before they were discovered.

There are stone walls in certain sections of New England, Virginia, and Kentucky, and other localities. In New England, the stones have been rounded by glacial action; in Virginia, they are fairly flat, and heavy projecting cap rocks are used; in Kentucky, the stone walls are often identical with those seen in the Cotswold hills in England, with the cap rocks standing on end. To supplement the height, in Virginia, many stone walls formerly had chestnut stakes and riders, which means that two stakes were driven in the ground opposite each other, inclining against the top of the wall, so as to form an "X." A rail was laid on this "X" forming the "rider," thus increasing the height of a four-foot stone wall by twelve to eighteen inches.

In stock countries, other than dairy countries, most stone walls to-day have one or more strands of barbed wire strung along them on stakes, to increase the efficiency of the fence where the old rail riders have rotted away.

It can be surmised that in a new country like America where naturally there was plenty of land, only the best of it was cleared and the swamps drained; consequently, the remaining woodlands are very large, and in many localities are almost continuous, only interspersed by cleared fields. In certain sections of New York State and New England, agricultural land before the opening of the West by the railroads, was more valuable than it is to-day. Much of this land, once cleared for pasture, now abandoned, has reforested itself, so that one sees amid new forest-growth the original stone walls built by the devoted labor of our forefathers, who doubtless thought they were creating capital out of the wildernesses. In many localities, especially near cities, where modern industrialism pays labor more than can be earned on rough farms, even the fairly good pasture land is rapidly growing up into pseudo-forests; hence, in some hunting countries that I know well, where fifteen years ago there were clean fields, to-day one rarely has unobstructed view for more than half a mile. For the future of riding to hounds in America, this is not a pretty picture, but it is the truth, and may well be taken into consideration by those interested in the maintenance of the sport or ambitious to inaugurate it in localities where it is not already in vogue.

A drag can be laid in a circuitous manner through open fields and over artificial jumps in many overgrown and wired-up countries, but, unfortunately, the wild fox can hardly be taught to run where riders to hounds would like to have him.

Any game that is worth playing at all ought to be worth playing well; hence, it may be advisable to seize the bull, as it were, firmly by the horns, in considering ways and means of making a country ridable where wire, in greater or lesser degree, prevents following of hounds. This procedure has generally become known as paneling, and must be done in every American country. In various localities, different types are used; in the Millbrook country, panels are almost exclusively made of four or five chestnut rails which rest on wire binders, holding two locust posts together; sometimes these panels are four or five rail-lengths in extent, but in many instances the unevenness of terrain makes it impractical to make a panel more than one or two rail-lengths wide.

Millbrook was for years perhaps the best-paneled country in America, and only through the devoted efforts of the master, Oakleigh Thorne, who held the office for nearly a score of years, was riding to hounds made possible in that country. At one time, the extent of paneled territory which was maintained under the supervision of the devoted Hunt secretary, the late D. U. Sloan, was between twenty and thirty thousand acres, and extended the longest way nearly twenty miles. The large Millbrook woodlands had rides cut through them, generally following old wood roads, so that *in toto* they extended up to perhaps one hundred miles. From six to ten men were constantly employed to maintain this paneling and to annually trim the fast-growing underbrush in the rides. It can be surmised that during the period of Mr. Thorne's mastership at least a quarter of a million dollars were spent in this way, without which expenditure there would have been no riding to hounds.

In certain sections of Virginia, what are known as "chicken-coop" panels came into use about twenty years ago. It is not certain who originated the idea, but they were used rather extensively by the late John R. Townsend, when master of the Orange County and Middleburg hunts. Their virtue rests in the fact that a single panel can be made of sixteen-foot boards—the distance between the ordinary posts in a wire fence; also, they can be placed over a wire fence without cutting it. This is done by drawing the staples on two posts, bending down the wire, and placing over it an inverted V-shaped coop made of boards which are fastened together on a framework of 2×4 joists. It is formidable-looking obstacle, although it hardly needs to be four feet high to prevent cattle from jumping it, because it is wide at the bottom, and cattle would have to jump wide as well as high to clear it. This they seem to dislike to do. Ridden horses jump this type of fence well, but from an aesthetic point of view it is anything but beautiful, and compared to a simple bar-way it is expensive. However, where landholders dislike to have their fences cut, it is easy to obtain permission to put up such a panel where ordinary paneling would be impossible.

Gates are sometimes provided in Virginia instead of panels; but, as the custom of the country is to have them five feet or more high, and the action of frost often dislodges the posts on which they are hung, it soon becomes impossible to open them from horseback. Although farmers like to have new

HUNT COUNTRIES AND QUARRY

gates put in, such means of progress across country are not supremely helpful when hounds are running.

In those sections of America where pigs are pastured with cattle and young stock, mesh or woven wire is almost universally used. Such wire as used in recent years has a mesh at the bottom only about four inches the smallest way. The size of this mesh increases towards the top, but even at the top it is difficult for the smallest hounds to get through at all—to hold swine such wire must be drawn tight to the ground at the bottom. It stands over four feet high, and nowadays usually has one or more strands of barbed wire stretched along the top of the posts to prevent cattle from leaning over the fence. One can easily imagine the agonized contortions hounds have to go through to get over such fencing. This type of fencing can be, and often is, paneled by the use of chicken-coop jumps, making it possible for mounted riders to get in and out of fields. However, what is frequently forgotten is the fact that it is impossible to panel such enclosures for *hounds*, and where the fields range from thirty to fifty acres, a pack following the natural line of the fox has no alternative, but must negotiate the wire as best they can. Where any amount of such wire exists, it is hopeless to attempt to have a pack hunt together as they would in natural country, for young or wire-shy hounds will soon be left. Many a hound has been lamed for life by such wire fences; on one occasion a beautiful bitch of mine hung by her hind leg for two days in the middle of a woodland where she could not be seen, and only by the vigilance of the huntsman was she at last discovered, nearly dead, and ruined for life. No doubt many hounds that have been lost while hunting have died in this manner. In such country as the Millbrook where no swine and few young animals are pastured, barbed wire is used rather than mesh wire, for it is much cheaper; consequently, in such country a pack of hounds is not impeded.

I have hunted two countries where there is practically no fencing. While this may not sound interesting to the hunt-to-jump advocate, *faut de mieux*, to anyone who likes to see hound work, such countries are ideal. One of these countries is Montauk Point, on Long Island, which is about ten miles long and, at most, three miles wide. Many years ago, it was used as a pasture land for young cattle, and in some sections it has a preponderance of natural grass land with small thick covers in the depressions from which foxes may be viewed away across the open, exactly as from the coverts in Leicestershire. If there were twenty miles square of such country, it would be delightful. The Point is flanked on one side by Long Island Sound, and on the other the Atlantic Ocean stretches away to the next hunting country—Ireland. Many amusing pranks do the Long Island foxes play in running the sandy beaches —not always conducive to the accounting for foxes. Frank Gray Griswold describes in his book, *Horses and Hounds* (1926), how, when he was master

HOUNDS AND HUNTING

and huntsman of the Queens County hounds (which preceded the Meadow Brook) nearly fifty years ago, the foxes played these same pranks on Rockaway Beach,—which vicinity has now become engulfed by the on-rushing city.

The gently rolling Overhills country of North Carolina presents a problem which perhaps exists in few other foxhunting centers. It is in the sandy coastal plain which so many centuries ago must have been the bed of the Atlantic Ocean. In most sections it is practically pure sand, underlaid by clay; except for isolated cotton fields here and there, it is entirely covered by a sparse growth of pine, interspersed by scrub oak. Where the pine trees predominate, the ground is covered with pine needles; other sections are covered with wiry bunch grass. There is no fencing, but ditches exist in some lowlying spots which in days before the Civil War were reclaimed from swamp land, by slave labor, for plantations. Although there is no wire, there is the unique problem of long, narrow swamps which fringe the numerous streams, and it is necessary to make crossings in these natural barriers by means of corduroy roads. From many high points in this country, straight rides have been cut seventy-five feet wide and miles in length. These rides, radiating from a given point, give delightful vistas through the woodland remindful of the rides in the French forests heretofore described, and are convenient both for shooting men and followers of hounds. Strange as it may seem, and in spite of the cover, one sees much hound work in this country, as referred to in Chapter VI, and a pack is, fortunately, in no danger of being "squandered" by mesh wire. The country about Aiken, S. C., which was successfully hunted for many years by Thomas Hitchcock, is not dissimilar.

Through the Middle West in recent years a number of hunts have been established. Some of them hunt foxes under the great handicap of wire; a number of them run a drag where all the fences must be paneled, which speaks well for the increasing interest in riding to hounds. There is a country in Kentucky which has great potentialities due to its fine visibility and excellent scenting conditions; it is nearly all grass, and has a certain percentage of stone walls, some of them free from wire.

In Oklahoma, there is a hunt which is unique, and that is Mr. Marland's Hounds. This hunt has been established in almost patriarchal manner by E. W. Marland for the diversion of his associates in the vicinity of Ponca City, which is now the centre of a great oil industry where only a few years ago Indians and cowboys pursued a chase of an entirely different character. Mr. Marland maintains a pack of beagles for the children, a pack for hunting hare (jack rabbits), and a pack for prairie wolf (coyote). The country consists of gently undulating plains covered with buffalo grass, dotted here and there by small coverts or fringes of trees along the water courses. Barbed wire fences enclose the enormous pastures which have been paneled for many miles in the run of wolves; wind and extreme dryness of certain seasons are the chief handicaps. Nevertheless, excellent hunting is often possible. *En passant*, this spot has been made a sporting oasis by the laying out of several polo grounds, a horse show ring, and all the necessary stables and kennels.

From Montreal, in Canada, where riding to hounds was inaugurated in 1826, south to Virginia, the matter of frost is a handicap. In the more northern countries, although it is too warm to begin serious hunting before the middle of September, winter oftentimes closes the season by the end of November, and spring hunting is out of the question owing to the deep-seated frost coming out of the ground, making going impossible. In normal years, even in Virginia, from the latter part of December to the middle of February, only on occasional days are hunting conditions good.

In some localities, through rigorous protection during the past ten years, wild deer have become a great menace, not only to orchards but to foxhunting. Before a pack can be stopped, deer will often run ahead of hounds straight away across rough country for many miles, ruining a hunting day and sometimes causing the loss of hounds. It might be explained that as there are no private deer parks where hounds may be walked among them as in England, it is nearly impossible to break hounds from running deer, which have a stronger scent than foxes.

In the matter of gaining permission to cross farm lands in America, the difficulties are not tremendous, for, unless actual damage is done, the farmer, once his understanding as to circumstances is clear, is prone to be interested in the spectacle of the hunt, and amused with its attendant incidents and accidents. In some districts this is saying much for his good sportsmanship, because in most parts the sport of riding to hounds in an organized manner is quite alien to what has ever been seen by him previously, and many of the people who hunt are quite unknown to him. Apropos, it is surprising how few people realize a point already touched on, namely, their obligations to the men who permit them to cross their property. In England, the case is somewhat different, where riding to hounds has been an institution and understood by all men for centuries. The master, or hunt committee, of an American country has much more to contend with between obtaining the good will of the landowners and buffeting the wire question than similar officials in Britain.

It is, indeed, a prodigious task to organize and properly maintain a hunt country in America, as any hunt country having sectors which because of wire, impenetrable woods or other cause one can not cross is seriously handicapped in that a day's sport may be ruined by hounds traversing territory where riders cannot follow. Organizers of hunts in America deserve the greatest credit and support, which infrequently is their reward for their hard work in the cause of the sport. There are often many things which they would like to see accomplished in their countries, but which are not done, because the constructive necessities cannot easily be understood by the ordinary follower of hounds. The latter frequently fails to realize the fact that just because he has seen pictures of hunts gaily galloping across beautiful English country such a picture can hardly be imitated in America to any degree except by an enormous amount of serious intent and vast expenditure, not to mention years of time spent in preparation.

It must be emphasized that there is much more in hunting across a country than an uninitiated observer who has only seen a hunt team in scarlet nonchalantly galloping around a show ring can possibly conceive. One must have a country with fair possibilities, constructive plans, and funds available for opening up the woodlands by means of rides, and for fighting the ruthless ogre—Wire; one must have the gift of initiative and determination to pursue religiously the attendant development and maintenance of the entire necessary regime; even then, there is still another all-important question to consider,—that is, the quarry.

Without suitable country the sport is impracticable, but without foxes or other quarry it is impossible. Therefore, it may be well to discuss at some length the hare and the fox, the only two kinds of quarry that can be suitably hunted on horseback in Eastern America. It has been explained that native hare, or cottontail rabbit, *Lepus sylvaticus,* may be hunted very satisfactorily on foot with beagles; but this quarry hardly gives sufficient points or long enough runs to be followed on a horse. If large hare universally existed in the eastern part of the United States, excellent sport might be enjoyed after this quarry in numerous localities, for hare naturally keep to the open fields, and their points are not so long as to require extensive country. Hence, in hare hunting, many of the topographical difficulties in following a fox would be obviated.

There are at present but few packs in America that hunt hare similar to the English hare, *Lepus europæus,* for the reason that these exist only in certain territories. One of these is Dutchess County, New York, where European hare are now numerous. In the past thirty years they have spread over an area of fifty or sixty miles from Millbrook, the location of the original importation, as mentioned in Chapter IV. It may reasonably be assumed that they will migrate all over Eastern America as the red fox and the English sparrow have done. Hare hunting originally began at Millbrook, in 1907, at the suggestion of that enthusiastic advocate of the ancient sport, O'Malley Knott, who as a boy had been properly "entered" with the South Mayo Harriers, in Ireland.

There are also hare on Nantucket Island, where with the permission of the Massachusetts Game Commission, in 1925, W. W. Justice, Jr., first put out the Western jack rabbit, *Lepus campestris.* Another importation followed in 1926, and a third lot in 1927. They have become acclimated, and are now reproducing themselves in a satisfactory manner. In thirty-eight days of hunting in the summer and autumn of 1927 with Mr. Justice's Harriers on the rolling moorlands of the central part of the Island of Nantucket, there were no blank days, which speaks well for the possibilities of the future of hare hunting in this location. Although the island is sandy, the scenting conditions seem to be fairly good, and summer hunting is possible on account of the comparative coolness of the atmosphere tempered as it is by the sea breezes. Mr. Marland, in his hunt country near Ponca City, in Oklahoma, maintains a pack referred to previously for hunting jack rabbits.

The fox in America is in most regions considered destructive vermin, to be exterminated if possible. In certain sections there is actually a bounty on the vulpine race; in vast areas he is ruthlessly trapped or shot in front of hounds, while only in a few localities is he legally protected. In Kentucky, where every other farmer owns hounds, the field trial associations are very influential, and foxes are protected by law and custom; this is also in a measure true in North Carolina. Broadly speaking everything is against the fox in most localities. The result is that in America foxes are often scarce; hence, for anyone interested in the organization of a hunt country, the fox supply must be carefully studied.

There are countries which are naturally good fox countries; that is, they have suitable coverts, suitable earths, and possibly a paucity of enemies; in some countries, topographical difficulties are detrimental,—such countries may have open plains which are ridable but have unridable rough hills adjoining. There may be plenty of foxes in these hills, but a few in the open vales, where it is impossible to find a fox if self-protection prompts him not to be there.

It must be remarked that in England the killing of a fox except by hounds is considered akin to murder. The result is, they are apparently not as wild as the American fox, and it is positive that they can get plenty to eat with much less effort, from the innumerable rabbit warrens adjoining the fox coverts. It is the logical deduction that the English fox cannot possibly compete in running ability with his American cousin, who every night has to travel untold miles in search of sustenance. In some American countries where farmers' hounds run loose the year round, foxes may be run by hounds every other night in the year; hence, they have little fear of hounds, and rarely go to ground until forced to do so. The circumstances in their struggle for existence obviously give them prodigious running ability.

It is probably little known in Europe that Eastern America is blest with two genera of foxes,—namely, the grey and the red. They do not cross, and usually inhabit different types of country, the grey living in dense swamps or rough mountainous districts, the red in more open plains.

HOUNDS AND HUNTING

The only genus of fox known by foxhunters along the Atlantic seaboard in the early colonial days was that wily sportsman, the grey fox, *Vulpes cinereo-argentatus*. He is found from Maine to Florida and westward to the plains. In the North he is to-day less frequently found than formerly, and is certainly much less numerous than the red fox, *Vulpus fulvus*. In the tidewater section of Virginia, and the rough peaks and slopes of the Appalachian Mountains he is plentiful: in such sections he vastly outnumbers red foxes. In the coastal plain of the Carolinas and southward, he is the only quarry for foxhounds. In the North, where dens abound, he will go to ground as red foxes do, besides climbing trees when pushed by hounds. In the Coastal Plain, where dens are few, I have never heard of a grey fox going to ground for refuge—tree climbing is his last resource. Apparently, the grey fox has its young in a nest on the ground as does the European hare, at least, this is true in such countries as lack natural dens or earths made by burrowing animals, such as ground hogs.

The origin of the red fox in America has been for many years the subject of intermittent discussion; hence, it may be well to clearly outline certain facts recorded by foxhunters, who have doubtless been the most numerous and interested observers. It is certain that the red fox of eastern America was imported from England, certainly to New York and Maryland (possibly to other states), at any rate, the gradual spread of red foxes can be easily traced.

In the American Turf Register for September, 1829, the following item appeared:

The red fox is supposed to have been imported from England to the eastern shores of Maryland by a Mr. Smith, and to have emigrated across the ice to Virginia in the hard winter of 1779–80, when the Chesapeake was frozen over.

The details of this importation to Maryland was verified by Colonel Skinner, editor of the Turf Register, to the effect that in the month of August, 1730, eight prosperous tobacco planters of Talbot County, Maryland, in discussing foxhunting over their bowls of mint julep, decided to import English foxes in order to duplicate in the new world the sport as they had enjoyed it in England. An order was given to the captain of the schooner "Monaccasy," who brought on his subsequent trip from Liverpool eight brace of red foxes consigned to Mr. Smith. Such interest was expressed in the arrival of the English foxes that a great ball was given, to which the gentry of the province were invited; match races between Virginia and Maryland horses were run on the following day, after which the red guests of honor were released.

The statement in the Turf Register led to an open forum in subsequent issues dealing with the spread of the red fox in eastern America. The summarized and apparently confirmed facts thus brought to light are as follows:

THE RED FOX (*Vulpes fulvus*) FROM IMPORTATIONS TO NEW YORK AND MARYLAND MIGRATED A THOUSAND MILES WEST AND SOUTH IN A HUNDRED YEARS.

THE GREY FOX (*Urocyon cinereo-argentatus*), INDIGENOUS TO THE UNITED STATES, CLIMBS TREES, AND IS A MOST DIVERTING SPORTSMAN.

HUNT COUNTRIES AND QUARRY

That, in 1789, the first red fox was killed in Perry County, Pennsylvania, and not a person present had ever seen or heard of an animal of the kind until a Mr. Lenarton, an old Jersey-man, pronounced it an English fox. He said the red fox was imported into New York from England by one of the first English governors, who was said to be a great sportsman, and turned out on Long Island, where they remained for many years, but at last made their way over the ice to the mainland and spread all over the country;

That, it is definitely known from the statement of George W. P. Custis, of Arlington, Virginia, the foxes hunted by George Washington near Mount Vernon "were grey";

That, previous to 1812, Dr. David S. Ker, of Virginia, had a pack of as well-bred "beagles" as ever opened. They were known to follow a red fox (Fredericksburg) to Port Royal and back, a distance of twenty-five miles;

That, the first red fox seen at Goochland, on the James River in Virginia, was in 1814, and "created a sensation among sportsmen";

That, in 1829, the red fox was migrating south and west. "They are now in almost every part of Virginia."

Records of hunting events which occurred near Philadelphia, in the year 1811, definitely state that both grey and red foxes were hunted. One particular account gives a vivid picture:

When the last mentioned fox was unkenneled, a part of the Company . . . left the main road for the wood. . . . The President and we kept the road at good speed until the wood was turned, when we entered a field. . . . A wide and deep ditch was before us, which it was necessary to pass. A flat planked bridge, known by the name of the 'Irish Bridge,' crossed it. On approaching it, it was perceived, a number of the planks had been removed . . . to prevent the straying of cattle, leaving an aperture of some eight or ten feet. . . . The horses were eager and mettlesome, and their riders elate and reckless of consequences . . . they were whipped and sprang handsomely over, not without some hazard. . . . It was a moment of high expectation and intense ambition, when,

'In vain the stream in foaming eddies whirls;
In vain the ditch, wide-gaping, threatens death.'

. . . A five or six-barred worm fence to the left of the wood, was afterwards cleared when the panting fox issued full in view, coursing the fields hard pressed by the clamorous pack, and the mounted pursuers to the halloa of Tally ho! *It was a fine prospect for a painter's pencil, and a most enlivening one to a sportsman. He sought refuge in the swamp, where he was soon overtaken, and proved to be an old one of the native family of the Greys.*

The more mischievous red-skin stock are imported rogues.

The Reverend Timothy Dwight, in the summer of 1810 (then president of Yale College) wrote in his Memoirs during a trip through Vermont that the red fox had first been seen there in that year.

Haiden C. Trigg, the famous breeder of foxhounds, records the following relating to red foxes in Kentucky.

In 1860, the red fox first made his advent into my section (Glasgow, Kentucky).

George L. F. Birdsong, another famous hound breeder, in writing to Mr. Trigg, describes the advent of the red fox into Georgia:

In 1840, when I got my dogs from Virginia and Maryland, there were no red foxes west of the Conee River, Georgia. They had migrated to the eastern banks of that stream. Since then they have crossed that stream and occupy the country between that stream and the Ocmulgee.

It is thus definitely established through the writings of contemporaneous foxhunters that the red fox from the first importations increased his kind and migrated a thousand miles or more towards the West and South, in about a century. These countries have natural rock dens as well as the holes of burrowing animals, which he could appropriate in manner similar to his usage in Europe. In such spots as lack burrowing animals and have no dens, he failed to go, as is instanced by my own knowledge of Harnett and Columbia Counties in North Carolina, which are without natural earths of any kind, and where there were no red foxes until imported there from other localities in 1920. Artificial earths were made for them, and they have gradually provided earths for themselves where tree stumps and roots have been burned out, or in subterranean water courses.

In some instances, it may be necessary to stock a country, especially in such localities where it is customary for foxes to be shot, or in any country having a temporary dearth of foxes through decimation by epidemics of mange, which occur even in the wildest regions. If dogs are affected by distemper, there seems to be no reason why foxes should not likewise be susceptible, although whether or not the wild fox is subject to such infections, it is difficult to say. In the Adirondack fox farms, I am told that hookworm has to be constantly fought, strange as it may seem.

Speaking of stocking hunt countries, this has often been done in England. One interesting consignment was in 1843, when the Duke of Richmond imported foxes from New York State. There are numerous instances of foxes having been brought from France to England, but as a rule they are imported from the north of Scotland.

Having visualized a ridable country, plenty of foxes, and a good pack of hounds that can drive them, it might be well to analyze for the benefit of the neophyte of what a really good hunt and a really good hunting day consists. Once upon a time, a lady was visiting in my household who had never hunted, but who rode well. I loaned her that perfect conveyance, *Commodore*

HUNT COUNTRIES AND QUARRY

Gaunt ('14), by *Sir Wilfred-Follow On*. I asked a good friend to pilot her. Twenty minutes after the meet, hounds found. She enjoyed a quick, short hunt, and within another twenty minutes hounds found again, and had a seven-mile point straight-away. Naturally, the budding Diana was thrilled beyond measure, but I warned her that to avoid disappointment she had best never hunt again, because she had been favored by the gods in experiencing such an event on her first day in the hunting field, and because she had yet to learn that in the elusive chase of the fox everything is not always rosy.

I can remember in one badly-managed country where I hunted years ago, foxes were so scarce and hounds so slack there was hardly a run of any kind two days out of three; yet, some people who did not know any better seemed to enjoy it. One can pick up almost any copy of The Field or Horse and Hound and read accounts of thrilling hunts with different packs, and on the very same page perhaps find that other packs have had several bad days in succession.

It is surprising how few people can give an accurate account of a hunt or the kind of season they have had. In order to do this, one must have some comparative point of view, a good eye for a country, and know the five essential fundamentals to be remembered in describing a hunt,—the point, the distance, the pace, whether the line of country covered was good or bad, and whether the quarry was accounted for. Several accounts of good hunts which may be taken as models have been used to illustrate various technical points throughout these pages. Sometimes when least expected, days occur when everything seems to "break right," hounds are right, foxes are found and accounted for in proper style. I shall never forget a few such days in Virginia, in 1916–17, the accounts of which, dug from the yellowing pages of my *Notitia Venatica* read as follows:

On September 27th at sunrise Hounds met at Kennels fit and ready after their summer's hunting from the Summer Kennels on the Blue Ridge Mountains. Carver cast eighteen couples in Sulphur Springs Wood but drew blank—hounds continued hunting westerly through the broom sage and small coverts until Old Welbourne Wood yielded a fox which fled westerly driven by a glorious burst of hound music. A beautiful exhibition of hound work now ensued. The pace while never too great for the warmth of the day was sufficient for a telling gallop and showed well the evenness in ability of the entire pack.

By Gochnauer's Ruins to Frazier's broom sage fields easterly to Old Welbourne and northerly toward Unison, when after two hours hounds ran into their fox on the Lacy Farm.

Sport of the highest order was continued two and three days a week during October until on October 21st at sunrise Carver cast hounds below the Hundred Acre on Beaver Dam Creek. With an exhilarating burst of music the pack went

HOUNDS AND HUNTING

away from Locust Grove Cliff, swinging easterly then westerly to the Kerick farm, then southerly—beautifully packed—across to Goose Creek Vale down which they ran and drove Reynard to earth in one and one-half hours on Mr. Fred's Cliff. A second fox was run to ground in forty minutes.

Drawing up Goose Creek the third fox of the day went away from Goodstone Ledges leading hounds in a circuitous run of an hour and thirty minutes through a beautiful galloping country before being killed near the point of first view.

Although the season continued dry and warm, early morning sport continued to be of the highest class.

On November 6th under a cloudy sky fifteen couples of hounds and a field of forty-odd met at Unison at 7 o'clock. A short run drove a fox to earth on Mr. Rust's at 8 o'clock. A second fox started in Locust Grove Cliff, after a loss, was viewed away by the Master and put the field through a process of elimination until after a steeplechaselike run of three to four miles reynard was driven to earth in Mrs. Piggott's Ledges on Beaver Dam Creek. A third fox viewed away on Millsville, set his head easterly toward Millsville Mill; swung lefthanded north and west to Philip's Corner—straight away across a beautiful line to Welbourne Vale to Stone Bridge, to Rattlesnake Mountain to Cromwell's Run to the C. C. Rumsey Estate, west again to near Five Points northly to Gatewood's Cliff where, after two hours of most marvelous hound work the pack was taken up. This last run was in the middle of the day—the ground being dry—Hounds ran for two hours a most difficult line of 14 miles. In one case three enormous wheat fields were crossed in succession while later the fox ran a stone fence, then a quarter mile of dusty road, and finally a second stone fence without Hounds making a loss.

Five thoroughbred horses only finished the day—35 to 40 miles having been covered, the Huntsman, the Joint Masters, Mrs. Charles Perkins and Mr. Irvin Beavers alone surviving of the Field.

Hunting continued without interruption by the weather until on November 13th—a foggy morning—fifteen couples of hounds killed in one hour and twenty minutes after a chase through a Beaver Dam Creek line of country.

Subsequently a second fox was viewed away by Mr. Fred on his Francis Mill estate which after a circuitous run in Goose Creek Vale of about four to five miles swam the Creek and took Hounds and Field a most unusual route through stable yards, pig pens, walking stone fences and frequented roads to the very edge of Middleburg village beyond which point he made good his escape. The point was six, the distance ten to twelve miles.

The third fox of the day started from Mr. Seipp's broom sage near Millsville, ran westerly across hill and dale to Cromwell Run Cliffs which being near Mr. Arthur White's stables a fresh lot of horses were sent for during a brief check, but before they could arrive hounds went away easterly at top speed across Mr. Bangs' beautiful galloping country, across Millsville Road, still on to Mr.

HUNT COUNTRIES AND QUARRY

Dudley's where Reynard finally went to earth, a run of about six miles in forty minutes—total distance for the day behind foxes of about twenty-five to thirty miles. Only the huntsman, riding the famous thoroughbred mare Gerome, *and the two Messrs. Norman finished the day without a change of horses.*

On December 6th, in a gale of wind, a rather extraordinary run of some ten miles took place. In writing to the Master of this run Mr. Charles E. Perkins said:

'The best run I have had in two seasons in Virginia. You will remember how difficult conditions were, and I can truthfully say I never saw hounds work a fox harder or better than the Piedmont did, and I have seldom seen conditions more trying. Besides the hounds, I have been particularly impressed with Carver's ability as a Huntsman. It must be a real satisfaction to you to have developed what are unquestionably the best pack of foxhounds in this country.'

December 13th gave the greatest day's sport ever known in the Piedmont country—four clean cut beautiful runs through delightful riding country lying between Francis Mill and Clifton Mill. Four foxes viewed away, four foxes run to earth—about twenty-five miles of galloping behind the pack—the shortest run no less than three to four miles, the longest twelve to fourteen.

A bit of snow on the ground, the most marvelous sky effects and views of the Blue Ridge Mountains in distant sunshine occasionally cut off by snow squalls.

Two ladies, Mrs. Thomas and Miss Ladenburg, went the whole route and finished the day.

On January 8th with a noon temperature of 48, the weather being clear and the going good, a fox found on Mr. Rust's took a line to Guinea Bridge, to Silcott Spring near Purcellville back through Mr. Piggott's through Mr. Pancoast's, through the new country, through Mrs. Dishman's to Mr. Costello's and was killed on Mr. Hall's. Every hound of seventeen couples up in the right place doing great work to the end of three and one-half hours' run. The point was seven miles—the distance about twenty-five.

January 29th—Temperature at noon 34 degrees. Hounds left Kennel at 12 o'clock. Conditions about as trying on hounds as possible, yet good sport was shown. A fox went away from Mr. Hartley's Cliff, straight to Goodstone, crossed through Benton, back to Mr. Fred's crossed next to Mountsville, back through Gochnauer's Cliff, up through Mr. Hartley's to Mr. Whitfield's and went to earth on Goodstone in 55 minutes. The second fox of the day was viewed away on Mr. Tabb's but ran to ground with the pack nearly on him. The third fox went away from the Misses Fletcher's, ran to Mr. C. Rector's, crossed the pike into Mr. Gatewood's, crossed the creek into Mr. Slater's, circled to the north of Rosehill into the big Cliff on Panther Skin, circled easterly through Welbourne, through Mr. Phillip's, to Millsville Farm, swam Goose Creek through Mr. Arthur White's and went to earth on Mr. Tabb's at 5 o'clock. The eighteen couples of hounds showed marvelous pack work considering conditions.

HOUNDS AND HUNTING

January 27th 17 couples met at Shamrock Hall. Wind was in the northwest blowing hard, and although the sun was shining, the ground did not thaw at all. Conditions most trying.

A fox was started about 2 o'clock in the afternoon near Rosehill House—hounds ran southerly up Goose Creek, gradually circling righthanded across Mr. Glascock's and Mr. Oxnard's, back to Rosehill, where the chase sank the hill, turning lefthanded up Panther Skin Ravine, northerly across Mrs. Fletcher's blue grass fields, past Clifton Mills, across Mr. Fletcher's to Blakely Grove School, whence hounds ran the road for over a mile, carrying the field at a good gallop, nearly all the way to Powell's Shop. Hounds circled righthanded across Mr. Frasier's, then lefthanded to the Blue Ridge and circled back across the estate of Mrs. Peach to General Buchanan's, where in a wheat field the pack was lifted at dusk, it was then freezing hard.

Hounds reached Kennels after dark.

The Master, Miss Harriman (Master of the Glen Arden), Miss Marion Hollins and five men alone survived the day. The point was six miles—the distance fifteen.

January 30th—Conditions excellent—going rather soft.

Three runs this day.

The first fox was viewed away on Mr. Fred's Millsville estate, went to earth almost immediately, but being dug out and liberated on Mr. Whitfield's, he put up splendid run across the estates of Messrs. Hartley, Goodwin, Benton and Parkins, swung righthanded in a big circle and ran to earth on Goose Creek near Francis' Mill in 40 minutes without a check. The second fox was viewed away in the near vicinity, but ran to ground on Mr. Whitfield's in 15 minutes. A third fox started on Mr. Hitt's Millsville property, first took a line westerly as far as Rosehill, circled sharp righthanded back easterly across Welbourne, Messrs. Phillip's, Hitt's, Neville's, Benton's and Parkin's, swung righthanded again across the same line of country, this time, however, setting his mask for the distant mountains, across Mr. Slater's and Mr. Fletcher's to Blakely School House, —westerly 9 miles was the point, into Clark County, where swinging lefthanded he was run to ground after dark. Of the field the Messrs. Norman and Dishman alone finished the day. The Huntsman's horse dropped dead, he taking the First Whip's horse—returned to Kennels with Hounds at 10 P.M.

L'ENVOI

And so, dear Boy, if the time and thought which has been given to the preparation of these pages may be productive of helpful suggestions to you, and perchance to your sister Diana (who soon will have grown old enough to be interested in the Chase, if heredity counts for aught), the effort will not have been in vain. After all, your real knowledge must come from the hard and relentless school of experience and be gleaned from wide-eyed discernment, constant study and intelligent application supported by unbounded optimism—an unwillingness to cry, "Enough." In this search for further learning you may well heed the terse truths of Gratian, that astute Spanish philosopher of the fifteenth century, among whose sayings is to be found the remarkable admonition: *'Tis a rare greatness to make use of the wise . . . . there is remarkable cleverness in studying without study, in getting much by means of many, and through them all to become wise.*

FINIS

Glossary

GLOSSARY

(Some expressions in this Glossary are used in Britain, but not in America and vice versa; some terms are practically obsolete, as they may be found only in ancient literature of the chase.)

ACCOUNT (FOR A FOX OR OTHER QUARRY)—Hunted game is said to be accounted for when killed or run to ground; the reverse of *lost*.

APPOINTMENTS CARD—See FIXTURE CARD.

AWAY (OF QUARRY AND HUNT)—See GONE AWAY.

BABBLER—A noisy hound; one which flings its tongue without cause when not on the line.

BAGGED FOX—See BAGMAN.

BAGMAN—A fox released when required; the term had its origin in the practice of some owners of English shooting estates who permitted their game-keepers to kill foxes, only to buy another when hounds met in the locality, on which occasion the fox would be dropped from a bag. In America, a bagman is generally referred to as a *dropped* or *bagged fox*.

BARBARY PACK—A scratch pack of hounds or other dogs, with sufficient nose to be useful in hunting.

BEAGLES—Small hounds, 11–15 inches high, generally used for hunting hare; also Kerry Beagles, the large black and tan hounds of Western Ireland.

BILLET—The droppings of the fox.

BLANK—A covert is blank or drawn blank when it holds no fox; a day is blank when hounds do not find.

BLIND COUNTRY—Where ground cannot be seen because of unkept fields overgrown with weeds or bushes.

BLOODED—Hounds are said to be blooded if they kill their quarry; a tyro is said to be blooded when he is anointed with fox blood at his first "kill."

BLUE TICK—A white hound which has small splashes of black hairs mixed with the white, sometimes giving the effect of blue.

BREAST HIGH—See SCENT.

GLOSSARY

Breeding—In-breeding, producing from closely related parents; line-breeding, producing from parents having common ancestry; cross-breeding, producing from parents having no common ancestry and of different type; out-crosses, the infusion of new blood in diluted measure in line-bred animals.

Brush—The tail of the fox.

Bullfinch—A hedge too high to leap clearly—riders have to bore through it; there is a ditch on one side or the other, sometimes on both.

Burning Scent—See Scent.

Burrow—The underground home of the rabbit or other animals. See Warren.

Burst—Often the first part of the run, if the hounds get away close to their fox; any fast part of a run.

Burst Him—A fox killed in the *burst*.

Bye (Day)—An extra hunting day not on the hunting fixture card.

Carries (of the Ground)—When it sticks to the fox's pads after frost.

Carry a Good (wide) Head—Of the hounds; keeping abreast while running a line.

Carry a Line—When hounds follow the scent; working a line.

Cast—To spread out in search of scent. Hounds either cast themselves or are cast by the huntsman.

Catch Hold—A huntsman is said to do this when he takes his hounds forward at a check, either to a halloo or for some reason of his own.

Cat Foot (of a hound)—A short-toed, round foot, as compared with the more elongated fox foot or hare foot.

Challenge—The first hound which speaks on finding the line *challenges*. See Scent.

Change—To leave the line of the hunted quarry for another.

Check (at fault)—An interruption to the run, the scent being temporarily lost.

Cheer—Any hunting cry to encourage hounds.

Chop—To kill a quarry soon after being found. See Mob.

Cocktail—Any horse not thoroughbred, and in England usually docked.

Cold (line)—The faint scent of quarry which may be from a few minutes to a few hours old, according to scenting conditions.

Conformation—Size, outline, and correlation of physical attributes; the particular structure of the body.

Counter—To follow the line of the quarry the wrong (reverse) way. See Scent.

Couples—A device of ancient origin consisting of a link with a swivel at each end attached to a ring, through which the strap-collars of the hounds are passed when coupling them together. A pack of hounds is

GLOSSARY

always referred to as being of so many couples (or couple), from the ancient practice of keeping hounds coupled until thrown off to hunt. See THROW OFF.

COURSE—To chase by sight and not by nose, as greyhounds coursing a hare.

COVERT (COVER)—A place where the fox is sheltered, whether wood, thicket, or gorse, etc. Such places, in England, have various local names,—holts, roughs, coppices, or copses, spinneys, shaws, etc. Artificial coverts are often planted, gorse, laurel, withies, hawthorn, etc., being used. Temporary coverts are also made of dead wood and bushes, and are called stick, faggot, or dead coverts.

COVERT-HACK—A horse used for riding to the place of meeting.

COVERT-LAD—See PAD-GROOM.

COW-HOCKS—Hocks coming too close together—a characteristic common to dairy cows.

CRASH—When the pack all give tongue together on finding a fox.

CROP—The whip used in hunting; it has a loop, called a keeper, at the top for the attachment of the thong. See WHIP.

CROPPER—A bad fall; the words *crumpler* and *crowner* are also used in the same significance, the latter generally with the addition of the epithet imperial.

CROSS-BREEDING—See BREEDING.

CROWNER—See CROPPER.

CRUMPLER—See CROPPER.

CRY (VOICE, TONGUE)—The method one hound has of telling another what is happening; the sound a hound makes when working the line of any quarry. It is different from the bark of common dogs, and varies materially at different phases of the chase. The sound made by hounds when they have run the quarry to ground is called, in America, a *den bark*.

CUB—The young of the fox.

CUB-HUNTING—Early season hunting. See Chapter VI.

CURRANT-JELLY—An English colloquialism referring to harriers and hare hunting.

DEN—The home of the fox.

DEN BARK—See CRY, MARK TO GROUND.

DEN DOG—A hound particularly keen on worrying at an earth, and who will give a peculiar cry (see CRY) which helps the huntsman in woodlands to locate the spot where the fox has gone to ground. An American expression.

DETERMINATION—The will to try, try, try. See STAMINA.

DEW CLAW—The false toe and claw on the forelegs of hounds, usually removed in England to enhance appearance, but retained in America on

GLOSSARY

the theory that they are of use in very rough country. To support this theory, it is a fact that the nails, or claws, naturally remain worn down. Dew claws on the hind legs of hounds are said to be an indication of impure ancestry.

DEWLAPPED—The dewlap is the pendulous skin under the neck, such as characterizes certain breeds of cattle.

DIP—To immerse hounds in a mild disinfectant, for the purpose of killing fleas or relieving skin irritations.

DOG FOX—The male fox.

DOG HOUND—The male hound.

DOUBLE—When the quarry turns short back on its course.

DRAFT—To remove hounds from a kennel or pack.

DRAG—The scent left by the fox on his return to his lair—synonymous with the American expression, "night line"; an artificial line, followed by drag hounds.

DRAG HOUNDS—Hounds used to hunt an artificial line.

DRAIN—Any underground passage for water into which the fox may run for shelter.

DRAW (DRAW A COVERT)—To search for a fox in covert.

DRAW BLANK—An unsuccessful draw. See BLANK.

DROPPED FOX—See BAGMAN.

DWELLING—Of hounds that lack the volition to get forward and linger unnecessarily long on the line.

EARTH—The hole of some burrowing animal, such as, badger in England and ground hog (woodchuck) in America, cleaned out and appropriated by the fox. The fox rarely, if ever, digs his own earth.

EARTH-STOPPER—A person employed to stop earths. It is done while the fox is abroad at night, and on his return he finds himself stopped out. In England, all earths are stopped in the district in which hounds are expected to be on any hunting day. See STOP.

ENDURANCE (OF A HOUND)—See GAMENESS.

ENTER—Young hounds when first put into the pack are said to be *entered*.

EYE TO HOUNDS—The art of watching the pack when hunting, and so following them intelligently.

FANFARE—French, from Spanish *fanfarra* (bluster); Arabian *farfár* (loquacious); a sounding or flourish of trumpets, as on entering the lists in a tournament; a lively piece played on hunting horns in France.

FAULT (AT FAULT)—See CHECK.

FEATHERING—Moving the stern from side to side; an act which indicates that the hound recognizes the scent, but not necessarily to a sufficient extent to speak to it.

FEEDER—Synonymous with KENNEL MAN.

GLOSSARY

Field—Followers of hounds other than master and hunt staff.

Find—Hounds are said to find when they first smell the line of quarry. In England, this is usually accompanied by a quick burst, the fox being viewed away from cover. In America, the circumstances are sometimes different. See Strike, Start.

Fixture Card—An announcement of dates, time, and places of meeting; sometimes called the "hunting appointments" card. (See page 158.)

Flash (of hounds)—Inclined to overrun the scent; a flashy pack is one that is inclined to be systematically wild, or one that is wild from lack of work; under certain conditions, such as, in a strong wind, the steadiest hounds will often be flashy.

Flewed—Hounds having low-hanging flews, or chaps.

Flighty—Uncertain and changeable, applied both to hounds and scent.

Fling—To drive to right or left in search of the line, at the least semblance of a check.

Foil (foils)—When an animal returns on its own tracks.

Foiled—A term applied to ground which has been much traversed by hounds, horses, cattle, sheep, &c.

Form—The seat, or kennel, of the hare.

Fox—*Canis vulpes*, order Carnivora; origin of word unknown, but suggested connection with Sanskrit *puccha* (tail), Dutch *vos*, German *fuchs*; called *Reynard* from *Raginohardus* (strong in counsel), also *Uncle Remus* and colloquially, in England, *Charles James*. Generally classified in the U. S. A. under two genera—the Red fox, *Vulpes fulvus*, of European origin (see Chapter X); the Grey fox, *urocyon cinereo-argentatus*, native of Eastern and Central U. S.; climbs trees. (See Notes, Chapter IV, page 68[1]). There is considerable variation in color and size both in red and grey foxes.

In England, it is said that originally there were two varieties of fox,—the "greyhound" and the "bull dog," the latter distinguished by its wider head and darker color.

Fresh (line)—The opposite of cold.

Full Cry—Originally alluding to the chorus of music from the pack; American hounds give their best cry at speed, as ancient hounds apparently did (see Cry, Chapter V); in England, "full cry" in many packs is somewhat of a misnomer in that modern English hounds are so deficient in cry that frequently when running close to their fox at speed they give little or no cry.

Gameness—Ability to stick; synonymous with endurance; the combination of stamina (or strength) and determination (or will).

Get Hounds' Heads Up—See Heads Up.

Giving Tongue—See Cry.

GLOSSARY

GONE AWAY—When the quarry has been found and the hunt goes away at speed.

GONE TO GROUND—Gone into a drain, earth, den, rabbit-hole, or other underground shelter.

HALLOO (HALLOA)—See VIEW HALLOO.

HARBOURER—The official in hunting the deer who knows where warrantable quarry may be found. See TUFTER.

HARE—For origin and kinds of hare see Chapter IV. See PUSS.

HARK FORWARD—A huntsman's cheer to encourage his hounds on the scent.

HARRIER—From med. Eng. *harien*, *harren*, to harry or worry game; to-day, medium-sized hounds, 18–20 inches, generally used for hare hunting; formerly used for miscellaneous quarry.

HEAD—See CARRY A HEAD.

HEADED (OF THE FOX)—Made to turn back.

HEADED TO DEATH—Killed unfairly when headed.

HEADS UP—When hounds in search of scent for any reason raise their noses from the ground.

HEEL—See COUNTER, SCENT.

HILL-TOPPER—See POINT-RIDER.

HIT OFF (THE LINE)—When hounds recover the line at a check.

HOICK (YOICK)—A cheer to hounds.

HOLD HARD—The warning to riders not to press too closely on the hounds.

HOLDING SCENT—See SCENT.

HOLD THEM FORWARD (OR BACK)—To take hounds on in search of a lost line.

HONEST—An honest hound is one that has no vices. See Chapter V.

HONOR A LINE—When a hound speaks on the scent of a given quarry.

HOUNDS—In England, hounds are to-day spoken of as if they were superdogs. To speak of a pack of *dogs* where hounds are meant would be considered the height of bad form. This was not true in the eighteenth century, *vide* Beckford. In rural America, one often hears the term *hound dog* used to distinguish a hound from an ordinary canine. In England, a *dog hound* means the male hound, and a *bitch hound* is the female of the species.

HUNTING—In England refers only to the chase with hounds and is never used where both dogs and the gun are employed, as is often the case in America.

HUNTING SENSE—See diagram and text, pages 76, 81.

HUNTSMAN—The individual who hunts a pack of hounds and who has charge of all activities in kennel.

IN-BREEDING—See BREEDING.

JACK HARE—The male hare.

GLOSSARY

Jumped—When a pack has been working a line slowly and suddenly makes its quarry go away at speed, they are said in America to have jumped their fox; or, the fox is said to be *up*.

Kennel—The fox's lair; formerly, a pack was termed a "kennel" of hounds.

Kennel Huntsman—In the case where the M.F.H. regularly hunts the pack, the professional who has the working supervision of hounds in kennel is called the kennel huntsman; under such circumstances, the kennel huntsman usually discharges the duty of first whipper-in when hunting. See Huntsman.

Kennel Man—A member of the hunt staff whose duties are confined to kennel work, such as, preparing hound feed, cleaning kennels, &c.

Kennels (kennel)—The place where hounds are kept.

Kill—When a pack kills its proper quarry.

Lair (kennel)—The vicinity where a fox generally lies above ground during the day.

Larking—Jumping fences across a hunt country when hounds are not running, or on non-hunting days.

Leveret—The young of the hare.

Lift—To take the hounds from a lost scent, with a view to hitting the line further on. A hazardous game to play, but sometimes very effective in certain countries with a clever huntsman.

Line—The track taken by any quarry and indicated to the hounds by means of scent.

Line-breeding—See Breeding.

Line Hunter—A hound which keeps close to the scent.

Livery—See Uniform.

Loss—Hounds are said to be at a loss when for any reason they can no longer follow the line.

Lost—See Account.

Lying—See Scent.

Main Earth—The fox's principal den and breeding place.

Manners—Obedience (of hounds) to voice and horn.

Mark to Ground—When hounds run a fox to ground and indicate their action by worrying at the earth and giving a peculiar cry known in America as a *den bark*. See Cry.

Mask—The fox's head (pate).

Meet—The rendezvous of those about to take part in the chase.

Mentality (of a hound)—See pages 76, 81.

Mew (Mue)—To shed, cast, or change. "The hart mews his horns," the deer casts his head, or sheds his antlers. From the French *muer*, and the Latin *mutare*, to change; of hawks, to moult. (*Master of Game*.)

[205]

GLOSSARY

Mews—London stables, originally aviaries where in medieval times falcons were kept while moulting.

M. F. H.—Master of Fox Hounds; M. H. may be used in other cases.

Mixer—An English tool used in stirring hound food.

Mob—To surround and kill a fox without giving him the chance of a run. See Chop.

Mouthy—See Noisy; of a hound that uses its voice falsely. See Chapter V.

Mute—Of a hound that does not speak on the line. See Chapter V.

Night Line—See Drag.

Noisy (of a hound)—Speaking without a scent. See Mouthy.

Nose—Scenting ability.

Out-cross—See Breeding.

Over It—See Scent.

Override—Of horsemen who press hounds too closely, especially at a check.

Overrun—Of hounds that do not check when they no longer scent the line.

Own (the line)—See Scent.

Oxer—Ox-fence; ox-rail; a strong hedge with a wide ditch, and a single rail about one yard in front of it. A double oxer has a rail on each side. Designed to keep cattle in pastures.

Pack—A number of hounds regularly hunted together, drafted for uniformity of ability and physical characteristics. A first-class hunt in England will regularly take out 17–20 couple and have 40–60 couple of all ages in kennels to draw from, depending upon the number of days per week they hunt.

Pack Sense—The trait in hounds of hunting in mass-formation, honoring each other's cry.

Pad—The foot of the fox.

Pad-groom—The groom who slowly rides the hunter to a meet, and who formerly brought back the hack. Also, covert-lad.

Pate—See Mask.

Pie—Badger pie: a hound color wherein the head, legs, under body and tail are cream or fawn, the ears and saddle shading into almost black hairs with lighter ends resembling in color the badger. Hare pie: same as badger pie, except that ears and saddle shade into brownish hairs with light ends resembling the color of the hare. These colors are often found in old-fashioned hounds in England, but rarely occur in American hounds.

Pink—The scarlet coat worn by foxhunters.

Point—The distance in a straight line between the two localities furthest apart in any hunt.

Point-rider (hill-topper)—One who rides not as the fox and hounds go, especially in rough country, but to points at which he hopes to pick up hounds.

GLOSSARY

Point-to-Point—A straight run. Most hunts now have point-to-point races during the season. The course is sometimes not flagged, and the competitors take their own line; but where a circuitous flagged course is used, "point-to-point" is a misnomer in the original English sense.

Potterer—A hound that dwells.

Puss—English expression for hare.

Put Down—To put to death.

Put-To—In England, gratings are placed against the ends of tile drains by the earth-stopper the night before hunting; hence—"drains put to."

Quarry—The hunted animal; originally the hounds' reward,—*quyrreye*, because eaten on the deer hide (*sur le quir*).

Rabbit-earth—A burrow, to which a fox often goes for shelter.

Rack—A way through a hedge.

Rat-catcher—Referring to one informally dressed when hunting.

Rate—To chastise an erring hound by word or whip.

Rat-tailed—Lacking long hairs on the tail.

Recovered—See Scent.

Refuse (of a horse)—To refuse a leap.

Ride—A lane cut through the forest.

Ringing-fox—One that runs in circles instead of going straight away.

Riot—When hounds run anything but legitimate quarry.

Rising—See Scent.

Roach-backed—An arch-backed hound.

Road-hunter—A hound which possesses the gift of being able to hunt a fox or hare on a road.

Rounding—The English practice of trimming the points of hounds' ears, theoretically to prevent them from being torn, and to give greater uniformity to pack appearance.

Run—The chase of the fox from finding to the kill; to run counter or heel; to run to earth; to run to ground; to run riot—to follow a wrong scent.

Scent—The odour given off by the fox by which he is found and followed by hounds. It is breast high, if so good that the hounds do not stoop to it; burning (or screaming), if very good or strong; flighty (or catchy), if variable; holding, if good enough yet not very strong; lying, when good and at the ground level; moving, if it is so fresh that it must be recent, and not a cold line or drag; recovered, if lost and found again; rising, when scent at the ground level seems poor but ground odours can be distinctly smelled by a mounted man; spotty, when scent lies unevenly.

When hounds speak on a scent, they own to it, speak on it, or challenge; when they go beyond it, they are over it; when they follow it the reverse way, it is heel, or counter; when they remain on it without fol-

GLOSSARY

lowing it, they dwell; when they first perceive it, they feel it, or hit it; and hit it off when recovered at a loss; if they hunt any other animal than that which is their proper game, they run riot; in England, when they lose it and stop trying they are said to throw up (that is, their heads).

Scoring—Hounds score when the whole pack speaks to a strong scent.

Scut—The hail of the hare or rabbit.

Second Horseman—A groom who slowly rides a second hunter from point to point that a follower of hounds may change from his spent horse to a fresh one.

Settle (to the line)—When at a find hounds coming from different joints pick up the line and go away together.

Sinking (of a fox)—Nearly beaten.

Skirter—A hound which jealously runs wide of the pack, allowing other hounds to do his work. See Chapter V.

Sling His Tongue—See Noisy.

Soft Mouth—Bugle-like, low-toned hound voice, as opposed to a choppy or squealing voice.

So-ho—The cry raised when a hare is viewed.

Speak(of a hound)—To cry when on the scent.

Splayed Feet—Loosely knit, flat feet.

Spotty—See Scent.

Spout—English expression for *rabbit-earth*.

Stained—Injured, as regards scent, by the previous passage of hounds, horses, cattle, &c.

Stamina (of a hound)—Endurance or physical strength to go on; physical ability to carry out *determination*.

Start—American expression for *find*. See Strike.

Staying (ability of a hound)—Gameness.

Steady (hound)—One that is not flighty, flashy, or dishonest. See Honest.

Stern—The tail of the hound.

Stick—Synonymous with being *game*; a hound to stick must have physical and mental attributes making it possible for him to keep trying.

Stooping (of hounds)—Putting their noses to the ground. See Scent. A hound is said to *stoop* to a scent when he has once taken to speaking on it.

Stop (earths)—When an earth-stopper closes the entrance of a fox earth by means of sticks or a stone.

Stop (hounds)—The act of the huntsman in calling hounds away from a hunted line with the assistance of his whippers-in. See Earth-stopper.

Stop-hound—A hound that squats to impart deeper-toned cry on finding scent.

GLOSSARY

STREAMING—Going across open country at great pace.

STRIKE (START)—American expression for *find;* a hound is said to strike on the taint of quarry which, however, may be cold or fresh. If a hound strikes on a cold line, he may follow that line for some time before he jumps his fox.

STRIKE HOUNDS—Possessing more keenness than others to find first traces of a cold fox line.

STUB-BRED (STUMP-BRED)—Foxes which in certain English districts have their young in bushes or stumps instead of underground; the old term was *stubbed*.

SWAY-BACK—The dorsal line of a hound that curves down rather than up.

TAIL HOUNDS—Hounds at the rear of the pack when it goes away, or at any stage of the hunt.

TAILING (TAILS OUT)—When through difference in ability, age, shape, and nose, hounds are unable to keep together and the pack straggles across country; usually indicative of a badly drafted pack; the opposite of *carrying a good head*.

TALLY-HO—The cheer announcing that the fox is viewed. See Notes, Chapter VI, page 140.[1] In America has arisen a unique colloquialism: a 4-horse coach is referred to as a *tally-ho,* due to the fact that the first English coach imported for amateur driving (about 50 years ago) was named, *Tally-ho;* subsequently, all 4-horse coaches were so designated.

THROW OFF (THROW IN)—To start the hunt by putting the hounds into a covert; the expression is derived from the ancient practice of taking hounds to a meet in couples—formerly a necessary procedure in woodland countries; when the hunt began, couples were thrown off. See COUPLES.

THROW UP—See SCENT.

THROWN OUT—Where a hound or horseman for any reason loses his position in a hunt.

THRUSTER (THRUSTING RIDER)—One who often makes himself a nuisance to the huntsman by overriding hounds.

TIE (TO THE LINE)—Of hounds that hunt the line closely and are sometimes difficult to lift.

TIMBER—A wooden fence, rail, stile, or gate.

TONGUE—See CRY.

TUFTER—Synonymous with French *limier;* one of a few couple of steady old hounds used by the harbourer to find a warrantable stag.

UNIFORM—Usually, the hunt staff is referred to as wearing *livery,* and qualified followers as wearing the hunt uniform. (Actors wear *costumes*.)

UP—See JUMPED.

GLOSSARY

Viewed Away (of the quarry)—When seen to go away from cover; a regular event in Britain, but rather an unusual possibility in America.

View Halloo—In some cases, a peculiar sort of scream used when a fox is viewed. The most usual cry is *tally-ho* (see Notes); a whistle is used by some hunt staffs for this purpose.

Vixen—The female fox.

Voice—See Cry.

Walk—Used in cases where puppies are put out on farms at an early age to be raised at liberty, to accustom them to farm animals and poultry.

'Ware Riot—The cry to the hounds when running riot.

Warrantable—A stag or hind, according to age and the season, considered proper to hunt. See Tufter.

Warren—A colony of rabbit burrows. See Burrow.

Whelp—A very young puppy.

Whip (crop)—The whip used in Britain has a right-angled crook on the handle, usually with corrugations on each side, for assistance in opening and shutting gates; also abbreviation for *whipper-in*.

Whipper-in (whip)—The huntsman's assistant in controlling hounds.

Whoo-hoop—The cheer announcing the death of the fox. See page 122.

Working a Line—See Carry a Line.

Worried—Torn to bits by hounds.

Yoick (yoicks, hoick)—An old hunting cry; verb, to cheer or urge on with a *yoick*. See Hoick.

Yoi-over—A cheer to hounds. See page 120.